Colin Platt was born in Canton, Ch... Balliol College, Oxford, became a res... in medieval archaeology at Leeds University, and took up a Leverhulme Research Fellowship in 1969. He is currently senior lecturer in history at the University of Southampton. He originated and was the founding editor of the journal *World Archaeology*, and his other published books include *The Monastic Grange in Medieval England* (1969), *Medieval Southampton* (1973), *Excavations in Medieval Southampton* (1975) and *Medieval England: a social history and archaeology from the Conquest to A.D. 1600*. His current research interest is the social history of medieval architecture and the arts.

Colin Platt

The English Medieval Town

PALADIN
GRANADA PUBLISHING
London Toronto Sydney New York

Published by Granada Publishing Limited
in Paladin Books 1979

ISBN 0 586 08272 7

First published in Great Britain by
Martin Secker & Warburg Ltd 1976
Copyright © Colin Platt 1976

Granada Publishing Ltd
Frogmore, St Albans, Herts AL2 2NF
and
3 Upper James Street, London W1R 4BP
1221 Avenue of the Americas, New York, NY 10020, USA
117 York Street, Sydney, NSW 2000, Australia
100 Skyway Avenue, Toronto, Ontario, Canada M9W 3A6
110 Northpark Centre, 2193 Johannesburg, South Africa
CML Centre, Queen & Wyndham, Auckland 1, New Zealand

Printed in Great Britain by
Fletcher & Son Ltd, Norwich
Set in Monophoto Ehrhardt

Contents

List of Illustrations   7

Preface and Acknowledgements   14

Abbreviations   17

1   **Urban Origins**   19

   Problems of scale; urban renewal in Anglo-Saxon England;
   fortification, the community and borough right; post-
   Conquest growth and the exclusion of the aristocracy; town
   plantations and grants of market as evidence of urban growth

2   **The Urban Landscape**   33

   Dominant influences on town plans – markets, defences,
   castles, abbeys; administrative and social influences, the suburbs; fortification; trading quarters; streets, paving and the
   prevention of encroachments; tenement plots; the first town
   houses; the partition of tenement plots and its effect on house
   plans; houses of *right-angle, parallel* and *courtyard* types; lesser
   town houses; cottages; sanitation; furnishings

3   **The Borough Economy: Growth and Decline**   93

   Local markets and distribution of goods; transport and fairs;
   England's overseas trade – wool and cloth, and the impact of
   changes in demand on the towns; other causes of economic
   recovery and recession in the late-medieval boroughs

4 **Borough Society** 115

Recruitment; replacement-rates and life expectations; country
properties; family and neighbourhood ties; the distribution of
wealth; lesser men and the crafts; trade regulation, the crafts
and borough government; class conflict; oligarchies; oppo-
nents of oligarchy

5 **The Borough Constitution** 151

The borough defined; early liberties and burgage tenure; the
fee farm and the commune; the charters of John; the Ipswich
charter of 1200; borough government and its officers; thirteenth-century administrative advance; the essential liberties
of the new town; seigneurial boroughs; incorporation and the
county boroughs; the boroughs as owners of property; charges
on borough finances

6 **The Church in the Boroughs** 179

Parish church origins, the proprietary church; the shedding of
advowsons; the parish church as public building; hospitals and
almshouses; the friars; parish fraternities; chantries and obits;
the chantry priest and the parish clergy; heresy

7 **The Early-Modern Borough: Continuity and Change** 211

Inflation, population growth, industrial change; the
Reformation in the towns; burgess investment in town properties; the Great Rebuilding; lawyers and gentry in the towns;
envoi

Notes 233

Bibliography 257

Index 269

List of Illustrations

1 The map of Britain, according to Matthew Paris; mid-thirteenth-century (B.M., Cotton Claud, D.vi, f.12v)

2 A section through the York defences, showing successive ramparts and walls (R.C.H.M.: Radley)

3 Late-Saxon Winchester, over the original Roman grid (Biddle)

4 Suffolk markets and fairs, to illustrate the concentration of grants of market in the period 1100–1350 (Scarfe)

5 Devonshire markets and fairs (Hoskins)

6 Hereford from the air, with the great triangular market-place (centre) and the cathedral (bottom left) (B.K.S. Surveys)

7 Hereford in 1800, with medieval street names (Lobel)

8 Nottingham in the early seventeenth century (Speed)

9 Gloucester as an example of continuity of planning, influenced by the defences (Hurst)

10 Chichester in the early seventeenth century, still influenced by the Roman plan (Speed)

11 New Winchelsea, a royal 'planted' town (R.C.H.M.)

12 Salisbury, the medieval city, showing the 'chequers', the open market (centre), and the cathedral (top right) (Meridian Airways)

13 Salisbury in 1800, with medieval street names (Lobel)

14 Ludlow, the medieval town, showing the castle (top left), the market (top centre), and the church (top right), with the later settled areas on the slope down to the river (Meridian Airways)

15 The growth, shown in plan units, of medieval Ludlow (Conzen)

16 Winchester in the early seventeenth century (Speed)

17 Stamford in the early seventeenth century, showing the typical spread of its medieval suburbs (Speed)

18 Troy ruined and reconstructed, French, late-fifteenth-century (Bodleian, Douce 353, f.43v)

19 The city of Campision, English, *circa* 1400 (Bodleian, Bodley 264, f.230)

20 The storming of the city of Baudas, English, *circa* 1400 (Bodleian, Bodley 264, f.222)

21 Kingston upon Hull in the early sixteenth century (B.M., Cotton Aug.I.i.83)

22 Sections through the late-medieval borough defences of Southampton and Coventry, both of which re-used the line of earlier works (Wacher and Hobley)

23 The city wall of York, looking towards Monk Bar (R.C.H.M.)

24 The fourteenth-century defensive arcade by Blue Anchor Lane, Southampton, incorporating late-twelfth-century house-fronts (Department of the Environment)

25 King's Lynn from the air, with the churches of St Margaret (top centre) and All Saints (bottom left), and with Hampton Court, the Hanse Steelyard and Thoresby College by the quay (R.C.H.M.)

26 A late-medieval dyehouse at Westwick Street, Norwich, showing changes in the plan over successive periods of use (Roberts)

27 Section through the make-up of Church Street, Oxford, showing the lines of successive gravel road surfaces over a layer of pre-Conquest paving (Hassall)

28 Section across Castle Street, Oxford, showing successive medieval road surfaces, cut by modern drains (Oxford Archaeological Excavation Committee)

29 Southampton, the medieval town, showing the broad central line of the High Street (Echo Commercial Photos)

30 The Shambles, York, early this century (R.C.H.M.)

31 Tenement plots on Southampton's High Street, as surveyed in 1845–6 for an unpublished sixty-inch Ordnance Survey map of the town (Ordnance Survey)

32 Remains of a lane, medieval town houses and a bakery, excavated in 1973 behind Goodramgate, York (York Archaeological Trust)

33 Built-up tenement plots in the parish of St Mary, Oxford, as mapped for Oriel College in 1814 (Salter)

34 Pits and beam-slots as evidence of early settlement west of the High Street, Southampton, subsequently overlain by large stone-built tenements and by a new east-west lane (Platt and Coleman-Smith)

35 Medieval rubbish pits and a nineteenth-century well in the back yards of High Street tenements, Southampton, excavated in 1968; scale in half-metres (Southampton Excavation Committee)

36 Late-twelfth-century burgess housing at Southampton (Faulkner)

37 The late-twelfth-century Music House, at Norwich. Plan and

section by H. J. T. Gowen; reconstruction adapted from the reconstruction by A. P. Baggs (Lipman)

38 The undercroft of the late-twelfth-century Music House, Norwich (Hallam Ashley)

39 The Jew's House, Lincoln, late-twelfth-century (Margaret Wood)

40 Carpenters at work: Noah building the Ark, French, early-fifteenth-century (B.M., Add. 18,850, f.15v)

41 Southampton burgess houses of the early fourteenth and the fifteenth centuries in French Street and the High Street (Faulkner)

42 Late-medieval *right-angle* houses of *broad* plan in Purfleet Street and Friar Street, King's Lynn (Parker)

43 Tackley's Inn, Oxford, a *double-range* tenement of *parallel* type dating to the late thirteenth or early fourteenth centuries. Shown in the alternative versions of the late W. A. Pantin (above) and of P. A. Faulkner (below)

44 The courtyard at Strangers' Hall, Norwich, fifteenth-century (R.C.H.M.)

45 31 North Street, York, during reconstruction in 1973, late-fifteenth-century (York Archaeological Trust)

46 Remains of late-medieval town houses, excavated in 1973, on the north side of St Peter's Street, Northampton; scales in half-metres (Northampton Development Corporation)

47 A late-fifteenth-century tenement at 16 Edmund Street, Exeter, now moved to a new site opposite the church of St Mary Steps (R.C.H.M.)

48 Late-fifteenth-century houses at 11-12 West Street, Exeter (Portman)

49 A late-medieval terrace development of six two-roomed cottages in Spon Street, Coventry (Jones)

50 A row of four cottages, of thirteenth- or early-fourteenth-century date, recently excavated on the Lower Brook Street site, Winchester (Biddle)

51 The wall-lines of four cottages of the thirteenth or early fourteenth century, showing during excavations on the Lower Brook Street site at Winchester, 1967 (Winchester Excavation Committee)

52 Late-medieval tenements at 31-4 Church Street, Oxford, excavated in 1968, showing the foundations of tenements next to the lane, and cesspits and wells in the yards to the rear (Oxford Archaeological Excavation Committee)

53 Garderobe arrangements at late-medieval houses in Catherine Street and Milk Street, Exeter (Portman)

54 A bed, English, fourteenth-century (Bodleian, Douce 88, f.144)
55 A wife wheedling her husband, French, late-fifteenth-century (Bodleian, Douce 195, f.118)
56 Derbyshire market-towns, with presumed market areas (Coates)
57 An apothecary's shop, French, *circa* 1300 (B.M., Sloane 1977, f.49v)
58 Bakers at work, French, fifteenth-century (Bodleian, Canon. liturg. 99, f.16)
59 The inland distributive trade of fifteenth-century Southampton
60 A waggon, French, *circa* 1300 (Bodleian, Douce 48, f.18v)
61 A supply waggon with spiked wheels, Flemish, mid-fourteenth-century (Bodleian, Bodley 264, f.83v)
62 The 'Gough' map, mid-fourteenth-century (Bodleian, Gough Gen. Top. 16)
63 A packhorse and driver approaching an inn, English, *circa* 1400 (Bodleian, Bodley 264, f.245v)
64 The overseas trade of late-medieval England
65 Merchants awaiting the arrival of ships, English, fourteenth-century (Bodleian, Bodley 401, f.55v)
66 Ships in front of a city, English, *circa* 1400 (Bodleian, Bodley 264, f.253v)
67 Dyers at their trade, Flemish, mid-fourteenth-century (Bodleian, Bodley 264, f.83)
68 English wool and cloth exports, 1349–1540 (Carus-Wilson and Coleman)
69 A shop front of *circa* 1500 at 11 Lady Street, Lavenham (R.C.H.M.)
70 The distribution of wealth, and its rate of growth, in late-medieval England (Schofield)
71 Little Hall, Market Place, Lavenham, fifteenth-century (R.C.H.M.)
72 Gildhall, Market Place, Lavenham, first half of the sixteenth century (R.C.H.M.)
73 Loading a ship at the quayside, Flemish, late-fifteenth-century (Bodleian, Douce 208, f.120v)
74 Late-fifteenth-century shops and tenements at Butcher Row, Shrewsbury, as they appeared at the beginning of this century (R.C.H.M.)
75 A fifteenth-century warehouse at Poole, now known as 'Town Cellars' (R.C.H.M.)
76 A tavern scene, Italian, late-fourteenth-century (B.M., Add. 27,695, f.14)

77 Illustrations from a medical treatise, late-thirteenth-century (Bodleian, Ashmole 399, f.33)

78 Physician and patient, French, end of fourteenth century (B.M., Royal 20 C.vii, f.78v)

79 Job feasting with his children, English, early-fifteenth-century (Bodleian, C.C.C. 161, p. 58)

80 Brass (1458) of John Forty, wool merchant, church of St Peter and St Paul, Northleach (R.C.H.M.)

81 Family alliances among the ruling class of medieval Southampton and of London (Platt and Williams)

82 Remains of a spiral staircase in a fourteenth-century tenement, excavated in 1972 at Grimsby Lane, Hull; scales in feet (Hull City Museums)

83 Brass (1401) of William Grevel, wool merchant, and his wife Marion, church of St James, Chipping Campden (R.C.H.M.)

84 William Grevel's house, Chipping Campden (R.C.H.M.)

85 The house at Coggeshall built by the heirs of Thomas Paycocke, clothier, who died in 1461 (R.C.H.M.)

86 The great door at Thomas Paycocke's house (R.C.H.M.)

87 Norwich in the early seventeenth century: a great provincial capital (Speed)

88 A metalworker and a smith, Flemish, mid-fourteenth-century (Bodleian, Bodley 264, f.171v)

89 Vestment-makers, Italian, *circa* 1400 (B.M., Add. 15,277, f.16)

90 The Merchant Adventurers' Hall, York (R.C.H.M.)

91 Undercroft of the Merchant Adventurers' Hall (R.C.H.M.)

92 The boy Jesus as an apprentice dyer, English, *circa* 1300 (Bodleian, Selden supra 38, f.27)

93 Central York and its Minster from the air (R.C.H.M.)

94 Musicians and dancers, Flemish, mid-fourteenth-century (Bodleian, Bodley 264, f.84v)

95 Ipswich in the early seventeenth century (Speed)

96 The great door of St Mary's Gild, Lincoln, late-twelfth-century (Margaret Wood)

97 Bury St Edmunds, with the abbey church (top centre), showing the chess-board planning of the streets (R.C.H.M.)

98 The probable disposition of tenement plots in medieval Hull, from the evidence of a rental of 1347 (V.C.H.: Stanewell)

99 Coventry in the early seventeenth century (Speed)

100 Bristol in the early seventeenth century (Speed)

101 Two of the gateways of late-medieval York (R.C.H.M.)

102 York in the early seventeenth century, with its many churches even after the mergers and closures of the Reformation (Speed)

103 Foundations of the church of St Mary, Tanner Street, Winchester, excavated in 1970; an earlier apsidal chancel underlies the late square-ended chancel extension; scale in feet and metres (Winchester Excavation Committee)

104 The church of St Pancras, Winchester, progressively enlarged on an early two-cell core (Biddle)

105 An ecclesiastical map of medieval Southampton, with a list of the principal recorded fraternities and chantries in the town

106 Procession round the church at Le Puy, Auvergne, Flemish, mid-fifteenth-century (Bodleian, Douce 374, f.15v)

107 The eleventh-century church of St Benedict, Norwich, as later extended and improved (Roberts)

108 A funeral procession of dogs and hares (B.M., Add. 49,622, f.133)

109 A preaching scene, French, late-fifteenth-century (Bodleian, Douce 195, f.139v)

110 The first Franciscans arrive in Flanders, Flemish or North French, *circa* 1500 (Bodleian, Douce 205, f.32)

111 Medieval burials excavated in 1973 below the floor of the former church of St Martin and All Saints, Oxford (Oxford Archaeological Excavation Committee)

112 Candlemas procession, French, mid-fourteenth-century (Bodleian, Douce 313, f.249v)

113 The Meyring Chantry (1500) at the church of St Mary Magdalene, Newark (R.C.H.M.)

114 John Greenaway's chapel (1517) at the church of St Peter, Tiverton (R.C.H.M.)

115 A late-fifteenth-century Doom, or Last Judgement scene, over the chancel arch at the church of St Thomas, Salisbury (R.C.H.M.)

116 A celebration of mass, with street scenes, Flemish, *circa* 1500 (Bodleian, Douce 112, f.21)

117 Gild and chantry chapels at churches in Coventry and Cambridge (V.C.H. and R.C.H.M.)

118 Population, wages and prices in late-medieval and early-modern England (Cornwall [revised]; Phelps Brown and Hopkins)

119 The market region of sixteenth-century Worcester, based on recorded debts to Worcester tradesmen (Dyer)

120 Shrewsbury in the late sixteenth century (B.M., Royal 18.D.III, f.89)

121 Scarborough in the early sixteenth century (B.M., Cotton Aug. I.ii.1)

122 A sixteenth-century house in Tudor Street, Exeter (R.C.H.M.)

123 14 Trinity Street, Cambridge, *circa* 1600 (R.C.H.M.)

124 The central stair and the chimney stack in houses of the mid-sixteenth and the early seventeenth centuries at Exeter and Oxford (Portman and Pantin)

125 The Feathers Hotel, Ludlow, early-seventeenth-century (R.C.H.M.)

Preface and Acknowledgements

This book, as it will quickly become obvious to the reader, has grown out of a more specialized study of the history and archaeology of medieval Southampton, on which I have been engaged for a period of almost seven years. It has taken its form from the range of problems that emerged as significant in Southampton, and its conclusions in each case have been tested against what I know of Southampton itself. Regrettably, the work has not equipped me, any more than did Professor Tait's over forty years ago, to attempt the still 'long overdue history of the English borough in the Middle Ages'. Indeed, in view of the very great bulk of sources yet to be explored, such an ambition may always elude the historian. Nevertheless, I believe that there is at least something that each specialist can bring to the illumination of a theme even as broad as this one. As an historian and an archaeologist as well, I have myself started from the conviction that the medieval English town should be seen not merely as a community of burgesses, progressing by the accumulation of rights, but also as an 'urban place'. It was not here that Professor Tait began.

I am conscious – very much so – of the great debt I owe in this book to the work of others, some of whom recur so regularly in my footnotes that they might almost be thought to have written the book themselves. I am particularly obliged also to Dr Keene and Professor Martin for permission to make use of their unpublished doctoral theses on Winchester and Ipswich, the first of which is shortly to form the core of Dr Keene's *Survey of Medieval Winchester*, a projected volume in Martin Biddle's series of *Winchester Studies*. Martin Biddle himself has helped me on other Winchester material, as have Alan Carter, J. P. Roberts and Barbara Green on Norwich, John Bartlett and Peter Armstrong on Hull, Henry Hurst on Gloucester, Tom Hassall on Oxford, John Williams on Northampton, and Peter Addyman on York. In the gathering together of the plates, I should mention especially the assistance of Dr W. O. Hassall and Miss Elizabeth Arkell at the

Bodleian Library, Oxford, and of Stephen Croad, John Hampton and Elaine Clayton, of the National Monuments Record, London. As always, I have been dependent on Alan Burn and Ron Smith, of the Southampton University Cartographic Unit, for a comprehensive redrawing of the figures.

These figures, for the most part, have been re-used from the works of others, and I am grateful in every case for individual permissions to republish them. My thanks are due to Martin Biddle for Figs. 3, 50 and 104 (*Antiquaries Journal*, 51[1971]; 48[1968]; 52[1972]); to Professor Carus-Wilson and Miss Olive Coleman for Fig. 68 (*England's Export Trade, 1275–1547*); to Bryan Coates for Fig. 56 (*Derbyshire Archaeological Journal*, 85[1965]); to Professor Conzen for Fig. 15 (*The Study of Urban History*, ed. H. J. Dyos); to Julian Cornwall for the population curve on Fig. 118 based on a revision of his estimates published in *Ec. H. R.*, 23[1970]; to Dr Alan Dyer for Fig. 119 (*The City of Worcester in the Sixteenth Century*); to Professor E. H. Phelps Brown and Sheila V. Hopkins, and to the editors of *Economica*, for the indexes of wages and prices on Fig. 118 (*Economica*, 23[1956]); to Patrick Faulkner for Figs. 36, 41 and 43 (originally published in my own *Excavations in Medieval Southampton, 1953–1969* and *Medieval Southampton*, and in the *Archaeological Journal*, 123[1966]); to Tom Hassall for Fig. 27 (*Oxoniensia*, 36[1971]); to Brian Hobley for the Coventry section on Fig. 22 (*Medieval Archaeology*, 5[1961], to Professor Hoskins for Fig. 5 (*Devonshire Studies*); to Henry Hurst for Fig. 9, based on plans not yet published by himself; to Stanley Jones for Fig. 49 (*Transactions and Proceedings of the Birmingham Archaeological Society*, 79[1960–1]); to Dr V. D. Lipman, Tony Baggs and the Norfolk and Norwich Archaeological Society for Fig. 37, part of which appeared originally in *Norfolk Archaeology* (*The Jews of Medieval Norwich*); to Mrs M. D. Lobel, the chairman and members of the Historic Towns Trust, and Lovell Johns Ltd for Figs. 7 and 13 (*Historic Towns*); to the late Dr W. A. Pantin for Figs. 43 and 124 (*Medieval Archaeology*, 6–7[1962–3]; *Antiquaries Journal*, 27[1947]); to Dr Vanessa Doe (Parker) for Fig. 42 (*The Making of King's Lynn*); to Dr Derek Portman for Figs. 53 and 124 (*Exeter Houses 1400–1700*); to J. P. Roberts and Alan Carter for Figs. 26 and 107 (*Norfolk Archaeology*, 35[1973]); to the Royal Commission on Historical Monuments for Figs. 2, 101 and part of 117 (*City of York*, vol. 2; *City of Cambridge*, vol. 2); to Norman Scarfe for Fig. 4 (*The Suffolk Landscape*); to Dr Roger Schofield for Fig. 70 (*Ec. H. R.*, 18[1965]); to Professor Pugh, Dr Allison, Dr Stephens and the Victoria History of the Counties of England for Fig. 98 and part of 117 (*City of Kingston upon Hull; City of Coventry and Borough of Warwick*); to John Wacher for the Southampton section in Fig. 22 (*Excavations in Medieval Southampton, 1953–1969*); and to Professor Williams for the London table in Fig. 81 (*Medieval London*). Full references to these works may be found in the bibliography, and they should be consulted wherever necessary to establish the basis upon which the graphs, tables, maps and other drawings have been compiled. The redrawn John Speed maps are from his *Theatre of the Empire of Great Britaine*, first published in 1611.

The copyright of the plates published in this book rests, in each case, with the photographers. For permission to reproduce them here myself, I am grateful to the British Museum for Figs. 1, 21, 40, 57, 76, 78, 89, 108, and 120–1; to the Bodleian Library, Oxford, for Figs. 18–20, 54–5, 58, 60–3, 65–7, 73, 77, 79, 88, 92, 94, 106, 109–10, 112, and 116; to the National Monuments Record (Royal Commission on Historical Monuments) for Figs. 11, 23, 25, 30, 44, 47, 69, 71–2, 74–5, 80, 83–6, 90–1, 93, 113–15, 122–3, and 125; to B.K.S. Surveys and Hereford City Council for Fig. 6; to Meridian Airways and the National Monuments Record for Figs. 12 and 14; to Echo Commercial Photos and Southampton Corporation for Fig. 29; to Mr Hallam Ashley for Fig. 38; to Mrs Kaines-Thomas (Margaret Wood) for Figs. 39 and 96; to Derek Portman for Fig. 48; to the Oxford Archaeological Excavations Committee for Figs. 28, 52 and 111; to Hull City Museums for Fig. 82; to the Southampton Excavation Committee for Fig. 35; to the Northampton Development Corporation for Fig. 46; to the Winchester Excavation Committee for Figs. 51 and 103; and to the York Archaeological Trust and its photographers John Bailey and Dave Jeffrey for Figs. 32 and 45.

I dedicate this book with gratitude to my wife, Valerie, and to our four young children, who have endured much in its making.

Abbreviations

B.M.	British Museum
Cal. C. R.	*Calendar of the close rolls preserved in the Public Record Office,* London, 1892– (in progress)
Cal. P. R.	*Calendar of the patent rolls preserved in the Public Record Office,* London, 1891– (in progress)
E. H. R.	*The English Historical Review*
Ec. H. R.	*The Economic History Review*
R.C.H.M.	Royal Commission on Historical Monuments
Statutes of the Realm	*The statutes of the realm, from original records and authentic manuscripts,* 11 vols in 12, Record Commissioners, London, 1810–28
T. R. H. S.	*Transactions of the Royal Historical Society*
V. C. H.	*The Victoria History of the Counties of England,* London, 1900– (in progress)

1 Urban Origins

No study of the English medieval town should begin without some cautionary words. Medieval England was never intensively urbanized. Estimates naturally vary, but, at one recent guess, as much as ninety-five per cent of its population might still have been rural as late as 1500, and these proportions were not to alter significantly for another two centuries at least.[1] Units of settlement which, for one reason or another, could be described as 'towns' were plentiful, but they were often very small. London alone, with a late-medieval population approaching 50,000, could compare with some of the greater continental cities. Among English provincial capitals, York had as few as 8000 inhabitants, whereas a quite substantial country town might muster three or four thousand at most.[2] Even this, of course, was unusual. A recent study of the lesser English country towns in the early sixteenth century led its author to conclude that 'with or without suburbs and rural settlements, towns of 1000 inhabitants or more were rare'. On the evidence of the subsidy returns of the 1520s, an average country town in southern and central England would have had a population of five or six hundred, not more.[3]

It was not just that the English town was small; frequently it also retained many rural characteristics that blurred its distinction from the countryside. Certainly it would be wrong, as we were warned long ago, to lay too much stress on the importance of 'fields and pastures' even to the eleventh-century borough, and it is no doubt true that at Canterbury, Ipswich and Norwich, as at other major urban centres, the concern of the burgesses in agriculture was small from an early date.[4] Nevertheless, husbandry was to continue an important element in the economies of many substantial country towns, among them Warwick and Leicester, Coventry, Worcester and Gloucester,[5] and for the smal-

1 The map of Britain, according to Matthew Paris; mid-thirteenth-century

ler market settlement it perhaps always retained its original dominant role. One such settlement was the borough of East Grinstead, in Sussex, where a taxation return of 1340 registered the ninth part of sheaves to be taken in tax at 60s 6d, as against a yield of only 20s 6d on the ninth of all other goods.[6] At other little market towns like Congleton, in Cheshire, and Oakham, in Rutland, husbandry was to be the part-time occupation of most local craftsmen, while amongst the burgesses, some at least were to be counted full-time farmers.[7]

To the foreign visitor, and in particular to the town-bred Italian, the small scale of English urbanization continued to be the cause of some surprise. When a Venetian nobleman came to England in 1500 or thereabouts, he found it, in his view, 'very thinly inhabited' with 'scarcely any towns of importance'.[8] His countryman, Girolamo Lando, a century later, summarized the true position very exactly. England, he reported, 'does not possess many large towns, which may be estimated to number twenty-four, a small number for its size, but has very frequent and populous villages and small towns.'[9] Of course, both commentators were Venetian, and both had belonged since birth to a long-established, highly urbanized society that had little in common with the pattern of living usual in the North. For them and for their kind, it was not just the scale of urban dwelling that separated one society from another: it was an entire philosophy of life. There was to be little at any time in England to match the devotion of the Italian to his *terra*. Citizenship, far from representing the inalienable emotional bond of the South, frequently came to be a condition in England the advantages of which would have to be weighed against its burdens. In late-medieval York, it was not uncommon for those considering seeking admission to the freedom to count carefully its pros and cons.[10] Peter Gotson, at Grimsby in 1390, steadfastly refused to become a burgess of the town, although formally required to do so in order to pursue his trade. Whatever the mayor might do about it, he claimed, he would continue to practise his craft within the liberty of Grimsby without seeking admission to a burgess-ship.[11]

To argue the restricted scale of urbanization in England, its frequent part-time quality and small emotional attachment, is not, however, to deny to the towns their importance in the economy, or their weight in the politics of the kingdom. From a very early date, when London spoke the king must listen attentively. Progressively, through the centuries, the share of the towns in the total lay wealth of England continued to rise steadily, at the expense of the surrounding countryside.[12] From

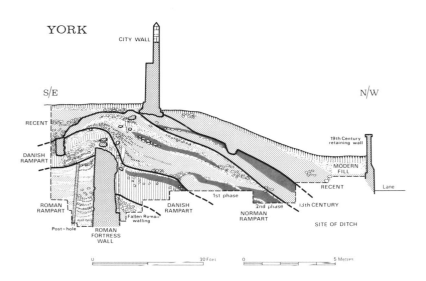

YORK

CITY WALL

S/E   N/W

RECENT

DANISH
RAMPART

19th Century
retaining wall

MODERN
FILL

RECENT

Lane

ROMAN
RAMPART

Post-hole

ROMAN
FORTRESS
WALL

Fallen Roman
walling

DANISH
RAMPART

1st phase

NORMAN
RAMPART

2nd phase

13th CENTURY

SITE OF DITCH

0   20 Feet   0   5 Metres

2 A section through the York defences, showing successive ramparts and
walls (R.C.H.M.: Radley)

wealth derived authority, of the kind that enabled the Cinque Ports in
the thirteenth century, with their indispensable naval resources, to ex-
tract further privileges for themselves from the king even when at their
most disorderly.[13] Inevitably, the king recognized his allies in the
towns, and their power grew with his own. Both processes were already
antique before the Normans came to England in the eleventh century.
They were rooted in the politics of an increasingly centralized kingdom,
and in the obscure and debatable movements of Dark Age and late-
Saxon trade.

The evidence is at best equivocal, but there seems increasing reason to
believe that trade in the North never died out wholly in the Dark Ages,
but rather changed its direction and its emphasis. It is one recent thesis
that as the rich consumers of the Late Antique world faded from the
North, it was more the demand for luxury products that failed than the
ability of traders to meet it. On this argument, population growth and
the new agricultural technology of the heavy plough and improved
harnesses generated an economic revival of great significance, to which
the record of 'Domesday Book' in the late eleventh century is already
ample testimony. But it was not a revival on late-Roman terms, and it

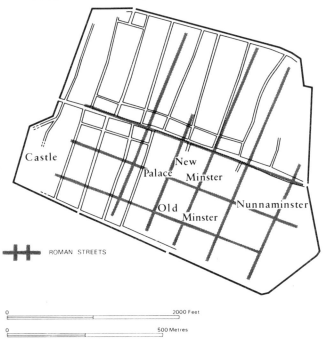

WINCHESTER

Castle

Palace

New
Minster

Old
Minster

Nunnaminster

ROMAN STREETS

0   2000 Feet

0   500 Metres

3 Late-Saxon Winchester, over the original Roman grid (Biddle)

no longer carried with it the same range of commodity exchanges that
had kept the antique trade routes open. For centuries, until the growth
of a new leisured aristocracy with a disposable surplus for the exchange
or purchase of luxuries, the primary products most in demand were
those that the locality itself could usually be expected to provide. In
such conditions a renewal of urban life could certainly occur, but its
growth was modest and it centred everywhere in the North on the
organization of local markets and on the promotion of no more than
regional exchanges.[14] Even at this period we may recall, of course, the
thriving trading centres at Dorestad, in Holland, at Birka, in Sweden,
and at Hedeby, on the Jutland peninsula.[15] Yet at these, too, the local
market function remained of great importance, and there is no reason to
suppose that the revival of the towns before the end of the millennium
in any way compared with the phenomenal urban expansion of the late
eleventh, the twelfth and the early thirteenth centuries, obeying differ-

ent market forces and meeting less restricted needs.

In Britain, the break with the Roman past was perhaps unusually complete, with predictable consequences in the towns. Nowhere has convincing evidence yet been recovered of an unbroken continuity of urban life in this former Roman province. Certainly, the bones of many Roman towns survived, to be made use of by their new English rulers as administrative centres and defended *enceintes*. But there is nothing to suggest that these towns remained in being as true 'urban places', and there is good reason on the contrary to believe that the royal and ecclesiastical uses to which, frequently, they were put, might actually have delayed their return to those primarily economic functions they were starting to resume no earlier than the late ninth and the tenth centuries. The well-studied former Roman settlement at Winchester is a case in point. To Bede, in the early eighth century, Winchester was known as a Saxon capital, the city of the *Gewisse*. Yet by 500, on the archaeological evidence, an Anglo-Saxon settlement had already been established at King's Worthy, within two miles of the town, and it has been suggested that this may have been only one of a ring of such primarily agricultural communities, to which the commercial and craft functions of the original urban nucleus were drawn as Winchester itself was steadily reduced to an administrative and an ecclesiastical purpose.[16]

However, although the renewal of urban life at Winchester cannot be dated much before the late ninth century, even if it is as early as that, for two full centuries already an active trading community had flourished at *Hamwih*, now Southampton, not many miles down-river to the south. The archaeological investigation of the Saxon levels at Southampton is not complete, but it has long been clear that the site is of exceptional importance, perhaps rivalling Dorestad or Hedeby. In striking testimony to an active trading life, the rich coin series from Anglo-Saxon Southampton begins before 700, to continue throughout the eighth and ninth centuries and to fade out only in the tenth. There is good evidence of metal-working at Hamwih, and of bone and textile industries. Houses and streets have been identified, while in overseas trade there are obvious links with Dorestad, on the Rhine, confirmed by the presence at Hamwih of Rhineland pottery and glass of ninth-century types, and by the ubiquitous quernstone fragments of Niedermendig lava found on every Hamwih site.[17] The urban quality of the freshly created Saxon community at Hamwih, sustained by industry and trade, need no longer be doubted. To our meagre evidence of continuing Dark Age trade, it has made a new, and an important, contribution.[18]

There are clear limits, of course, to the comprehensiveness of this pre-Conquest urbanization, but it is not just in terms of the development of local markets or of continuing overseas trade that we may recognize a 'relatively well advanced urban order' within the Anglo-Saxon period.[19] As Professor Loyn has shown, on the evidence of that early-tenth-century list known as the 'Burghal Hidage', the association of the kings of Wessex with a considered programme of fortification in their dominions was of vital importance to the development of those characteristics distinctive of the 'free' royal borough.[20] By reserving, even in the greater franchises, his rights over the burhs, or fortified places, as an element in the system of national defence, the king began a close association with his developing boroughs which was to be continuously beneficial to them both. It is clear that not all of the burhs developed as urban communities, and that some were conceived from the start merely as fortresses. Yet it is significant that when Ethelred and Ethelfled, between 885 and 900, built their burh at Worcester, they did it expressly for the protection of 'all the folk', and that its elements included a market with streets both within and without the burh.[21] At Worcester, as probably at many other similar centres, it was the provision of fortifications, with communal responsibility for manning and maintenance, that hastened the development of the borough. Traces of such Saxon urban defences, with all that these may be taken to imply, have been identified at Hereford, Warwick, Lydford and Tamworth; commonly they take the form of substantial ditches and ramparts, sometimes revetted in stone. Where former Roman defences survived in reasonable order, as they must have done at both Exeter and Winchester, the original stone walls were repaired.[22]

Quite possibly, as has been argued recently, the reorganization of at least some of these borough defences was accompanied by a comprehensive re-planning within the borough itself, to be followed by fresh urban growth. At Winchester, the archaeological dating of several streets, at least two of which were sealed beneath the primary earthworks of the Norman castle, has suggested not only that the basic lay-out of the main streets of the medieval city was of Saxon, probably tenth-century date, but that the entire rectilinear street system of Winchester may be datable as early as the last years of the ninth century or the first years of the tenth, at which time it was established in accordance with a deliberate plan (Fig. 3).[23] In this context, it is not without significance that the true 'urban' development of Winchester, following its prolonged life as an administrative and ecclesiastical centre, has been dated by its excavator no earlier than the tenth century.[24]

Such a quality of 'urban' life, suggested by association of the inhabitants in communal programmes of rampart-building and maintenance of the defences, and perhaps implicit also in the deliberate planned layouts of some of the Burghal Hidage towns, may be recognized again in the concern displayed in borough documents of the tenth century for property rights of all kinds, including the right to collect market tolls. Already, that is, by the tenth century, borough courts had developed to handle the affairs of the townsmen; there were royal officials, the portreeves, to collect the dues of the king in the towns and to watch over the preservation of his rights there; a concept of borough-right was developing as something quite distinct from the land-right of the more conventional rural kind.[25] We can discover little of those associations of townsmen, the 'men of credit', who carried such programmes through, who witnessed documents, confirmed trading contracts, and made it their business to be present at the *burghemot*, or borough court. But it is not unlikely, as Professor Loyn suggests, that they came together in the fellowships, or gilds, that are known to have characterized borough society in a number of pre-Conquest towns.[26] If indeed they did so, they would have anticipated an arrangement that would become familiar throughout England in the twelfth and thirteenth centuries as the burgess members of the gilds merchant took over in many boroughs the further responsibilities of urban administrators. They would have found, in free association, the elements of a communal voice.

It is possible, certainly, to overrate the effect of the Norman Conquest on the development of the boroughs, as Professor Carl Stephenson unhappily did in the thirties.[27] Increasingly, continuity has become the theme of historians and archaeologists alike. Nevertheless, it is an undoubted fact that the Normans quite commonly practised deliberate borough colonization of their own, whether from nothing, as in the conquest and settlement of Glamorgan,[28] or in the encouragement of additional settlement of a colonizing kind in major existing towns, at which new groups of French traders were established. Significantly, too, there is important linguistic evidence of a heavy borrowing of French vocabulary in the language of commerce and borough affairs. It parallels similar borrowings in the spheres of government and the law, but is not matched at all in farming or in fishing where English influence remained dominant.[29] Later there would be other borrowings: in charters of liberties, in the names and functions of borough officers, and in exper-

SUFFOLK

Before 1100 (including presumed markets)

Beccles

Hoxne
Eye
Blythburgh
Dunwich
Bury St Edmunds
Kelsale
Stowmarket
Haverhill   Clare
Ipswich
Sudbury

N

1100 – 1350

Belton
Flixton
Oulton   Lowestoft
Bungay   Carlton Colville
Brandon   Homersfield   Kessingland
Lakenheath   Brampton   Covehithe
(Whittingham)   Westhall   Sotherton
Market Weston   Redgrave   Fressingfield   Wissett
Worlington   Botesdale   Burgate   Wingfield   Halesworth   Reydon
Stradbroke   Southwold
Laxfield   Bramfield
Exning   Wyverston   Mendlesham   Earl   Middleton
Moulton   Soham   Saxmundham   Leiston
Barrow   Haughley   Debenham   Benhall
Ousden   Onehouse   Framlingham   Sizewell
Hawkedon   Felsham   Needham   Earl Stonham   Kettleburgh   Aldringham
(Thurston)   Market   Hacheston
Gt Bricett   Ringshall   Clopton   Pettistree
Gt Thurlow   Lavenham   Bildeston   Witnesham   Grundisburgh   Orford
Long   Brent Eleigh   Woodbridge
Melford   Kersey   Gt
Hadleigh   Bealings
Kirton   Bawdsey
Stoke-by-Nayland   Shelley   Shotley   (Croxton)
Bures St Mary   Nayland   Walton
Erwarton

After 1350

Mildenhall

Ixworth   Westhorpe

Wickham Market   Aldeburgh

Stratford St Mary

| 0 | | 15 Miles |
| 0 | | 20 Km |

26

imental political systems, like the commune. Yet what, overall, these point to may be less the importance of the cataclysm at the Conquest itself than the abiding influence of both Anglo-Norman and Angevin continental connections at a time when towns everywhere in the North and the West were startlingly on the increase.

Undoubtedly, a good part of this fresh spurt of urban growth owed itself to the resurrection of the international luxury trades, in fine cloth, for example, or in wine, which had been largely in abeyance since the collapse of the Roman economy in the West. An exclusive aristocracy had begun to re-shape itself, with refined tastes and with the resources to gratify them.[30] But connected with this, and certainly as important, was a general return to those other conditions which could give body to an urban revival: in effect, a rising population, a measure of international peace, and the establishment of good order locally on the initiative of emergent national kings. It is no accident that the towns and the king grew together. As the king's power spread out along his roads, across his forests and into his boroughs – the sites of his castles and his courts – he found natural allies in the burgesses. It was in the twelfth century that the king, for the first time, recognized the gild merchant as a trading association in the boroughs; it was in that century, too, that he began to grant its members comprehensive exemptions from local tolls on the roads and waterways throughout his kingdom. That prodigious rise in the wealth of the king, placing him once and for all over his aristocracy as patron extraordinary in his dominions, derived in significant measure from his towns.

The separation of the king from the higher feudality had its own equivalent in the towns. Typically, the town of Domesday England was still dominated by its local aristocracy, and there were large holdings within it in the hands of great landowners, including the Crown and the Church. There might already have been sokemen, probably burgesses, at Stamford in the late eleventh century, 'who have their lands in demesne and seek lords where they will'. Yet at Stamford, too, there were important landowners: Queen Edith with seventy 'messuages', or tenements with their adjoining land, the Countess Judith with fourteen, and the abbot of Peterborough with ten messuages of his own and a mill.[31] At contemporary Leicester, it has been remarked, many of the houses in the Domesday borough were appurtenant to rural manors.[32]

4 Suffolk markets and fairs, to illustrate the concentration of grants of market in the period 1100–1350 (Scarfe)

While at Warwick, in 1086, if the king had 113 houses in the borough, his 'barons' had 112; each of these men, furthermore, had other property in the surrounding shire.[33]

Very probably, however, the hold on the towns of the aristocracy was weakening even as 'Domesday Book' itself was compiled. At Warwick, the survey recorded nineteen burgesses, each with a messuage in the borough, 'with sake and soke and all customs', in effect with all the juridical rights of a freeholder. They constituted a distinct group, conceivably the original body of that burgess aristocracy that would soon come to dominate the town.[34] In the next decade, a Gloucester survey of 1097–1100, if read with the Domesday record, points to the existence of an active market in town houses, or burgage tenements, still the interest of rural landowners but freely negotiable property, open to purchase and investment.[35] Free transferability of land in the boroughs, as soon as it became generally recognized and exploited by the burgesses themselves, would be the essence of burgage tenure, the most valuable privilege they possessed.

The dispossession of the local aristocracy, a withdrawal rather than a rout, may have spread over a large number of years, but by the thirteenth century it was normally complete. In the twelfth-century boroughs, it could not have been difficult to find parallels to the knightly Dunning family, with its long-lasting interest in Cambridge.[36] There were the Cauvels, for example, at Canterbury, and the family of John, son of Vivian.[37] But the Dunnings were to find themselves in financial difficulties by the mid-thirteenth century, as would their exact contemporaries and probable equivalents, the Bulehuse family of Southampton.[38] And it was the burgess dynasties of the Chiches, of Terric the goldsmith and others, who ran thirteenth-century Canterbury, just as it was the Flemings, the Bonhaits, the Barbfletes and the Isembards, who were the masters of contemporary Southampton.

With the expansion of international trade, and with the great fortunes that men of ability could make in it, a new professionalism had entered the boroughs. The careers of burgess and squire, as Miss Cam remarked of the Dunnings, are not necessarily compatible.[39] Furthermore, they would become less so throughout the twelfth and thirteenth centuries as commercial expertise mounted and as the pressure of business affairs kept men ever more closely to the towns. In the late Middle Ages, the attractions of a country estate as investment, and the lure of gentility, might draw the wealthier burgess out into the countryside again, significantly reducing the life-span of his dynasty in the borough. Yet this had

not always been so. Property-holding in the shires, although not unknown among thirteenth-century burgesses, was not an important social
or economic preoccupation of their class. At no time in the Middle
Ages, that is, were English burgess dynasties to last as long as in the
period between John's charters, in 1200 or thereabouts, and the Black
Death, in 1348–9. Such family continuity, promoted by intermarriage
among dynastic lines, reflected a profound satisfaction with urban living
that can have come only from a unique combination of independence
and economic success. It coincided precisely with that point in the
history of the English boroughs at which the urban tradition, in its
fullest sense, had come at last into its own.

There are two obvious guides, both of them very convincing, to the impact
of the urban expansion that everywhere characterized England in the
twelfth and thirteenth centuries. One of them is the known incidence of new
town foundations, reaching a peak in these centuries; the other is the spread
of market rights.

To take a single county, the Domesday record for Devonshire shows
it to have had only the four towns at Exeter, Barnstaple, Lydford and
Totnes, with a fifth emergent borough at Okehampton. Yet by 1238 a
dramatic change had occurred. In that year, no fewer than eighteen
Devonshire boroughs sent delegates to meet the king's justices; there
had been thirteen successful borough foundations since the last count in
1086.[40] What had happened in these centuries over the kingdom as a
whole was very little different. Deliberate town plantations in England,
as Professor Beresford has shown, increased in number from immediately after the Conquest. Before 1100, twenty-one new towns had
been established in England, with a further nineteen settled during the
first three decades of the twelfth century. In Wales, over the same
period, there were eighteen new town plantations.[41] The foundation of
new towns, although it fell off appreciably during the civil wars of
Stephen's reign, continued throughout the twelfth century, reaching
new peaks in the decade 1191–1200 and again in the two decades 1211–
1230. In all, there were some forty-nine new town plantations in the
years 1191–1230, after which numbers would fall and failures rise as the
country became saturated with boroughs.[42]

Clear and useful distinctions can be made between the types of borough foundation that characterized the recognizable peak periods.
Before 1100, in what Professor Beresford has termed the 'conquerors'
decades', the interest of the king himself in the new foundations was

The map shows Devonshire markets and fairs with the following locations marked:

Ilfracombe, Combe Martin, Marwood, Pilton, Barnstaple, Newport, Bishop's Tawton, N.Molton, SOMERSET, Clovelly, Northam, Bideford, Hartland, S.Molton, Bampton, Buckland Brewer, Great Torrington, Rackenford, Holcombe Rogus, Canonsleigh, Chulmleigh, Witheridge, Sampford Peverell, Tiverton, Uffculme, Hollacombe, Cullompton, Sheepwash, Hatherleigh, Bradninch, Broadhembury, Holsworthy, North Tawton, Bow, Langford, Awliscombe, Crediton, Honiton, Okehampton, Axminster, South Zeal, Strete, Ottery St.Mary, Whitford, Exeter, Clyst St.Mary, Aylesbeare, Sidbury, Colyton, Lydford, Moretonhampstead, Topsham, Newton Poppleford, Brentor, Kennford, Woodbury, Seaton, Sidmouth, Kenton, Bovey Tracey, Chudleigh, Highweek, Tavistock, Teignmouth, Newton Abbot, Ashburton, Bradley, Stokeinteignhead, Buckland Monachorum, Denbury, Kingskerswell, Bere Ferrers, Buckfastleigh, Ipplepen, Cockington, CORNWALL, Totnes, Paignton, Tamerton Foliot, South Brent, Berry Pomeroy, Plymouth, Plympton, Ermington, Modbury, Moreleigh, Dartmouth, Aveton Gifford, Kingsbridge, Dodbrooke, West Alvington, East Portlemouth

0 — 20 Miles

0 — 30 Km

● Market and Fair
○ Market only
▲ Fair only

5 Devonshire markets and fairs (Hoskins)

significantly higher than it ever would be again. Reflecting the importance to the Crown of widespread burgess support, one in three of the planted towns was to be a royal foundation, while some eighty per cent of the boroughs created were established in the shadow of fortresses. Through the reign of Henry I, although more than half of borough plantations continued to be sheltered by castles, the proportions of royal to baronial foundations were changing in favour of the latter. Already, that is, the emphasis on the town as an instrument of government was fading. Many, and shortly most, of the new towns of the mid-to-late twelfth century grew up unprotected by a castle, Boston and Lynn being typical of the new ports of this tradition, and St Neots of the market towns. In a period of quickening trading exchanges and of relatively easy profits, the commercial success of plantations such as these could not fail to encourage many imitators. By the end of the twelfth century, seigneurial foundations were commonplace, as they were to continue to be through the following decades of the early-thirteenth-century boom.[43] Mistakes, of course, were made, and Moreton-in-Marsh (Gloucestershire), Bretford (Warwickshire), and Broadway (Worcestershire) have been instanced as examples of these.[44] Nevertheless, on the whole, the confidence of the landowners was justified, and their expectations were at least partially fulfilled. Chipping Sodbury and Stratford-on-Avon, Northleach and Chipping Campden, would each have repaid the lord's initial investment many times over.[45] As successful market towns, they brought rents and dues to the landowner far in excess of any agricultural profits he might otherwise have derived from the land.

It was the acquisition, above all, of market rights that constituted for many of these speculative plantations the first step towards borough status. Not all markets were located at towns, and the grant of market privileges was no certain guarantee of success. Nevertheless, the creation, or the recognition, of markets by the king was essentially part of the general urbanizing process, and it reached its peak in the reigns of Henry III and Edward I, just when the towns themselves were at their most vigorous. In two recent studies of market creations, in Derbyshire and then in Staffordshire, the same overall pattern has emerged. Of the markets and fairs of Derbyshire recorded before 1350, as many as two-thirds of the total number had been recognized by the king before 1275, a good half of these grants of market rights bunching together in the quarter-century 1250–1275. By the middle of the fourteenth century, and probably for some decades before this, the twenty-eight market towns of Derbyshire had come to constitute a 'comprehensive network of trading centres', serving, every populated region of the county (Fig. 56).[46] In Staffordshire, similarly, the overwhelming majority of the markets in the county had come into existence before 1350. Just as in Derbyshire, most had been recognized by Henry III and his son, the peak in recognitions occurring in the 1250s.[47]

While Domesday, it must be said, is no fair record of the spread of markets and fairs in late-eleventh-century England, it is instructive, all the same, to set the approximately fifty markets and two fairs of the

Domesday record against the 1200 or so settlements in England and Wales that were to acquire market rights from the king between 1227 and 1350.[48] Probably, the first figure is incomplete; certainly, the second is inflated by the inclusion of communities too small to be considered as towns. But however we view it, what the contrast illustrates unquestionably is a flowering of trade on a local level quite as dramatic as the contemporary resuscitation of international exchanges which was bringing certain great ports of the realm into prominence. We shall always know less of the market dealings of St Neots, for example, than of shipping movements at Bristol and Southampton; there was not the same reason to record them. Yet it was this growth of trade everywhere in England, and at all levels, that inspired the widespread transformation of the semi-rural to the wholly urban community, and that fuelled the surge into independence of the towns.

2 The Urban Landscape

All towns display, to a greater or lesser degree, the influence on their plans of distinctive individual dominants, whether natural, cultural or economic, and no town can be quite like another. However, if there was one factor most influential in the shaping of our older towns, this must surely have been the junction of antique routes, a crossing of the ways at which a market might grow up and flourish. In point of fact, the great majority of English town plans may be seen to be 'market-based',[1] and it is common in these for the intersection, or converging, of major trackways to have determined not merely the siting of the borough, but also how its streets and its markets should be disposed. It was, thus, on the lines of the principal approach roads to Hereford that its first Saxon defences were penetrated by gateways, and it was to be on the stretch of level ground at the junction of these roads that the great market of Hereford (Fig. 6) was re-sited shortly following the Conquest. Inevitably, the tenements of Hereford's early citizens first clustered in the vicinity of the market, to spread out in later years along the line of the streets which converged on it (Fig. 7).[2] Favourable communications were what gave the re-sited borough of Salisbury (Fig. 12) its decisive advantage over the neighbouring settlement at Wilton.[3] And it was good communications again, at a meeting of the ways, that promoted the growth of early-medieval Nottingham, determining the plan of its spacious funnel-shaped market-place (Fig. 8), and encouraging the king to grant it far-reaching privileges, among these the requirement of Henry I that the men of the shires of Nottingham and Derby should come first to Nottingham to market, rather than take their custom elsewhere.[4]

It is, however, in the smaller towns that the essential dominance of the market stands most clearly revealed. The Northumberland borough of Alnwick, originating in a fortress, then came to take its final form from the triangular space, later to become the market-place, created by the intersection of three important roads some way to the south of the

castle. For centuries, there was to be little more to the borough than a cluster of houses at the castle gate, with a great concentration of burgess dwellings by the market-place itself, or along the three major traffic roads that entered it.[5]

The simple radial plan, at Alnwick as elsewhere, focusing on a central market-place and church, gave to the burgesses the advantage of house frontages, if not always on the market-place itself, at least on a road that approached it. And if, as would be the case in many of the later towns, settlement stretched along an existing road rather than about a junction of different ways, the same impulse to share out the most valuable frontages drove men to settle in a continuous line along the road, and only rarely in subsidiary streets behind it. Thus developed the basic linear plan, with its single main street broadening sometimes into a rectangular market-place and sometimes into a V-shaped market with church or market-hall at the end, that would come to be most characteristic of the English country town. It can be seen, for example, at the successful new borough foundation at Market Harborough, developing in the late twelfth century, with its wide main street and the church sited at one end.[6] In such a town, and in its many parallel foundations elsewhere, the burgage plot would be narrow in frontage, though deep. The street would be as long as it needed to be to give each man his opening in trade.

The highway town, with its extended linear plan, had grown only for the purposes of trade. It was undefended and usually, of its nature, undefendable. But the town at a junction of the ways, often of much earlier foundation, had frequently begun life as an administrative or a religious centre, and it continued to be influenced by these requirements. Both Hereford and Nottingham, important market centres though they became, matured as tenth-century burhs, while Hereford, going back much further even than this, had been the seat of a bishopric since as early as the late seventh century. For them, and for others like them, the plan of the borough might be determined by more than commercial needs. Borough defences, whether inherited or supplied, would contain growth and shape it; in many, a castle, a cathedral or an abbey might need to be accommodated, or might itself form the nucleus of the plan. Among the most interesting, and certainly the earliest, examples of such conditioning are the very common survivals in towns

6 Hereford from the air, with the great triangular market-place (centre) and the cathedral (bottom left)

HEREFORD

0   500 Feet

0   200 Metres

PORT FIELDS

Frogs Lane

Hospital Lane

Frere Lane

Catts Lane

Bye St. without the Gate

Wydemarsh St.

Bowsey Lane

Wydemarsh Street

Malieres Street

Jews Street

Bishopsgate St. or Bye St.

Olde Street

Bewal Street

Frenschemanne Street

Coken Row

Middle Row

Eigne Street

High Street

Butchery

Grope Lane

Guildford Street

Behyndethewall Lane

The Market

Norton

Aley

Hungreye Street

Bythebroke Street

Wroterhale Street

Brode Street

Black Lane

Plow Lane

Broad Caboches Lane

Milk Lane

Oldeschole St.

Behyndethewall Lane

Canons Street

Schire Lane

West Gate St.

Middle Row Kings Ditch

Little Lane

Castle Street

Sortordes Lane

Castle Street

Wyebridge Street

Pipewell

RIVER WYE

Rodipol Way

Brutton Street

N

of Roman origin of elements of the Roman plan (Fig. 9). There is nothing in this to establish continuity of settlement on such sites, for it is plain that the Roman grid plan, in each case, was unknown to those who re-settled the sites after a period of disuse. Yet what they demonstrate very clearly is the powerful influence on later planning of a dominant surviving feature: in this case, of the Roman defensive circuit, and particularly of the placing of its gates. There are gates and main highways, obviously Roman in origin, in Winchester (Fig. 3), Canterbury and Gloucester (Fig. 9), in Chester, Colchester, Chichester (Fig. 10), Exeter and Bath.[7] And the simplicity of the Roman grid-type layout, already suggested by the surviving lines of highway, rampart or wall, recommended it again to later settlers. It was precisely those characteristics that it owed to its Roman planners that the monk Lucian admired in late-twelfth-century Chester: its two straight streets, originating in Roman gateways and determined by the lines of Roman roads, with the fine open crossing at the middle where stood the medieval market. They recalled to Lucian irresistibly the symbolism of the Cross and of the four Evangelists.[8]

Although clearly for different reasons, the straightforward grid, or chess-board plan, as adopted in the lay-out of new settlements, would always retain its attraction. It was used, on one theory, by the Wessex kings in the setting-out of their principal burhs.[9] And in those post-Conquest foundations with a sound expectation of growth, it was frequently resorted to again. It was with the king's determined backing that New Winchelsea (Fig. 11) and the north Welsh planted towns grew up on chess-board lines, attracting sufficient new settlers to pack the vacant lots. At New Salisbury, it was the re-siting of the cathedral down by the river that was the most powerful inducement to settlement. Begun in 1220, it was accompanied by the systematic laying-out of a fine new grid-plan city, instantly commercially successful, in which the *insulae*, or blocks enclosed by the streets, were themselves to become known as 'chequers' (Figs. 12 and 13).[10]

Although Ludlow (Fig. 14) has frequently been cited, with Bury St Edmunds (Fig. 97), as an early example of such planning,[11] it is probably better to take it now as an illustration of that other characteristic urban development pattern, the market centre that grew up in the shadow of a castle. The grid at Ludlow, it has recently been argued, is

7 Hereford in 1800, with medieval street names (Lobel)

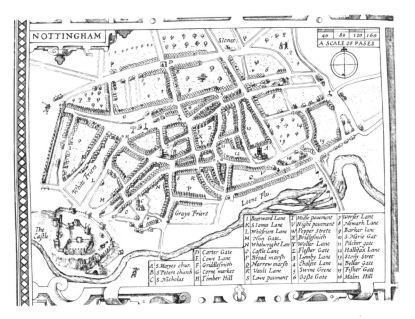

NOTTINGHAM

A SCALE OF PASES

A	S.Maryes chur.		I	Bearward Lane
B	S Peters church		K	S Iames Lane
C	S Nicholas		L	Whitfriers Lane
D	Carter Gate		M	Mun Gate
E	Cowe Lane		N	Whelwright Lan
F	Gridlesmith		O	Castle Lane
G	Corne market		P	Broad marsh
H	Timber Hill		Q	Narrow marsh
			R	Vault Lane
			S	Lowe pavment
T	Midle pavment		7	worser Lane
V	Highe pavment		8	Newark Lane
W	Pepper Strete		9	Barker lane
X	Bridlesmith		10	S.Marie Gat
Y	Weller Lane		11	Pilcher gate
Z	Flesher Gate		12	Hallifax Lone
1	Lymby Lane		13	Story Strete
2	Choler Lane		14	Bellar Gate
3	Swine Grene		15	Fisher Gate
4	Gosse Gate		16	Malm Hill

8 Nottingham in the early seventeenth century (Speed)
9 (opposite) Gloucester as an example of continuity of planning, influenced by the defences (Hurst)

likely to have developed through at least five distinct phases, each identifiable in a separate unit in the plan (Fig. 15). Of these, the second phase would have been the most important in the development of the borough economy, for it consisted of the laying-out of a large street market and associated burgage plots along the flat top of the ridge, on the end of which the castle was sited, and it probably included the building of the church, towards the eastern end of the street. Subsequently, there was to be a regularly planned southwards extension of the whole body of the town, down the slope towards the river, perhaps of the thirteenth century and identifiable as phase four. It followed an earlier third-phase movement further along the ridge from the church, and was itself succeeded by a fifth phase of post-medieval development, south of the castle, at the south-west corner of the town.[12]

At Ludlow, in a situation for which there are many obvious continental parallels, the building of a castle had attracted further settlement, initially at the castle gate in what has been recognized as the classical 'suburban' pattern. The town had then grown unit by unit to fill out a

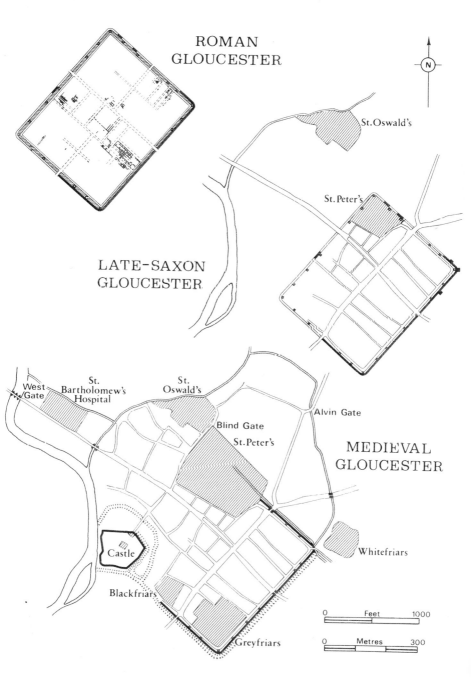

ROMAN
GLOUCESTER

N

St. Oswald's

St. Peter's

LATE–SAXON
GLOUCESTER

West
Gate

St.
Bartholomew's
Hospital

St.
Oswald's

Alvin Gate

Blind Gate

St. Peter's

MEDIÆVAL
GLOUCESTER

Castle

Whitefriars

Blackfriars

Greyfriars

0   Feet   1000

0   Metres   300

10 Chichester in the early seventeenth century, still influenced by the Roman plan (Speed)

plan which, superficially, has the appearance of a single-phase development. At St Albans, it was a great Benedictine abbey, reformed in the third quarter of the tenth century, that gave its original purpose to the town and dictated its subsequent shape. The large triangular market-place at St Albans, subsequently partially built-over in a not uncommon instance of market colonization, dates back to the deliberate late-tenth-century development of St Albans by its abbots. It is on the north precinct wall of the abbey that the base of the triangle abuts; along its sides were disposed the earliest burgage plots, multiplying northwards along the main approach road to the abbey, as the number of settlers grew.[13]

Where the placing of a castle or an abbey failed to influence the earliest plan of a borough, the subsequent insertion of one or other of these might have gone far to transform it. At Oxford and at Exeter, at

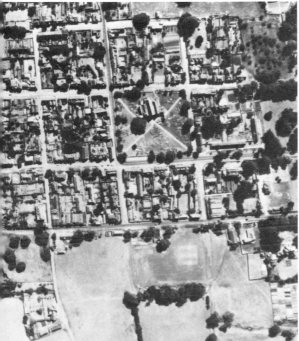

11 New Winchelsea, a royal 'planted' town (R.C.H.M.)

12 Salisbury, the medieval city, showing the 'chequers', the open market (centre), and the cathedral (top right)

SALISBURY

N

Castle Street
Scots Lane
Endless Street
Rolveston
Mylkmonger Street
Chipper Street
Gigore Street
Wyneman Street
Market Place
Carter Street
Butcher Row
Old Poultry
Winchester Street
The Ditch or Trench
Brown Street
Culver Street
High Street
New Street
New Street
Love Lane
St Martin Street
Feren Street
St Mary's Cathedral
Drakehall Street

0   600 Feet

0   150 Metres

14 Ludlow, the medieval town, showing the castle (top left), the market (top centre), and the church (top right), with the later settled areas on the slope down to the river

13 (opposite) Salisbury in 1800, with medieval street names (Lobel)

Wallingford, Wareham and Chichester, new castles of the late eleventh and early twelfth centuries required the destruction of pre-existing houses. Work on the castle at Winchester, begun in 1067, has recently been shown to have destroyed at least one entire street of tenements, and there is a suggestion of similar clearance below the bailey defences of the post-Conquest fortress at Southampton.[14] By 1086, Domesday tells us, over forty houses had been demolished at Canterbury to make room for the Conqueror's castle. Yet it was not this so much as the steady expansion of religious institutions in the city that distorted Canterbury's plan. To quote Dr Urry, there are now 'many canonical or academic lawns', at Canterbury, Oxford and Cambridge, which were 'originally streets of houses'.[15]

While it is true that prominent natural features – a river, a water-front, a flat space, or a ridge of well-drained gravel – were never unimportant

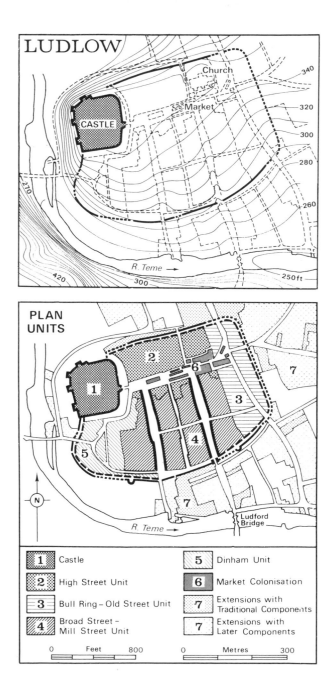

LUDLOW

Church

Market

CASTLE

340

320

300

280

270

260

R. Teme →

420

300

250ft

**PLAN
UNITS**

2

6

7

1

3

4

5

7

N

7

Ludford
Bridge

R. Teme →

1	Castle		**5**	Dinham Unit
2	High Street Unit		**6**	Market Colonisation
3	Bull Ring – Old Street Unit		**7**	Extensions with Traditional Components
4	Broad Street – Mill Street Unit		**7**	Extensions with Later Components

0   Feet   800   0   Metres   300

in the shaping of a town plan, it should be remembered that towns are the most artificial of all human creations and that they reflect, more than anything, the social habits of the men who made them. Vital though the existing watercourses were to the economy of King's Lynn, and influential though they must have been in its planning, the borough could scarcely have taken the form that it did had it not been divided, for administrative purposes, into three distinct units. At the centre, the original settlement had its market and its priory church. In the mid-twelfth century, its extension to the north, promoted by the bishop of Norwich and under his lordship, grew up with a market and a chapel of its own. Not very much later, in the early thirteenth century, the first two units merged, but a third unit, at South Lynn, remained administratively distinct until as late as 1555. South Lynn, without the market and other privileges of the consolidated borough to the north, lagged behind its neighbour commercially, although, even so, by the fifteenth century it had wealthy traders and a merchant gild of its own.[16] Such a bit-by-bit development, with important economic and social consequences, would be characteristic too of Bristol, where there were major suburban expansions at Redcliffe and Temple Fee (Fig. 100).[17] At Coventry, it was the separate administrative development of the parts of the prior and the earl that for a long time governed its growth (see p. 168).

Inevitably, such administrative distinctions, wherever they existed, could not have failed to be reflected in the developing plan of a borough, but there were other social considerations also, more pervasive than these, that might govern such things as the placing of a religious institution or a hospital, and that would determine the character of a suburb. It may be that too much emphasis has been placed on the peripheral siting of friaries, either just within or immediately outside the defended circuits of many English towns. They were there, for example, at Gloucester and at Hereford, at Nottingham, Reading and Salisbury,[18] but had probably come to be so more for reasons of available space than as a consequence of any deliberate preference for poor areas. More certainly contrived were the remote situations of the leper hospitals, established outside the settled limits of many English towns to isolate the victims of a complaint thought to be contagious and very common in the twelfth and thirteenth centuries. The lazar house at Cambridge, we are told, stood at the 'remotest corner' of the territory of the borough.[19]

15 The growth, shown in plan units, of medieval Ludlow (Conzen)

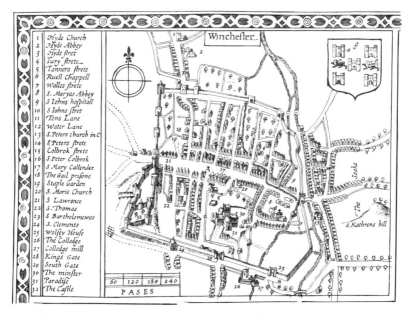

16 Winchester in the early seventeenth century (Speed)

It was matched by Exeter's hospital of St Mary Magdalene for lepers, sited half a mile outside the gates of the city,[20] by London's many lazar houses, ringing the city and placed on the line of its major exit roads,[21] and by similar extra-mural establishments at Leicester[22] and at Gloucester,[23] at Grimsby,[24] Stamford[25] and elsewhere.

There was an element, too, of deliberate exclusion in the development of the typical suburb. Certainly, not all suburbs were the resort of the poor and the unenfranchised. At Canterbury, from the twelfth century and even before, the suburbs had housed an important sector of the city's population for which there was room, had the desire been there, within the existing walls.[26] And in fourteenth-century Warwick, as the tax records clearly show, it was in the suburbs that the wealthy chose to establish themselves, attracted there by the borough's extensive suburban fields.[27] But the case of Warwick was exceptional, and even there this weighting in favour of the suburbs need not have persisted very long. By the sixteenth century, and probably before, the balance had swung back to the town. Of the nine wealthiest men in Warwick, assessed for the subsidy of 1543, all lived in the town wards and none in the suburbs. Only the suburb at Bridge End had remained reasonably

46

prosperous; at West Street, the proportion of low to middling taxpayers was just about average for the borough; at Smith Street and at Saltisford, there were unusually high percentages of taxpayers of the lowest class.[28]

At Winchester, identical tax records have been employed by Dr Keene to demonstrate that the suburbs, although populous, were poor. While, that is, the Winchester suburbs (Fig. 16) are likely to have held between them somewhat more than a third of the entire population of the city, their share of its wealth was restricted. In 1340, there were no wealthy taxpayers at all in the suburb called the 'Soke', outside the east and south gates of the city, and over the suburbs as a whole, the incidence of the poor, or the relatively poor, was higher than within the walled area. By the sixteenth century, when these become measurable again in the subsidy assessments of the 1520s, neither the proportion of suburban to city dwellers nor their relative wealth had shown any signs of change.[29] Where, as at Leicester, suburban growth was rapid, this was not to accommodate the wealthy. Only some seventeen per cent of the taxpayers at Leicester in 1269–71 are identifiably suburban, as against as much as forty-five per cent in 1524–5, but at no time did these numbers include the more substantial men of the borough. Not every Leicester suburban dweller was poor, of course, and some suburbs were noticeably worse off than others. Yet it would be true to say of the suburbs in general that while being the most densely populated area in late-medieval Leicester, they were also its poorest sector.[30]

Just how densely populated and how poor such suburbs were, it is usually impossible to say, for the unassessably poor had no reason to feature in the records. Yet there are occasions, too, when the very silence of the records may itself be considered significant. At Southampton, no special distinction was made, in the subsidy returns of 1524, between the inner and the outer wards of the borough (Fig. 105). However, it was All Saints, the only ward to stretch beyond the walls into the suburbs of Southampton, that held the highest proportion of taxpayers assessed at the lowest rate. Similarly, at Portswood, a distant suburb which alone of the suburban areas had its own section in the accounts, the wealthiest taxpayer, Robert Baker, was assessed at no more than £7, where assessments of £20 and over were common within the borough; of the total of twenty-one taxpayers assessable in Portswood, fully eighteen were rated at no more than £1. Seventy years before, the terrier of 1454, a very full list of the properties within Southampton's walls compiled as an aid to the apportionment of

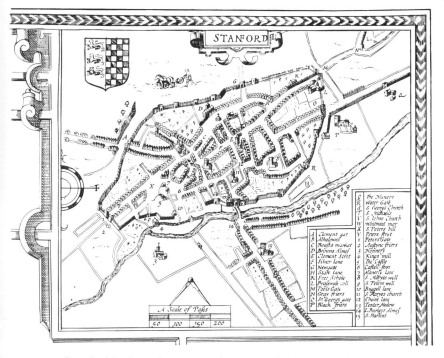

The legend on the map reads:

STANFORD

A Clement gat
B Althalowes
C Beasts market
D Brouns Almes
E Clement Stret
F Silver lane
G Newgate
H Stane lane
K Free Schole
L Brasenose coll
M Tyste Gate
N Gray friers
O St Georgs gate
P Black friers

E The Nunery
K Water Gate
S S Georgi Church
T S Michaels
V S Johns Church
W Whitmeat mar
X S Peters hill
Y Peters fret
1 Peters Gate
2 Austyne friers
3 Nonnery
4 Kings mill
5 The Castle
6 Castell fret
7 Waverly lane
8 S Maryes well
9 S Peters well
10 Buggell lane
11 S Maryes church
12 Chaine lane
13 Tenter Medow
14 L Burleys Almes
15 S Martins

A Scale of Paſes
50   100   150   200

17 Stamford in the early seventeenth century, showing the typical spread
of its medieval suburbs (Speed)

defence charges, had already shown that whereas six per cent of the then
occupied properties in the walled borough were to be ranked as 'capital'
tenements and some sixty per cent as either tenements or 'small' tenements, only thirty per cent could be described as cottages. Conceivably, the poorest dwellings at Southampton were not listed in the
terrier, as not liable to defence charges in the town. Yet the document
itself is exceptionally complete, sufficient evidence for a convincing map
to be compiled of the tenement pattern in the late-medieval town, and
the small total of cottages recorded there can suggest only that the
labouring poor lived, for the most part, outside the defended *enceinte* of
the borough, and that the very poorest, unidentifiable in any surviving
record, are likely to have done the same. On this and other evidence, the
rich in medieval Southampton, at least from the building of its first
systematic defences, undoubtedly avoided the suburbs.[31]

It was this relative poverty of the majority of the suburbs that

18 Troy ruined and reconstructed, French, late-fifteenth-century

prevented their systematic development. Characteristically, they stretched out in an untidy ribbon along the lines of the principal approach roads (Figs. 17 and 99), clustering in particular about the enlarged open spaces that were usually to be met with at the gates. Although commonly within the franchise of the town, the suburb stood physically in relation to its begetter rather as did the surrounding countryside, firmly excluded by its walls. Indeed, if the rich and middling burgesses of a town like Southampton were to choose to live within the walls of their borough, it was only partly because they welcomed the security such fortifications could provide. For them, as for many in their situation, the borough defences would have stood as a permanent reminder of an important legal and social distinction, built up over many years and at great cost, between the town and the countryside beyond. No suburban dweller in medieval England could have been unaware of the potential disadvantages of his situation.

19 The city of Campision, English, *circa* 1400
20 The storming of the city of Baudas, English, *circa* 1400

Typically, it was their walls that the men of London and of Canterbury, of Oxford, Colchester and Shrewsbury, chose to depict on their seals. In contemporary art, it was the wall of a city which identified it (Figs. 18–20).[32]

The fortification of the English boroughs, although never as complete nor as sophisticated as that of their equivalents on the Continent, is not without an interest of its own. In the first place, it was perhaps more general than is often acknowledged, for there were no fewer than 108 towns in England and Wales that acquired fortifications of their own. In the second, whether or not a borough was fortified might depend less on considerations of defence than upon the nature of its allegiance. Broadly, it was the privileged royal borough that was defended, and the seigneurial borough that frequently went unwalled.[33]

Well illustrating the attractions of a work that had more than military objectives to recommend it, the great fortified circuit of Coventry (Fig. 99) was constructed only after the borough had secured its independence. Over the 200 years it took to complete, the Coventry defensive system absorbed much of the surplus revenue of the borough, but it stood, even while building, as a notable expression of corporate independence and pride. Promising security and good government, it attracted trade to the town.[34] In contemporary Hull, it was precisely

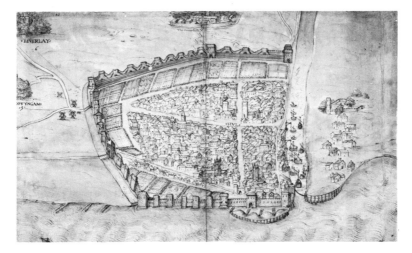

21 Kingston upon Hull in the early sixteenth century

this quality in the enhancement of trade which was advanced by the burgesses in 1321 as their first reason for walling the town.[35] Prosperous, like Coventry, while other towns were suffering a decline, Hull built itself, through the second half of the fourteenth century, a massive circuit wall studded with interval towers (Fig. 21), one of which has recently been excavated. Constructed of locally manufactured bricks, it was probably the first major public work in medieval England to have been carried out in this new material.[36]

Where Coventry and Hull were able to complete their walls, there were many more towns in medieval England that started their circuits than were ever able to finish them. The stone wall, although certainly projected at Ipswich, was probably never begun; it would have replaced the rampart and ditch defences which the burgesses had put up early in the thirteenth century, shortly after receiving their charter.[37] At King's Lynn, too, the ramparts were never wholly replaced, while on the stone wall itself the quality of workmanship noticeably deteriorated as, over the years, it was extended.[38] It was not so much that the burgesses lost their enthusiasm for walls, as that they could not generally afford them. Early rampart and ditch defences, of eleventh- or twelfth-century date, have been identified at a number of towns,[39] and there are cases also of surviving Roman defences, with late-Saxon earthworks at least one of which, at Hereford, was massively revetted in stone.[40] But the building

51

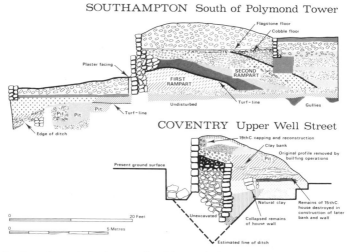

SOUTHAMPTON South of Polymond Tower

Flagstone floor
Cobble floor
Plaster facing
SECOND RAMPART
FIRST RAMPART
Undisturbed
Turf-line
Gullies
Turf-line
Pit
Pit
Pit
Edge of ditch

COVENTRY Upper Well Street

19thC. capping and reconstruction
Clay bank
Original profile removed by building operations
Present ground surface
Pit
Natural clay
Remains of 15thC. house destroyed in construction of later bank and wall
Unexcavated
Collapsed remains of house wall
Estimated line of ditch

0   20 Feet
0   5 Metres

22 Sections through the late-medieval borough defences of Southampton and Coventry, both of which re-used the line of earlier works (Wacher and Hobley)

23 The city wall of York, looking towards Monk Bar

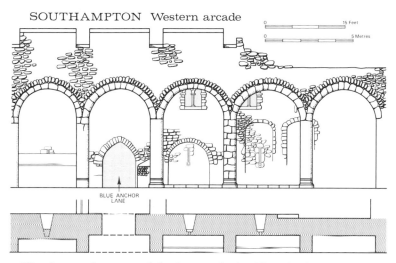

24 The fourteenth-century defensive arcade by Blue Anchor Lane, Southampton, incorporating late-twelfth-century house fronts (Department of the Environment)

of a full set of masonry defences, however desirable this might be, was a task of a different order, and every kind of economy was attempted. The progressive enlargement of a defended area, seen at Bristol (Fig. 100) and matched in many cities on the Continent,[41] was rarely sought in England. If a line of Roman or Anglo-Saxon defences already existed, it was re-adopted, with few exceptions, by the medieval wall; if a new programme of works were attempted, it might exclude, as in early-thirteenth-century Southampton, an important area of settlement.[42] England, as Girolamo Lando was later to observe, 'truly enjoys remarkable advantages with the sea as its wall and moat'.[43] Accustomed to the benefits of stable government, and unused to civil disorder, the towns found it hard, as Edward III would discover, to take seriously the task, and the burden, of fortification. A recent programme of repairs to the walls which had been carried out at Gloucester with reasonable efficiency so long as the emergency lasted, had then been allowed to lapse. In 1360, Edward expressed himself 'much surprised', for he held it advisable, as he carefully explained, that the city should be 'well fortified in time of peace as of war'.[44]

If the purpose of Gloucester's wall had been military alone, nobody might have doubted the justice of the king's complaint. However, it is probably true to say that a wall that was incomplete or ruinous, for the

53

purposes it was called upon to fulfil, might have served the average town at least as well as one that had been properly maintained. Few towns took as long as Coventry to complete their walls, but, for all except those directly hurried by the king, it was a wearisome and piecemeal process, spreading, usually, over a period of five decades or more.[45] The flimsiest barrier was already enough to protect the town's rights in its tolls, and there was little to speed the work. Murage, or wall-building, moneys, rarely sufficient for the task in hand, had frequently to be dissipated on repairs. The walls themselves, constructed in short annual stints, were ramshackle and given to collapse. In instructive contrast, the difference between the fine work on the king's gatehouse in Southampton and the shoddy workmanship and plainly inadequate foundations of the town wall has been revealed by recent excavations. Where the king's overseers at the castle had been careful to ensure high standards of stonework and design, it is abundantly clear that the borough officials had skimped and saved wherever they could on the construction of Southampton's town wall (Fig. 22). For centuries, little but its own weight, and the support of an adjoining much later building, stopped Arundel Tower, at the north-west corner of the town, from slipping down its bank into the sea. Further south, along the line of the wall, the façades of surviving houses, dating back to the late twelfth century, had been incorporated in the fourteenth-century arcade (Fig. 24). Parts of other houses, further south again, were left standing intact in the body of the wall as an additional economy in its construction.[46]

Unimportant though the town wall may frequently have been as a military obstacle, there can be no doubt of its vital contribution to the plan of the town, or of its effect on the fortunes of individual trading areas. The borough of Alnwick, although fortified only in the fifteenth century with a wall that was noticeably short-lived, still shows in its plan the line of the former defences, preserved in the peripheral streets that ring the medieval town.[47] Older defensive circuits were, of course, even more influential, dictating not merely the alignment of the streets but also their value for trading. Winchester's High Street, linking the two main gates of the city on a former Roman line, remained its principal trading sector. Inevitably, licences to sell on the High Street were more expensive and more difficult to obtain than those on the many side-streets, known as 'blind' streets, that were blocked at the far end by the wall. In encroachments, too, on the line of the streets, the same effects were visible. On the High Street, encroachments on which were strictly controlled from a very early date, the house frontages at Winchester can be shown to have moved little, if at all, from the eleventh until the twentieth centuries. In contrast, on the side-streets, where controls were applied less strictly, frontages at the more popular end of the street, towards the High Street, moved appreciably forward over the years, creating a characteristic funnelling of the streets outwards towards the walls, where their closing had stifled development or had prevented it ever occurring.[48] A much later closing-off of the waterfront in four-teenth-century Southampton, blocked from the sea by a wall, brought a once prosperous sector of the borough, the site of many fine houses, to a condition of permanent decline.[49] No doubt for fear of just such a consequence, an equivalent waterfront at the Norfolk port of King's Lynn, with its important warehousing and wharves (Fig. 25), was never adequately fortified.[50]

Crucial in determining the speed of the response to a new obstacle, such as a wall, was the habit of every medieval burgess of living where he would trade. Characteristically, the failure to distinguish a residential from a commercial sector in the town made of each street a market of its own, the better for being more accessible. And in each of these markets, as is still true today, specialization by trade might occur. Such specialization, it has sometimes been said, was less a characteristic of the later medieval town than of the earlier; and perhaps, to a limited extent, this was so. But at no time was the grouping of the more important trades and crafts in the medieval town confined only to those industries like cloth-making which depended, for example, on an accessible supply of running water. In almost every English town, the small specialized market kept individual trades together, and at the general market, also, grouping by speciality was just as likely to occur. At Salisbury market, later colonized by permanent stalls and shops (Fig. 13), there came to be a Butcher Row, a Pot Row, a Cordwainer Row, an Ironmonger Row, a Wheeler Row and a Fish Row.[51] Elsewhere, individual markets might be scattered through the town. There were separate markets for corn, hay and livestock in thirteenth-century Stratford-upon-Avon, and probably for poultry and dairy produce as well.[52] The street markets of medieval Ipswich (Fig. 95), although within the same general area of the town, gathered separately to dispose of corn and bread, dairy products, apples and wine, meat, poultry, fish and pies, timber and cloth.[53]

It had been noted by FitzStephen of late-twelfth-century London that 'those engaged in business of various kinds, sellers of merchandise, hirers of labour, are distributed every morning into their several localities according to their trade'.[54] And while there may have been

some dispersal of the London trades in later centuries, as is thought to have occurred at Oxford,[55] a degree of occupational zoning remained throughout the Middle Ages a characteristic of trade in the capital. It was with Walbrook Ward, for example, that the skinners were long associated, having vintners, cordwainers and other trade groups as neighbours.[56] Nor would it be the unexpected concentration of shops but their wealth that would cause an Italian visitor, late in the fifteenth century, to observe that 'in one single street, named the Strand, leading to St Paul's, there are fifty-two goldsmiths' shops, so rich and full of silver vessels, great and small, that in all the shops in Milan, Rome, Venice, and Florence put together, I do not think there would be found so many of the magnificence that are to be seen in London.'[57]

In general, however, the concentration of trades was by quarter rather than by street, and it could be dictated by specialist needs. In fifteenth-century Salisbury (Fig. 13), whereas the weavers and tuckers chose usually to live in St Martin's Ward, the dyers concentrated particularly in Market Ward, by the river Avon, and a similar riverside location in New Street Ward evidently suited the skinners, the tailors, the saddlers and the curriers.[58] From the twelfth century or earlier, it was the plentiful supply of fresh running water which attracted the dyers and tanners to the Brooks area of medieval Winchester;[59] there were fullers settled by the river at Stratford, King's Lynn and Alnwick;[60] and at Norwich, recent excavations at Westwick Street, by the river, have uncovered the remains of a long-lived late-medieval dye-house (Fig. 26).[61]

Where natural advantages drew particular trades, others were more consciously directed by social pressures or municipal fiat. That 'generalized pattern of zoning by occupation', which is said to have been characteristic of medieval King's Lynn, was altering in the sixteenth century and before, to the exclusion of the industrial craftsmen.[62] And everywhere the banishment of the unsocial crafts took effect in the later Middle Ages. The butchers, the fishmongers and the tanners, notorious offenders in matters of public hygiene, were assigned specific localities where their trades could do least harm. Nothing more is heard, after the early fourteenth century, of the 'street of the smiths', once the northern end of Southampton's High Street,[63] and the potters too, as much a fire

25 King's Lynn from the air, with the churches of St Margaret (top centre) and All Saints (bottom left), and with Hampton Court, the Hanse Steelyard and Thoresby College by the quay

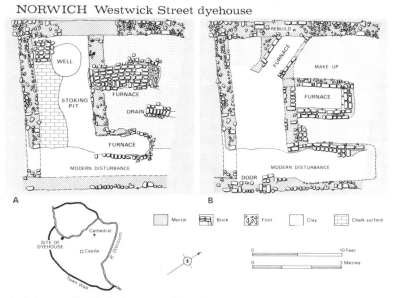

26 A late-medieval dyehouse at Westwick Street, Norwich, showing changes in the plan over successive periods of use (Roberts)

risk as the smiths, were commonly excluded, at least in the later period, from the more densely populated areas in the towns. At York, it was not just the availability of a suitable raw material that kept the tile-makers outside the city walls, in Bishops Fields; nor this that kept the tileries and the lime-kilns outside Hull.[64] Such potters' kilns as have been excavated at Doncaster and Chichester have been found located in the suburbs.[65]

The banishment of the noxious trades was one thing. But the usual purpose of municipal authorities was to concentrate trade rather than to disperse it, and it was to this end that they concerned themselves, from a very early date, with the maintenance of at least those principal thoroughfares on which the trade of the borough first centred. It was the discouragement of trade that worried those who sought, in late-medieval Southampton, to compel all householders with frontages on the main streets of the borough to contribute to the renewal of the paving: English Street, French Street and Bull Street had become 'full perilous and jepardouce to ride or goo theryn'.[66] Nor were these new concerns.

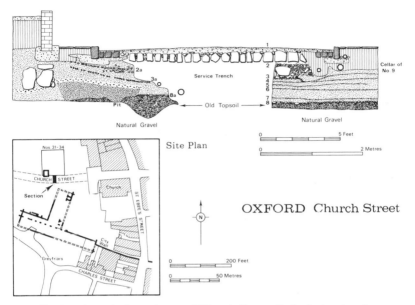

27 Section through the make-up of Church Street, Oxford, showing the lines of successive gravel road surfaces over a layer of pre-Conquest paving (Hassall)

In 1286, four citizens of Lincoln had been commissioned to 'arrange for the paving of the high road running through the said town, taking care that the better sort who have tenements on or abutting upon the said road contribute thereto in proportion to their tenements'.[67] And already, before the Conquest, the earliest surface of Church Street, Oxford, identified in recent excavations in St Aldate's, was stone-paved, in contrast to many of its identifiable successors (Fig. 27).[68] Usually, the material for road surfacing and repairs at Oxford was gravel (Fig. 28). At Winchester, it was a spread of small flints over chalk, on top of which rubbish accumulated swiftly. In scarcely more than a century and a half of use, an early street found sealed below the remains of the castle at Winchester had built up an accumulation no less than five feet in thickness, within which eight successive road surfaces have been identified.[69] It was a problem which continued to concern the more active borough authorities, with varying degrees of success. Even London, with its relatively sophisticated hierarchy of scavengers and rakers,[70] failed to meet it entirely. It was in November, just when conditions were at their worst, that Andreas Franciscus wrote of London:

28 Section across Castle Street, Oxford, showing successive medieval road surfaces, cut by modern drains

All the streets are so badly paved that they get wet at the slightest quantity of water, and this happens very frequently owing to the large numbers of cattle carrying water, as well as on account of the rain, of which there is a great deal in this island. Then a vast amount of evil-smelling mud is formed, which does not disappear quickly but lasts a long time, in fact nearly the whole year round.[71]

Of course, nobody welcomed such conditions in the towns, and efforts were made constantly to remedy them. The provision of adequate paving, and its subsequent protection against feckless carters with overheavy loads or with iron-shod wheels on their carts, was to become the concern of almost every late-medieval municipal authority, and increasingly, too, the towns were to recognize the failure of the policy that had placed the burden on the individual householder. In a striking instance of the extension of municipal concerns, the appointment of a salaried paviour at Southampton in 1482 followed swiftly on the acknowledgement of the town's right to charge householders the cost of paving repairs: he was to survey the state of the paving, to effect repairs where necessary, and to collect his expenses from the householder.[72] Nottingham's municipal paviour, appointed in 1501, was to be assigned the yearly wage of 33s 4d and a gown. He was to draw his supplies of stone and sand from the borough chamberlains, and would 'make and mend all the defaults in all places of the said town in the pavements'.[73]

As important in the preservation of the main thoroughfares was the

29 Southampton, the medieval town, showing the broad central line of the High Street

prevention of permanent encroachments. Noticed already at Winchester, where the effects are still observable on the city's plan (see pp. 54–5), such action continued to be needed so long as street trading was practised in the boroughs and as the distinction between temporary stall and permanent shop persisted ill-defined. It was perhaps to guard against such encroachments that the bishop of Worcester, in laying out his new borough of Stratford-upon-Avon, provided for streets fifty feet wide, or more, and it certainly illustrates the dangers of which he and others must have been aware, that it was precisely the most important of these streets, itself ninety feet wide and the principal thoroughfare of the town, that sprouted a permanent row of shops down its middle.[74]

Permanent encroachments of this kind, a form of market colonization, were to occur in many of the market streets of English towns, becoming a feature, for example, of early-modern Briggate, the original market thoroughfare of Leeds.[75] Yet it was, too, the continuing market purpose of other similar streets that operated to keep them wide and clear. The fine proportions of Southampton's High Street (Fig. 29), and of its extra-mural extension Above Bar, testify to the lasting importance of this imposing thoroughfare to the commercial life of both the medieval and the modern town. It was on the High Street, at St Lawrence church door, that the principal market was located in medieval Southampton, to be moved southwards in the sixteenth century, still along the line of the

30 The Shambles, York, early this century

31 (opposite) Tenement plots on Southampton's High Street, as surveyed in 1845-6 for an unpublished sixty-inch Ordnance Survey map of the town (Ordnance Survey)

same street, to more commodious covered quarters in Holy Rood. And it was here, on the High Street or just off it, that the butchers and the poulterers, the smiths, the innkeepers and many of the wealthiest merchants of Southampton chose, at one time or another, to settle.[76] When, in the late fifteenth century, William Worcestre paced out the streets of Bristol, he recorded widths at several of these of just over fifty feet, and at many others of thirty-five feet or more.[77] And while it is true that there were lanes and alleys in medieval Bristol as narrow as eight or nine feet and a few not much wider than six, the essential quality of the borough's plan, as at many lesser towns, was the comparatively open structure that it owed to its broad market streets. The jury which spoke of thirteenth-century Winchester as if its whole street system were its market-place,[78] came very close to the truth. It was Winchester's market function that had contributed to the shaping of the original city, and it was its markets that kept it so.

In much the same way, it was the continuing value placed on market street frontages that determined both the plan of the original burgage plot and the nature of the house, or houses, set upon it. Characteristically, the burgage plot was much deeper than it was wide, giving a

SOUTHAMPTON

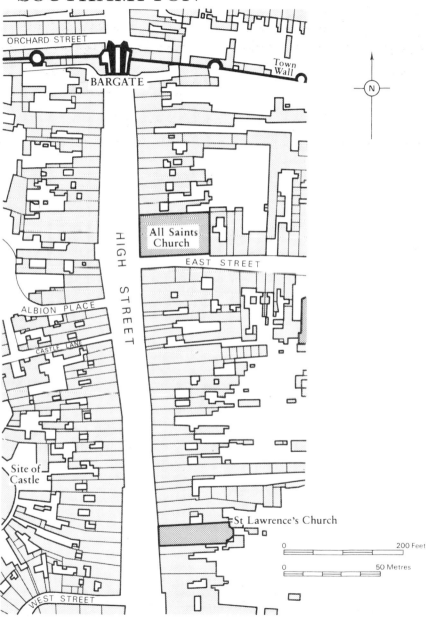

ORCHARD STREET

Town Wall

BARGATE

N

HIGH STREET

All Saints Church

EAST STREET

ALBION PLACE

CASTLE LANE

Site of Castle

St Lawrence's Church

WEST STREET

| 0 | | | 200 Feet |
| 0 | | | 50 Metres |

ratio of depth to width which, at Alnwick at least, was generally in excess of 6:1.[79] Such a deliberately drawn-out plan, with its narrow trading frontage, was not to be found as regularly on the less frequented back- and side-streets of the towns, and at all towns the shape of an individual plot might be distorted by an existing natural feature such as a stream, a gully or a cliff, or by the intrusion of a church, a monastic precinct or a castle. Nevertheless, the clear advantage of the rectangular over any other plan, presenting the short side to the street, was as obvious in favoured built-up areas of the medieval town as it continues to be in similar conditions today. In 1155, the king himself would recognize this when he determined his tariffs at Scarborough: 'And they shall pay to me yearly, for each house in Scarborough whose gable is turned towards the street four pence, and for those houses whose sides are turned towards the street, six pence.'[80]

Plots might be narrow in most medieval towns, but they were not, by the same token, small. The little we know of the earliest burgage plots is enough already to suggest that some, at least, were large.[81] And in later generations, certainly, generous allocations of land to new settlers characterized many of the speculative new town plantations of twelfth- and thirteenth-century England. Late in the twelfth century, the burgesses of Stratford-upon-Avon were attracted there by tenement plots almost sixty feet by two hundred; while at contemporary Burton-upon-Trent the chosen dimensions were nearer seventy feet by four hundred, and half-acre plots were far from unusual in many other Midland towns.[82] Inevitably, some subdivision of the original plots occurred within decades of the first settlement. At Banbury, a small episcopal borough of twelfth-century foundation, many plots had already been divided by 1225, this crowding of the central area of the borough testifying to its immediate commercial success.[83] Yet in many cases, among them Stratford again, the large burgage plots of the original allocation of lands remained substantially intact throughout the Middle Ages or, if divided, were partitioned only in half. Mason's Court, one of the great houses of fifteenth-century Stratford, was built along the street frontage, not at right-angles to it. Its central hall, with flanking wings, covered a total frontage of just over fifty feet, only a little less than the three and a half perches of the original twelfth-century plot.[84]

32 Remains of a lane, medieval town houses and a bakery, excavated in 1973 behind Goodramgate, York

OXFORD Oriel College Tenements

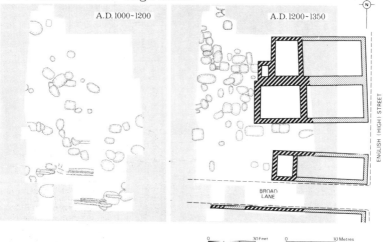

34 Pits and beam-slots as evidence of early settlement west of the High Street, Southampton, subsequently overlain by large stone-built tenements and by a new east-west lane (Platt and Coleman-Smith)
33 (opposite) Built-up tenement plots in the parish of St Mary, Oxford, as mapped for Oriel College in 1814

Mason's Court is not unique. It belongs to that category of English town house described by the late Dr Pantin as of 'extended parallel' plan,[85] and is matched at Stamford, in Lincolnshire, as at several other towns, where the parallel plan remained, despite its extravagant use of street frontage, the more popular.[86] Nevertheless, it was the plot running back from the street, characteristically both long and narrow, that more usually set the pattern for development in the towns, and it was to this that the rural hall-house, in a number of ingenious ways, would have over the years to be adapted. It was the hall, essentially, that remained throughout the Middle Ages the basic element of all but the most diminutive of town houses. And it was by solution of problems of lighting and access to this hall that the typical town-house plan evolved, responsive continually to the narrowing of plot frontages, as the better favoured trading area in each town became more crowded.

When, in the earlier period, plot areas had been large, there was little to govern or to standardize building practice upon them. At the end of the eleventh century, a substantial house on Tanner Street, in Winchester, might still be built parallel to the street, in contrast to the

35 Medieval rubbish pits and a nineteenth-century well in the back yards of High Street tenements, Southampton, excavated in 1968; scale in half-metres

right-angle tenements succeeding it, and it was only in the next century that the large open yard behind the house was developed.[87] Open yards, with traces of livestock enclosures, have been identified, too, in the earliest levels at Southampton and King's Lynn.[88] They belong to communities still strongly rural in their habits, which would be replaced in the late twelfth and thirteenth centuries by men of a markedly more urban disposition. It was early in the thirteenth century that great stone houses began to be built along the line of the High Street at Southampton, crowding the sites and cutting across the remains of earlier settlement (Fig. 34). Usually, they were set with their gable ends facing the street, and they were equipped in each case with a small yard at the side or to the rear, useful only for the disposal of rubbish (Fig. 35). In the story of urban beginnings at Southampton, even that rubbish is significant. The broken pottery alone would be sufficient to tell us that the trading emphasis of the port had begun to swing from Normandy and the Rhineland, predominantly to south-west France. But still more interesting is the bone and botanical evidence. The bone recovered from twelfth-century pits in Southampton has usually derived from large joints or even whole carcasses, suggesting butchery and per-haps stock-keeping on the sites. In the thirteenth century, as butchery

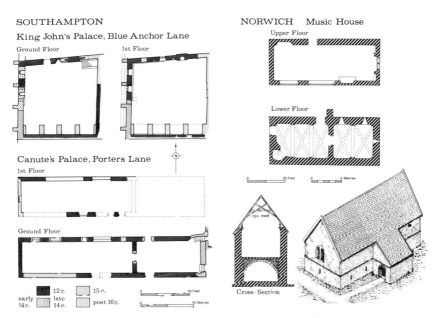

SOUTHAMPTON

King John's Palace, Blue Anchor Lane

Ground Floor   1st Floor

Canute's Palace, Porters Lane
1st Floor

Ground Floor

early 14 c.   12 c.   15 c.
late 14 c.   post 16 c.

NORWICH   Music House

Upper Floor

Lower Floor

15c. roof

Cross-Section

36 Late-twelfth-century burgess housing at Southampton (Faulkner)
37 The late-twelfth-century Music House, at Norwich. Plan and section
by H. J. T. Gowen; reconstruction adapted from the reconstruction by
A. P. Baggs (Lipman)

became a specialized trade, concentrating in markets of its own, the size
of the joints was reduced and the choice of meats widened appreciably.
The same enlarged choice, with evidence of increasing trading contacts
with the South, may be found in the botanical remains. Seeds of elder
and of nettle were the best that a twelfth-century pit could produce. By
the middle of the thirteenth century, the burgesses of Southampton
could afford to indulge more extravagant tastes. Along with the pottery
and the bone in their rubbish pits, there were the remains of grapes, of
figs and of walnuts, all very probably imported. From local markets,
they had purchased a variety of regional produce, including raspberries
and strawberries, sloes, cherries, plums and hazelnuts.[89]

Although little is known of the earliest burgess dwellings at
Southampton, except that they were of timber-frame construction in-
filled with wattle and daub, there are still survivors of their immediate
successors. Stone buildings of the late twelfth century remain on Porters
Lane and on Blue Anchor Lane, down by the shore. Another was
recently excavated on Cuckoo Lane, behind the surviving town wall

38 The undercroft of the late-twelfth-century Music House, Norwich

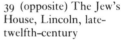

39 (opposite) The Jew's House, Lincoln, late-twelfth-century

which incorporates part of its structure, and a fourth, on the High Street, was recorded before demolition. While not unlike the contemporary 'upper-hall' manor-house of the countryside, these are yet distinctively urban buildings. Each incorporated both the dwelling of the merchant and a space for a warehouse or shop. At Porters Lane, the building usually known as 'Canute's Palace' is an 'upper-hall' house of classic pattern, with the hall and chamber of the upper floor repeated exactly down below; to it, a separate warehouse attaches at the eastern end, with a chamber over it, which may have served originally as a counting house (Fig. 36). Of the other three houses, all of which were probably double-range buildings with their gables against the street or the quay, none show any evidence that the ground floor had other purposes than warehousing and display. Over it, the dwelling quarters on the first floor were approached by an external stair. They consisted of a hall and a chamber, or chambers, divided from each other by the central spine wall which supported the junction of the two gables. At each house, the kitchen, for which there is no structural evidence remaining, is likely to have been a separate building in the yard.[90]

Nothing connects these Southampton houses with the Jewish financiers allegedly the builders of equivalent houses elsewhere, nor is there,

of course, anything essentially Jewish about the plan of a house of this type. One of those with a probably authentic Jewish connection is the 'Music House' at Norwich (Fig. 37), now sometimes known as 'Jurnet's House' after the Jew who may have built it. Measuring 18ft 9in by 52ft 6in internally, the Norwich Music House is not unlike the western residential block of the Porters Lane house at Southampton. But it is entered by way of an external ground-floor porch, for which there is no comparable evidence at Southampton, and it is by a newel stair, set in the thickness of the wall, that the two lower chambers of the Norwich house are connected with its great upper chamber, or hall (Fig. 38).[91]

In the same tradition, there are fine early stone houses at Lincoln (the 'Jew's House' (Fig. 39) and 'Aaron the Jew's House') and at Bury St Edmunds ('Moyses Hall'), nor is there any reason to doubt that the fashion was more general than this. At Canterbury, certainly, by the early thirteenth century, there were thirty stone houses or more, some of them very large.[92] And it was the size as well as the expense of such houses that attracted the attention of contemporaries. For many years, the 'great stone houses' of Richard of Leicester, an early-thirteenth-century notable of Southampton, remained a landmark in the port. Other stone houses had been built by his associates, Master Roger, the

40 Carpenters at work: Noah building the Ark, French, early-fifteenth-century

41 (opposite) Southampton burgess houses of the early fourteenth and the fifteenth centuries in French Street and the High Street (Faulkner)

brother of Gervase, Walter le Fleming, a shipowner, John de la Bulehuse, of a long-lived family line, and the Norman, Roger de Tankerville.[93]

No doubt, the conversion to building in stone had something to do with fire precautions. It had been urged for this reason in fitz Ailwin's London building assize of 1189, and there had been London citizens before this date who had sought to secure their goods in stone buildings roofed with tiles.[94] But there were other reasons, too, for deciding upon such an expensive and showy material, not least of these personal prestige. The major campaign of stone-building in the towns coincides with the confirmation of their liberties, and it was as short-lived as the excitement itself. Nevertheless, before it ended, the burgesses of Southampton had had the opportunity to display, for all to see, the motives that had driven them to such perfectionism. In wishing to honour the Franciscan friars who had settled in their town in 1233/4, they had set about the building of a new stone 'cloister', against the stern principles of the order. Almost immediately, they were to watch it demolished on the command of Albert of Pisa, the provincial minister, to be replaced by humbler quarters of timber, wattle and daub.[95]

The austerities forced on the wealthy burgesses of Southampton were

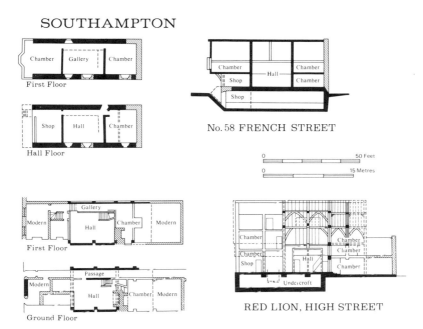

No. 58 FRENCH STREET

RED LION, HIGH STREET

elsewhere unavoidable from the beginning. Whereas there is a growing body of evidence, both in the towns[96] and in the countryside,[97] for an increase in the use of stone for building from early in the thirteenth century, complete stone buildings of the Southampton kind can never have been more than rarities. At Southampton itself, the timber-framed structure and external stone cladding of 58 French Street (Fig. 41) probably represent a very common solution to the problems of fire and expense.[98] At Canterbury, at least one of the early stone houses mentioned in the rentals was constructed partially of timber,[99] and at other towns, while stone might be used in the construction of a hall, the shops and other chambers that fronted or adjoined it were more commonly finished in timber.[100] Indeed, it was in this mixed tradition, part timber and part stone, that the town house typically evolved. In later years, it was to be by sophistication of carpentry, above all, that the best use would be made of town plots (Fig. 40).

It was the partitioning of plots, already becoming a reality in the thirteenth century and very common in the later Middle Ages, which forced a re-thinking of the typical town-house plan. Sometimes it can be watched in detail, as at the messuage called 'Peperestede', in the parish of St Mary Tower, Ipswich, first partitioned in 1324 and then re-divided some forty years later.[101] More often, it can be recognized only as an accomplished fact, the explanation, for example, of that division of properties in late-medieval Swansea which secured that of all the tenements assigned in 1400 to Elizabeth, dowager-duchess of Norfolk, almost twice as many were half-burgages as were whole, and there were many quarter and other fractional burgages as well.[102] Nevertheless, whatever the form partitioning would take, what it demonstrates most clearly is the continuing importance of a good street frontage, against which all other considerations were secondary. It was to obtain maximum value from the frontage that almost every partitioning expedient was devised. And it was this, of course, that was most clearly reflected in the late-medieval town-house plan.

Two obvious solutions presented themselves. The first, and always the more popular, was a straightforward parcelling-up of the available frontage, narrowing the plots to the rear. It was this that led to the building of houses of *right-angle* type, with a gable or no more than a short wing facing the street. They are assignable to Dr Pantin's *narrow* or *broad* plan categories, depending on whether there is a gable or a wing at the front. The second solution, adopted in some larger properties, was the partitioning of the frontage alone, to form a number of separate shop units, each of which would be let or even sold on its own. Behind these shops, the tenement could be kept independent, making full use of the width, as well as most of the depth, of the original burgage plot, It was this that contributed to the emergence of the *double-range* and *courtyard* plans, especially suitable for houses of *parallel* type.[103]

One example of the *narrow* plan house of *right-angle* type is the early-fourteenth-century building at 58 French Street (Fig. 41), Southampton, already cited above (p. 73) to illustrate an economical combination of timber construction and stone. A three-part house of six bays, 58 French Street has a central two-bay hall with equal-length chamber blocks at either end, the whole being set on a vaulted undercroft of stone. As was usually the case with such buildings, the hall was open to the roof, communication between the two upper chambers, at front and back, being by way of a side gallery. Next to the street, both the front part of the undercroft and its overlying ground-floor chamber had probably been designed as shops, while the equivalent ground-floor chamber at the back may have served as a counting-house. Like the hall,

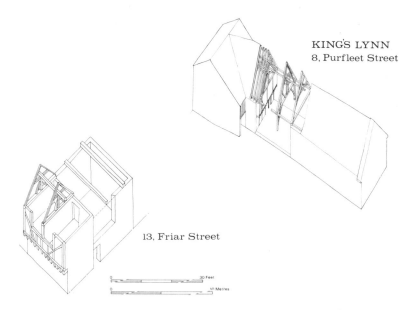

KING'S LYNN
8, Purfleet Street

13, Friar Street

0 _____ 30 Feet
0 _____ 10 Metres

42 Late-medieval *right-angle* houses of *broad* plan in Purfleet Street and Friar Street, King's Lynn (Parker)

both upper chambers were unceilinged and open to the rafters.[104]

At French Street, where the plot was wide enough to allow it, entrance to the hall could be by way of a side door, in addition to whatever access there might be through the ground-floor shop at the front. But this, on crowded urban sites, was not always a workable plan, and a common variant in the late-medieval town, making full use of the whole available frontage, may be seen in another Southampton building, the fifteenth-century burgess tenement now the Red Lion (Fig. 41), on the High Street. The Red Lion, which is set on an earlier stone-built undercroft, is a good example of a timber-framed town house of the more sophisticated kind, three-storeyed and formerly jettied at the front in two stages. Like the French Street house, which it resembles in many particulars of its plan, it is of six bays, the unusually high central hall being open through the full three storeys to the roof. In this case, however, access to the hall was blocked on both sides by existing tenements, and the house had to be provided with an entrance passage running the whole length of the building and supporting, through the hall, a connecting gallery from which access could be had to both first

75

OXFORD Tackley's Inn

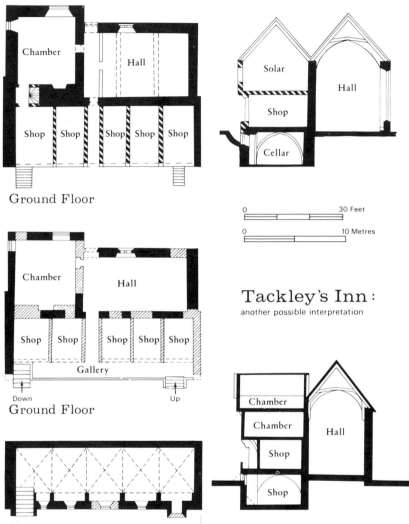

Ground Floor

Chamber
Hall
Shop Shop Shop Shop Shop

Solar
Hall
Shop
Cellar

0   30 Feet

0   10 Metres

Ground Floor

Chamber
Hall
Shop Shop Shop Shop Shop
Gallery
Down   Up

Undercroft

Tackley's Inn:
another possible interpretation

Chamber
Chamber
Shop
Hall
Shop

43 Tackley's Inn, Oxford, a *double-range* tenement of *parallel* type, dating to the late thirteenth or early fourteenth centuries. Shown in the alternative versions of the late W. A. Pantin (above) and of P. A. Faulkner (below)

44 (opposite) The courtyard at Strangers' Hall, Norwich, fifteenth-century

and second-floor chambers. At the Red Lion, there was no basement shop, the space being entered from the far end, away from the street, and being usable only for storage.[105]

As with other houses of its type, of which there are many surviving examples, the Red Lion at Southampton demonstrates two important complementary tendencies in late-medieval English town-house architecture, the one being to widen the structure to take full advantage of the entire available street frontage, the other being to increase its height. Southampton's High Street was lined with such houses, as 'fair', as the young Edward VI would note, as any that London could offer.[106] But the *narrow* plan was not everywhere as generally in use as it came to be in late-medieval Southampton, and at King's Lynn, for example, the preference would seem always to have been for *right-angle* houses of *broad* plan, with a short wing fronting on the street. The street-front range of such a building, as was probably the case at 8 Purfleet Street (Fig. 42), would have included a shop, or a workroom, on the ground floor, with a chamber above it, and with a passage through to the rear of the tenement, on the side. The hall, accommodated in the long range behind, which was set at right-angles to the line of the street, commonly abutted directly on the rear of the street-front range, or it might be elaborated, as at Purfleet Street, in a three-part arrangement, with

chambers at either end. Beyond the hall, at the far end from the street, it was not unusual in King's Lynn houses of this type for the domestic range to be extended further into a warehouse which, if the plot were wide enough, might be placed at right-angles again to the line of the hall and chamber block, thus closing-off that end of the court that was furthest from the street.[107]

The best surviving example of this more elaborate plan at King's Lynn is Hampton Court, a great tenement down by the quays (Fig. 25). Whereas at Purfleet Street there had been space only for a single shop and the entrance passage on the street frontage, at Hampton Court a range of shops could be accommodated on the ground floor of the street-front wing, and this was to be an important feature again of houses of *parallel* type, both of the *double-range* and *courtyard* plans. Early *double-range* houses, with shop and hall adjoining and both parallel to the street, have been excavated recently at Winchester.[108] But the best-known example of the type is the much larger, and later, Tackley's Inn (Fig. 43), an Oxford tenement of the early fourteenth century which may, indeed, have had shops on two levels in the street-front range, five at ground level, or just above it, and one below in the undercroft.[109] At Tackley's Inn, the upper chambers, or solars, above the shops were

45 (opposite) 31 North Street, York, during reconstruction in 1973, late-fifteenth-century

46 Remains of late-medieval town houses, excavated in 1973, on the north side of St Peter's Street, Northampton; scales in half-metres

probably intended to be let out separately with them. Slightly off-centre, between the second shop and the third, a passage led through to give access to a parallel hall at the back; coinciding with the line of the screens passage, it separated the hall from its attached two-storeyed chamber block.[110]

In effect, at Tackley's Inn a conventional fourteenth-century two-part house, with a hall open to the rafters and chamber block set at one end, had been placed up against the back of a well-designed commercial range which exploited fully the available length of street frontage. And it was by altering the plan only slightly that the same purpose could be achieved at a house of *courtyard* plan, siting the hall, as at Salisbury's Balle's Place, on the other side of a court which separated it from the shops of the street-front range.[111] In such an arrangement, the hall would have its usual two-storeyed chamber block at one end; next to the street, shops shared a separate building with the main gateway of the tenement, through which access could be gained to the central court. Whereas Balle's Place has now been demolished, a more complete example of the same plan survives in the fifteenth-century Norwich building known as Strangers' Hall (Fig. 44). At Strangers' Hall, the original two-part hall and chamber block, with its not much later cham-

ber block added to the other end of the hall, is set well back from the street, separated from it by a courtyard and by a street-front range of shops pierced by the gate of the tenement. Very probably, it was by the mid-sixteenth century at latest that the central court at Strangers' Hall had come to be fully enclosed.[112]

Houses of *courtyard* plan, extravagant in plot use and often handsomely built, stood at the top end of the scale of burgess housing. Near its bottom were the lesser buildings, still something more than cottages, in which shopkeepers, master craftsmen and minor borough officials must commonly have made their homes. The accommodation such houses offered was essentially very simple, and it ran to a standard form. Surviving fifteenth-century building contracts, which have been preserved for houses of this kind in London, Bristol and Canterbury, vary only slightly in their specifications. In London, by a contract of 1410, three houses were to be built together in Friday Street as parts of a single development. Each was to have a shop on the ground floor, fully fitted and ready for business; on the floor above, there was to be a hall, a larder and a kitchen in each case, with a principal chamber, a retiring-room and a privy on the next floor up again. Very similar in its arrangements was the Bristol house for which a contract was negotiated on

48 Late-fifteenth-century
houses at 11–12 West
Street, Exeter

17 November 1472. Again built on three floors, it repeated the pattern of a ground-floor shop, a first-floor hall, and bedchambers on the floor above. The Canterbury houses, built at the end of the century, although humbler in conception, provided very similar accommodation. In a block of four, each house had its ground-floor shop on the street front, with adjoining stores and with a hall and kitchen to the rear; on the first floor, a chamber was reached by a stairway from the hall.[113]

Of surviving examples of such smaller houses, one of the better known is now 13 Friar Street (Fig. 42), King's Lynn, described and illustrated by Dr Parker. Strictly a *right-angle* house of *broad* plan, the Friar Street tenement repeats the essential elements of all such urban housing, disposed in the manner characteristic of King's Lynn. On the ground floor, it had a shop at the front and a hall at the rear; above the shop, there was a single great chamber, later divided in two; lighting to the hall was provided by a large window on the side-passage wall, and it was this passage that gave access to the hall from the street.[114] Better preserved than Friar Street and perhaps also more truly representative of its class, are surviving late-fifteenth-century houses at Exeter, each on a diminutive plot with accommodation arranged on several floors. The house formerly at 16 Edmund Street (Fig. 47) and now moved to a new

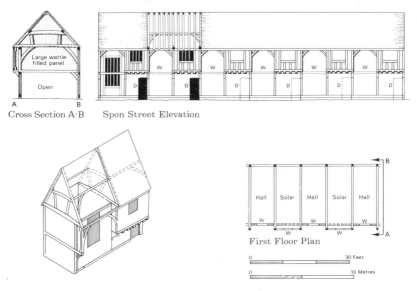

Cross Section A-B   Spon Street Elevation

First Floor Plan

site opposite the church of St Mary Steps, Exeter, is a fine timber-framed structure jettied in two stages. Its ground floor, little more than ten by fourteen feet in area, was shared by a shop and a kitchen; over it, there was a hall on the first floor and two chambers on the second floor, the whole topped by a cockloft in the gable of the roof. At 11 West Street (Fig. 48), Exeter, a very similar corner house offers the same accommodation on a slightly larger scale: shop and kitchen on the ground floor, hall on the first floor, a pair of chambers on the second. Next to it, 12 West Street (Fig. 48) has an extra storey but is set on a still smaller plot, only 10ft 4in wide internally. Here, too, there would have been a shop and probably a kitchen on the ground floor, with the hall above, and with one or two chambers on each of the floors above that.[115]

In several English towns, rows of cottages, each unit on a plot as small as those of the Exeter houses, were to become a feature of the later-developed areas. At York, such development had begun at least by the early fourteenth century, and it took the form of substantial investment in terrace-type buildings, of which examples are known at Goodramgate and at St Martin's Row, in Coney Street. The Goodramgate terrace,

49 (opposite) A late-medieval terrace development of six two-roomed cottages in Spon Street, Coventry (Jones)

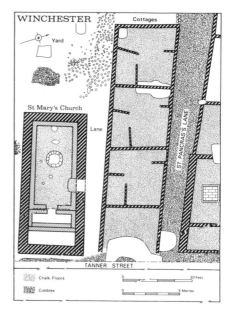

50 The wall-lines on the Lower Brook Street site at Winchester, 1967

also known as Our Lady's Row, was built in or shortly after 1316, to provide an income in rentals for a new chantry dedicated to the Virgin. It was sited along the southern side of the cemetery of the church of Holy Trinity, and was a long, narrow building, measuring 130 by 16 feet, under a single roof. In 1585, when described again, Our Lady's Row included nine separate housing units, six of them 'tenements' and the remaining three 'cottages'.[116] At St Martin's Row, a very similar development in Coney Street for which a building contract survives dated 1335, each house was to have a ground-floor chamber, with an open hearth and with a door and window on the laneside wall. The chambers above, jettied forwards in each case a distance of two feet over the lane, were to be supplied with windows on the other side of the building, overlooking the church of St Martin. Overall, the length of the row was agreed at 100 feet, its width to be eighteen feet at one end and fifteen feet at the other.[117] Six fifteenth-century cottages, again built in a row using the same simple two-room plan, have survived at St James's Street, King's Lynn.[118] In late-medieval Winchester, although nothing now remains of them above ground, cottage rows of up to this number are known to have been put up by speculators.[119]

Population pressure in the more favoured towns is likely to have

83

51 A row of four cottages, of thirteenth- or early-fourteenth-century date, recently excavated on the Lower Brook Street site, Winchester (Biddle)

encouraged the speculative builder, and the cottage rows, some of which have survived along the approach roads to the medieval centre of Coventry, are one of many tributes to the borough's then wealth. An exceptionally complete six-unit range of timber-framed houses on Spon Street, Coventry, may be taken to illustrate a type of which there are several other surviving specimens on Spon Street itself, as well as on Much Park Street, just within Coventry's walls, and on the road to Leicester, just outside them. In the Spon Street terrace, according to a recent interpretation, each cottage unit consisted of a ground-floor hall, open to the roof across one half only of the building, with an upper chamber over the other half, floored to the line of the middle roof truss. Below the chamber, it has been suggested, a cross passage ran through from the street door to the yard, separated from the hall by a partition. With great economy of detail and of space, the width of each cottage was kept to a bare seventeen feet (Fig. 49).[120]

Austere in finish and restricted in floor area though these Spon Street cottages undoubtedly were, they nevertheless included all the essential

52 Late-medieval tenements at 31–4 Church Street, Oxford, excavated in 1968, showing the foundations of tenements next to the lane, and cesspits and wells in the yards to the rear

elements of good-class artisan housing, and they were positioned, furthermore, on an important approach road to the borough. Evidently, neither these nor others of their kind were intended for letting to the very poor in the borough, who may have settled in decaying tenements abandoned for better quarters by the wealthy, squatted in disused defensive towers on the circuit of the walls, or built themselves hovels on unwanted plots in some of the remoter suburbs. Some traces of these last may yet be found by careful excavation of former suburban plots. But only at Martin Biddle's Lower Brook Street site, in Winchester, have there been any real indications so far of what such basic housing might have been like. It was in 1967 that a short row of four flimsily built cottages (Fig. 51) was uncovered during excavations on the Brook Street site, just to the north of the church of St Mary, Tanner Street, and adjoining St Pancras Lane. Of thirteenth- or early-fourteenth-century date, they were simple single-cell units, each about seventeen feet square. In three of them, traces of partitioning, identically placed, suggest the internal division of each unit into a living-chamber, or 'hall',

EXETER

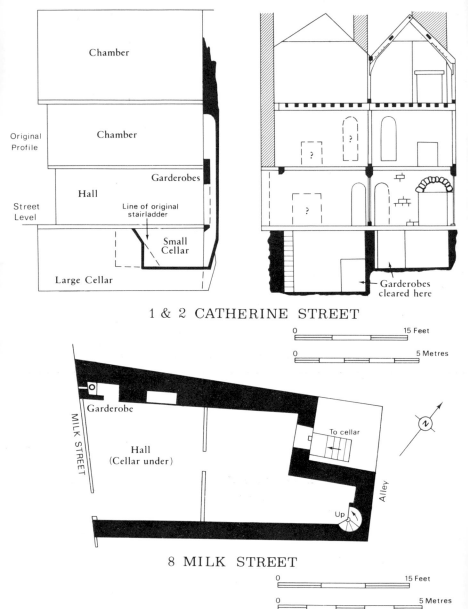

Chamber

Chamber

Original Profile

Garderobes

Street Level

Hall

Line of original stairladder

Small Cellar

Large Cellar

? ? ?

Garderobes cleared here

1 & 2 CATHERINE STREET

0   15 Feet

0   5 Metres

Garderobe

MILK STREET

Hall
(Cellar under)

To cellar

Alley

N

Up

8 MILK STREET

0   15 Feet

0   5 Metres

a bedchamber scarcely larger than a cubicle, and an entrance passage next to the door into the lane (Fig. 50).[121] As part of a deliberate terrace development, they are still, perhaps, some distance from the houses of the really poor. But in their reduction to its most basic of the standard medieval town-house plan, they stand at the end of a very long line. It is perhaps unlikely that we shall ever see further down it than this.

Whether on the Brook Street or other evidence, there can be little doubt that the poor, in the English boroughs, lived in conditions that were both crowded and insanitary. Yet for others, only slightly better served by fortune, the typical borough of the later Middle Ages was not after all such a bad place in which to settle, and it is certainly true that, throughout the period, standards of cleanliness and of municipal hygiene were rising. Town authorities, from the thirteenth century, had concerned themselves with the paving and the cleansing of the streets; there were public latrines, we know, in late-medieval London, at Leicester and at Winchester, at Hull, Southampton and Exeter;[122] and there were to be supplies of fresh water, brought by pipe or open conduit as a public facility, at London, Exeter, Southampton and Bristol by the fourteenth century, at Gloucester and Hull by the fifteenth.[123] Voicing a distaste for the insanitary conditions which, even before the onset of plague, had led to the association in the public mind of filth with disease in the towns, Edward III, in October 1332, ordered the citizens of York to clean their streets and, once clean, to keep them so. It was his wish, he declared, to 'provide for the protection of the health of the inhabitants and of those coming to the present parliament'; he had done this on account of the 'abominable smell abounding in the said city more than in any other city of the realm from dung and manure and other filth and dirt wherewith the streets and lanes are filled and obstructed'.[124] It was Richard II, his fastidious grandson, who was later to be responsible for what has been described as the 'first urban sanitary act', of 1388.[125]

Such public concern undoubtedly followed the cultivation of nicer private habits. In town houses of the thirteenth century and after, there is a growing body of archaeological evidence for the provision of drainage systems of a relatively sophisticated kind,[126] and it was in the thirteenth century again that the larger burgess houses, in Southampton

53 Garderobe arrangements at late-medieval houses in Catherine Street and Milk Street, Exeter (Portman)

Obi p.c.

and elsewhere, were first provided with stone-built cesspits of their own.[127] Commonly, from the fourteenth century, building contracts specify the provision of adequate cesspits at town houses, with or without the overlying garderobe. A tavern in Paternoster Row, London, for which the contract is dated 1342, was to have a pit in the corner of the cellar, seven feet square, to take the waste from the garderobe, or privy. And when, again in London, arrangements were made in 1370 to build a range of eighteen shops, they were to be provided with ten stone-lined pits for the privies, eight of them to be shared between the shops and each to be ten feet deep.[128]

There are good examples of domestic garderobes, built into the thickness of the stone rear walls, at two fifteenth-century burgess houses in Catherine Street, Exeter. Scarcely more than cupboards at the back of each hall and first-floor chamber, they were served by shafts running down into specially-constructed pits in the cellars below; at least one of these cellars had evidently been built expressly for cleaning out the pit. In what must have been in every way a more convenient arrangement, the garderobe of another Exeter house, at 8 Milk Street, was placed in the north wall of the hall, next to the street, from which it could be cleared, and onto which a small slit window opened (Fig. 53).[129]

No doubt, regular cesspit cleaning would do much to keep the privies sweet, but it was probably the growing practice of night cartage of filth that did most to freshen living quarters in the better houses of the towns, holding the worst odours at bay. Cesspit digging, as the archaeology of the English towns is beginning to show, fell off noticeably in the fourteenth century, coinciding with the worst of the plagues, nor was it to be resumed on any considerable scale until the sixteenth century, at earliest.[130] Since the late twelfth century, below-ground pollution had been a recognized danger in the towns. An unlined cesspit, by the terms of fitz Ailwin's London assize of 1189, was required to be set at least a foot further away from the neighbour's boundary than a cesspit lined with stone.[131] But the most effective reforms in the boroughs were brought on by the terror of plague, and it was belief in the role of odours in the transmitting of disease that particularly encouraged their banishment. Levinus Lemnius, the sixteenth-century Dutch physician, was no critic of English society, which he found almost universally pleasing. Nevertheless, his professional opinion of the health of his hosts, whom he found 'freshe and cleane coloured', is probably worth

54 A bed, English, fourteenth-century

𝔇 u wult par auœ̃ture fans.

55 A wife wheedling her husband, French, late-fifteenth-century

attention. Much of this he attributed to a wholesome diet, traditionally rich in fine roasts, but he noted, too, how the 'neate cleanlines, the exquisite finenesse, the pleasaunte and delightfull furniture in every poynt for household, wonderfully rejoysed mee; their chambers and parlours strawed over with sweete herbes refreshed mee; their nosegays finely entermingled wyth sundry sortes of fragraunte floures in their bedchambers and privy roomes, with comfortable smell cheered mee up and entirelye delyghted all my sences.'[132]

Levinus Lemnius visited England at a period of notoriously conspicuous consumption when, as one contemporary was driven to observe, the household effects of his countrymen had 'growne in maner even to passing delicacie'.[133] Yet this is not to say that the house of the English burgess had been poorly equipped before. We possess, in a Latin-English schoolroom vocabulary of the early fifteenth century, a list of the furnishings thought appropriate for the hall: they included a trestle and a standing table, a long settle, a chair, benches and stools, with a screen, fire-irons and bellows, basins, cushions and tapestry covers for the bench and the back of the chair.[134] And for the rich man, this was just a beginning. The inventory of Richard Toky, a London grocer who died in 1391, shows him to have lived in a house of conventional plan and of probably unremarkable scale: in his chamber, he had had to find places for four beds and a cradle, with the other essential fittings of the apartment. Yet where, evidently, Toky had spent his money was on the hangings and the curtains, the cushions and the chair-covers of the hall and his personal chamber, and on fine clothes, plate and jewellery for himself.[135] With others of his fellowship in London, he would have made his house brilliant with colour: its walls brightly painted, its tapestries, hangings and the many soft cushions of its hall alive with representations of dragons, unicorns and other mythical beasts, of lions and peacocks, eagles, boars and dolphins.[136]

Richard of Southwick, burgess of Southampton, who died almost exactly a century before, had been able in his own generation to indulge very similar tastes. Among the objects recovered in 1966 from the pit alongside what was probably his tenement were finely painted wine jugs from south-west France, lustrewares from Spain, glass from Venice, silk from Persia, and wooden vessels and other articles from the Low Countries or possibly the Baltic. In Richard's tenement, the windows were glazed, the floors were of inlaid tile, the roof furniture was flamboyant, and the drain was well-finished in stone. Richard had fed well on the products of the South, and had come to appreciate good wine. In a nice cosmopolitan touch, his pet had been a Barbary ape.[137]

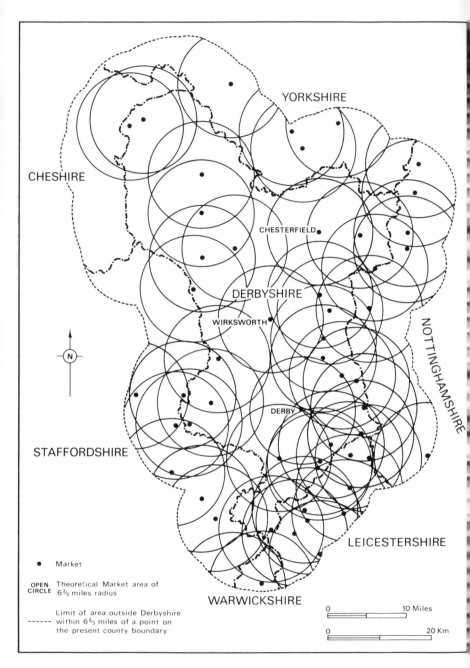

CHESHIRE

YORKSHIRE

CHESTERFIELD

DERBYSHIRE

WIRKSWORTH

NOTTINGHAMSHIRE

DERBY

STAFFORDSHIRE

N

LEICESTERSHIRE

● Market

OPEN
CIRCLE Theoretical Market area of
6⅔ miles radius

------ Limit of area outside Derbyshire
within 6⅔ miles of a point on
the present county boundary

WARWICKSHIRE

0   10 Miles

0   20 Km

56 Derbyshire market-towns, with presumed market areas (Coates)

3 The Borough Economy: Growth and Decline

The one thing that all boroughs had in common was, of course, their function as a market. In a primarily agricultural society, such as England would remain throughout the Middle Ages, what determines ideally the distribution of markets is the amount of time it may take to come in to the market from an outlying area, to dispose of produce, and to complete the journey home again before dark. This is certainly how Henry Bracton viewed it in the mid-thirteenth century,[1] and it is the limited 'reasonable' journey of no more than twenty miles in all that must explain the proliferation of local markets in medieval England (Fig. 56), some of them very small but many the basic nuclei for prospering market towns. Essentially, then, it was the distance that a man could walk, there and back, limiting his ability to exercise choice as to where to dispose of his produce, that determined the placing of our towns. And it was this captive local trade that kept them solidly in being, whatever the state of national finances, from their foundation through to the present.

For certain commodities, especially foodstuffs, trade would always be intensely local. Movements of grain, for example, although exports were not unknown, would usually be short-distance, and livestock too, while capable of moving great distances on the hoof, might have been found for sale at every local market, as would dairy produce, fruit and vegetables, alongside locally made household goods, fuels, skins, and certain varieties of cloth.[2] By modern standards, every medieval community of any size was exceptionally well equipped with specialized craftsmen, employed in a wide variety of trades and removing, by their presence, the need for long-distance exchanges. It is not, perhaps, that self-sufficiency was ever deliberately sought by the English boroughs, for channels of trade within the kingdom remained open and well-used throughout the Middle Ages. Yet in the small, relatively newly created borough of Stratford-upon-Avon in the mid-thirteenth century, there were weavers, fullers and dyers in residence, tanners and shoemakers,

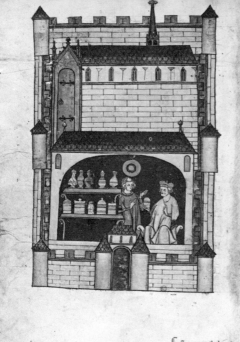

57 An apothecary's shop, French, *circa* 1300

58 (opposite) Bakers at work, French, fifteenth-century

Ci commence le livre.

glovemakers, tailors, carpenters, tilers, coopers, smiths and locksmiths, with two millers, a wheelwright, an oil-maker, a rope-maker, and at least one butcher, baker and cook.[3] Of the trades recorded at twelfth- and thirteenth-century Coventry, an expanding urban community at an important junction of routes, there were sixteen different occupations assignable to the wool and cloth trades, fifteen to the victualling trades, twelve to the metal-working trades, eight to the leather and fur trades, and four to the building industry. Among miscellaneous craftsmen at Coventry in those centuries, there was a wheelwright, a bowstring-maker, an engine-maker, a fletcher, a basket-maker and a wig-maker; there were two parchment-makers and two charcoal-burners, three turners and three scribes, six coopers and eight carters.[4] In the records of medieval London, over 180 trades are named.[5]

In the nature of things, and this was only partially a reflection of the state of the waterways and roads, certain commodities could travel only just so far. The brokage books of fifteenth-century Southampton, a record of the carts and pack-horses entering and leaving the town, complete with destinations, may be analysed to show that the usual limits for the carriage of coal and building materials seldom rose above twelve miles; that household goods, iron and fish travelled perhaps

94

thirty miles at most; that the bulky but valuable trade in wine could extend as far north as Oxford, a distance of over sixty miles, whereas dyestuffs, less cumbersome and still more costly, might be taken by road to Coventry and Leicester in the north, and at least as far as Honiton and Exeter in the west (Fig. 59).[6] Special purchases, regardless of bulk, naturally made their own rules. The obedientiaries of Durham Cathedral Priory, although they were accustomed to shop locally for many goods at Durham market, thought nothing of travelling as far as Boston, in Lincolnshire, to make their bulk purchases at the fair.[7] And they could do this precisely because there were others on their route as interested as themselves in the maintenance of the roads, bridges and waterways without which trade would have come to a halt. The citizens of York, among others, were to exhibit continuing concern to preserve access by road and by river. In the words of a York jury of the late fourteenth century, the river Ouse was a 'highway', of great importance not merely to York but to the whole of the county and to the towns and territories further north.[8] It was to the upkeep of the bridges over the Ouse that the revenue from the new city lands was to be assigned after 1392, and York citizens were to show themselves generous both in this and in the following century in the allocation of money in their wills to

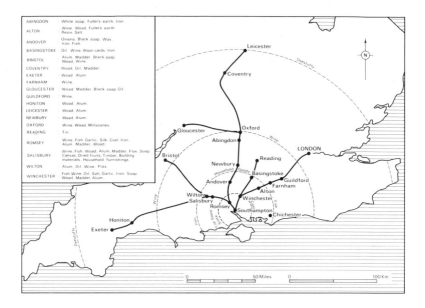

ABINGDON	White soap. Fuller's earth. Iron.
ALTON	Wine. Woad. Fuller's earth. Resin. Salt.
ANDOVER	Onions. Black soap. Wax. Iron. Fish.
BASINGSTOKE	Oil. Wine. Wool-cards. Iron.
BRISTOL	Alum. Madder. Black soap. Woad. Wine.
COVENTRY	Woad. Oil. Madder.
EXETER	Woad. Alum.
FARNHAM	Wine.
GLOUCESTER	Woad. Madder. Black soap. Oil.
GUILDFORD	Wine.
HONITON	Woad. Alum.
LEICESTER	Woad. Alum.
NEWBURY	Woad. Alum.
OXFORD	Wine. Woad. Millstones.
READING	Tin.
ROMSEY	Wine. Fish. Garlic. Silk. Coal. Iron. Alum. Madder. Woad.
SALISBURY	Wine. Fish. Woad. Alum. Madder. Flax. Soap. Canvas. Dried fruits. Timber. Building materials. Household furnishings.
WILTON	Alum. Oil. Wine. Flax.
WINCHESTER	Fish. Wine. Oil. Salt. Garlic. Iron. Soap. Woad. Madder. Alum.

the maintenance of the bridges and the roads.[9] Downriver, at Hull, it had been one of the king's first moves, on his acquisition of the port, to improve its approaches by road, while subsequently the burgesses of Hull would be fully as zealous as their fellows in York in the protection of navigation on the Ouse and in the financing, by bequest, of repairs to the roads in the vicinity.[10]

Inevitably, the travel literature of medieval England seldom neglects to comment on the foulness of the ways, but, as Professor Stenton once remarked, 'no system of communications is ever unreservedly praised by those who have to use it',[11] and the English system, for all its defects, was never so bad as to discourage a heavy traffic of its own. By the middle of the fourteenth century well-established carting routes radiated from London.[12] They are clearly shown on that unique contemporary record known as the Gough Map (Fig. 62), the compiler of which, although he missed some major routes of which there is other good evidence, knew the kingdom well. Not only was he concerned to show the roads themselves and the towns and cities along the way, but, to make his map more useful, he ventured also on the computation of distances between each major point, a reasonable though rarely an accurate guide.[13] Furthermore, although his purpose had chiefly been to

59 (opposite) The inland distributive trade of fifteenth-century Southampton

60 A waggon, French, *circa* 1300

chart the overland routes of the kingdom, he was careful to sketch in also its principal waterways, for these were equally important in transport. When the bursar of Durham went shopping for the priory at Boston Fair, the route he chose to bring back his purchases made use of both rivers and roads. From Boston, they travelled by boat to Lincoln then overland by cart to Torksey, from which they could again make use of water transport on the navigable Trent and the Ouse; at Aldwark, near Boroughbridge, they took to the roads again, to complete the journey to Durham by cart.[14]

It was this mobility of both purchaser and seller, over comparatively long distances wherever the profits were sufficient to warrant it, that made possible the development of the fairs in England as a medium for trading exchanges of the more valuable or the more sophisticated kinds. As early as 1220, attendance at the great fairs at Boston and Lynn, St Ives and Winchester had been counted an allowable excuse for non-attendance at the portmanmoot of Leicester,[15] and it was to those that most men went if they could. But the greater boroughs everywhere, including Leicester itself, had fairs – sometimes several – of their own, and movement between these, except in the deepest winter months, could hardly have been other than continual. In Derbyshire alone, no fewer than twenty-four market towns and boroughs had fairs, totalling

p oz illir de fa terre vous vonra bon lover
p lus oz ne porteroient · xxiiij · fommier
·z· fe nel voles prendre a celer ne vous quier
l anural vous deffie · z tuit fi chenalier

61 A supply waggon with spiked wheels, Flemish, mid-fourteenth-century
62 (opposite) The 'Gough' map, mid-fourteenth-century

between them 120 fair-days in the county. For these, the most popular months were July and September; none were timed to occur between early December and late April.[16]

Although it was in the twelfth and more particularly the thirteenth centuries that the English fairs flourished and multiplied, their importance, with certain notable exceptions, remained high throughout the Middle Ages. At St Giles Fair, Winchester, the profits of the bishop were never greater than at the date they were first recorded, in the reign of Richard I, after which they would go into a decline.[17] But the experience of the greater fairs, suffering from the privileged position in the export trade of newly created staple towns, was not shared, Professor Gross has argued, by the lesser.[18] Late in the fifteenth century, the burgesses of Southampton would still find it worth their while to go to the expense of securing letters patent from the king, confirming them in their fair at Trinity Chapel, by the Itchen.[19] And the continuing value of Sturbridge Fair, near Cambridge, is underlined by the persisting and bitter dispute between the burgesses of Cambridge and the University,

Covit len font de la cite de cali

both claimants to the profits of its court, active from the reign of Richard II and not finally resolved in the burgesses' favour until Elizabeth's judgement of 1589.[20] Indeed, many years were still to pass before the reshaping of the road system in the eighteenth century, and the coming of canals and railways in the nineteenth, would finally outmode the fair. In the Middle Ages certainly, and only to a slightly lesser degree in the early-modern period, the fair had held the key to trading exchanges on a more than regional level. When Edward III, in the mid-fourteenth century, established the fairs of Bordeaux, he saw them still as the most certain recipe for economic revival in the most important of his overseas possessions. It was as late as the sixteenth century that these fairs were to reach their peak.[21]

It would not be difficult to reconstruct in detail a list of the commodities exchanged at such fairs. One, among many, could be compiled from the preferential tariff negotiated by the men of Salisbury at Southampton in 1329, granting them especially favourable terms on a wide range of

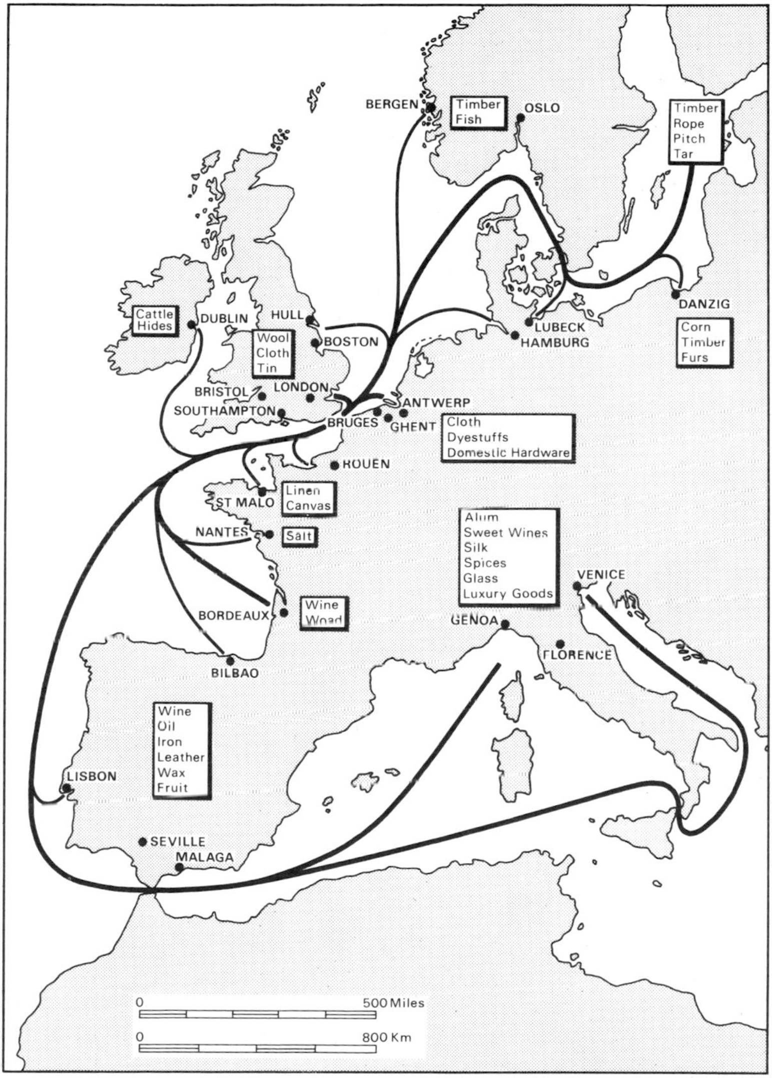
BERGEN
Timber
Fish
OSLO
Timber
Rope
Pitch
Tar
DANZIG
Corn
Timber
Furs
Cattle
Hides
DUBLIN
HULL
Wool
Cloth
Tin
BOSTON
LUBECK
HAMBURG
BRISTOL
LONDON
ANTWERP
SOUTHAMPTON
BRUGES
GHENT
Cloth
Dyestuffs
Domestic Hardware
ROUEN
Linen
Canvas
ST MALO
NANTES
Salt
Alum
Sweet Wines
Silk
Spices
Glass
Luxury Goods
VENICE
BORDEAUX
Wine
Woad
GENOA
FLORENCE
BILBAO
Wine
Oil
Iron
Leather
Wax
Fruit
LISBON
SEVILLE
MALAGA
0
500 Miles
0
800 Km

64 The overseas trade of late-medieval England

63 (opposite) A packhorse and driver approaching an inn, English, *circa* 1400

65 Merchants awaiting the arrival of ships, English, fourteenth-century

groceries, spices and wines, dyes and cloth, building materials and household goods of every description, many of them imported and all of which would subsequently have been found in the fairs and markets of Wiltshire and the West Country.[22] But the briefest study of these lists would be enough to show that a wide difference existed between the variety of goods received into the towns and the comparatively restricted nature of the commodities they could offer in exchange. In local markets this might have mattered very little, being perhaps always a characteristic of such trade; however great in variety the goods might be, they were small in value and insignificant in the total economy. In those towns concerned in overseas trade, whether as manufacturing centres or as ports, the imbalance could prove more serious.

England, throughout the Middle Ages, was known for the fine quality of its wool, that 'veritable golden fleece' that Girolamo Lando would praise.[23] In the fourteenth and the fifteenth centuries, in particular, it became an important exporter of cloth. Yet while the trade was a valuable one, the envy of many foreign rivals, it stood virtually alone: if it failed, there were towns in England that would be left with no other resort. Individually, there was little that any of them could do about it. The supply of the raw material, wool, was relatively inelastic. It could

66 Ships in front of a city, English, *circa* 1400

not be raised quickly to meet increased demand, especially if pasture were already in short supply, nor could recovery be expected to be swift from a setback such as the outbreak of scab in the 1270s. Furthermore, an awkward characteristic of the trade was that its prices, at least in the short term, were dictated not by supply, as was always the case with cereals and other foodstuff prices, but by demand. Alterations in that demand, frequently a direct consequence of political action beyond the control of the merchants, could splinter personal fortunes and temporarily ruin the trade. In practice, it was not just the weather, or an outbreak of scab, that the farmer or the merchant had to fear, but the king and his enemies as well.[24]

So important were fluctuations in the wool and cloth trades to many English towns, that they may often be taken as general indicators of economic progress or decline. Early in the fourteenth century, for example, it was the rise in wool prices that was probably one cause of inflation on a national scale.[25] In the individual cloth-producing centre, labour troubles or technological advance might swiftly bring about the decline of a once-flourishing industry, while sudden variations in overseas demand put pressure on the best-laid economy. Not all towns had an interest in the trade, but there were few completely untouched by it.

C uide moi donc prendre goiselet au broi
D abilone est si fort ne truent prince ne roi
R e mes le dieu du ciel qui tout a desous soi
R aburzadan a dit au message en secroi

67 Dyers at their trade, Flemish, mid-fourteenth-century

Among those most firmly committed to the manufacture or the market-
ing of cloth were the greatest towns and cities of the realm.

Their concern may, indeed, have been as old as the communities
themselves. It is possible, as has been argued recently, that wool was
already sufficiently important in the eleventh century to explain the
kingdom's wealth.[26] And whether or not this was so, there can be no
doubt of the existence of a local cloth industry in mid-twelfth-century
Lincoln, which the king would make special provision to protect.[27]
Large-scale manufacture of cloth, a reality at Lincoln well before the
end of the century, is identifiable also at other provincial centres some
years before 1200: at York, Beverley and Newcastle in the north, at
Leicester, Northampton, Stamford and Oxford in the central counties,
at Winchester in the south, and at Marlborough and Exeter in the
west.[28] Late in the eleventh century, the Flemish cities had obtained
their first privileges in England, and there were Flemish merchants in
the kingdom certainly from the early twelfth century, purchasing wool
for the cloth industry at home. They would be joined in the next
century by the Italians, when there would also be Frenchmen, Germans

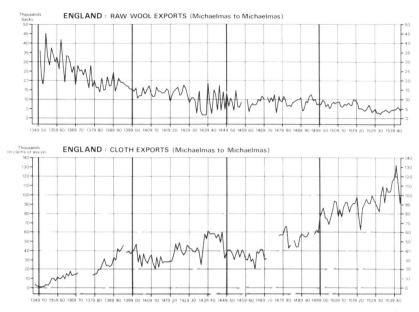

68 English wool and cloth exports, 1349–1540 (Carus-Wilson and Coleman)

and Spaniards engaging in the trade.[29]

The rising demand for English wool derived in general from the requirements of a growing population everywhere in Europe, and in particular from the success of the Flemish and Italian textile industries, which absorbed much of what England could produce. At Winchester, known also for its cloth industry, it was the wool trade, through the thirteenth and early fourteenth centuries, that built the fortunes of many local families. Likewise, there were substantial burgesses in late-thirteenth-century Southampton who owed much of their prosperity to wool, as there were, too, in London and in provincial centres as far afield as Shrewsbury or Ludlow.[30] But the high quality of the English wools, which continued to guarantee their market overseas, was not matched in locally produced cloth. With the exception of Lincoln and a few other centres, among them Beverley, Stamford and Northampton, the English cloth towns became known rather for the manufacture of second- or third-grade cloths: burels and russets that might serve to clothe an army or be given by the king in alms, but which could scarcely compete with the finer textiles imported increasingly from Flanders.[31]

69 A shop front of *circa* 1500 at 11 Lady Street, Lavenham
70 (opposite) The distribution of wealth, and its rate of growth, in late-medieval England (Schofield)

Whereas there is no way of determining the precise scale of the Flemish invasion of the English cloth market, it is probable that the import of Flemish textiles, rising slowly in quantity through the twelfth and early thirteenth centuries, had reached a significant level by the mid-century, to dominate certain sectors of the English market before its end.[32] Undoubtedly, the setting up of new fairs throughout England in these centuries facilitated Flemish commercial penetration, and it was this, among other things, that contributed to the difficulties experienced by many English cloth-producing centres some decades before 1300. In addition, social tensions brought about new and destructive alignments. On the one side, the craftsmen fullers and weavers were being driven by the denial of privileges into attempts to organize their crafts, to restrict hours and to raise charges. On the other, the capitalist entrepreneurs, usually the dyers and the burellers, in the face of increasing opposition, were tempted to look outside the towns for other reserves of labour in the countryside.[33] The building up, by the application of urban capital, of what had long been a traditional rural craft, introduced a new com-

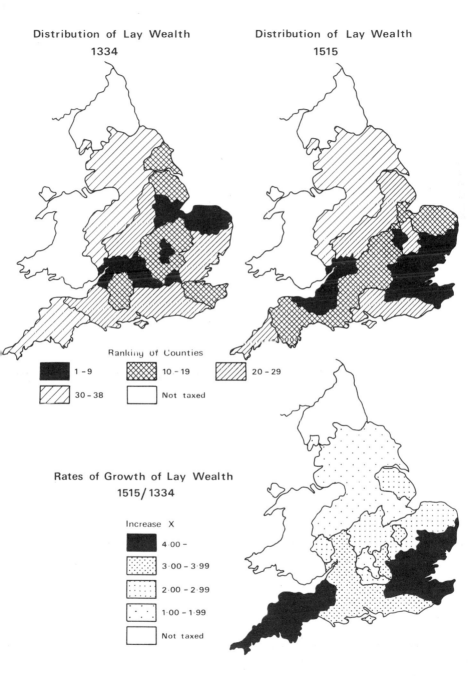

Distribution of Lay Wealth
1334

Distribution of Lay Wealth
1515

Ranking of Counties

1 – 9   10 – 19   20 – 29

30 – 38   Not taxed

Rates of Growth of Lay Wealth
1515/1334

Increase X

4·00 –

3·00 – 3·99

2·00 – 2·99

1·00 – 1·99

Not taxed

71 Little Hall, Market Place, Lavenham, fifteenth-century

petitive element into the weakened industry. There had been fulling mills in rural areas at least since the late twelfth century, and many more would be built in the thirteenth. While not, perhaps, the elements of an early 'industrial revolution', they could not have developed in the absence of a firmly based rural craft, producing cloth for a market larger than the immediate locality.[34] From the late thirteenth century, the contribution of fresh urban capital, now available on a considerable scale, was to build yet more mills and to make possible for the first time the penetration by the country industry of those distant markets long familiar to the entrepreneur and industrialist in the towns. At no point was the urban cloth industry wholly replaced, and at many towns it was not even seriously threatened by its growing rural equivalent. But some centres, including Oxford, Northampton, Leicester and Stamford, suffered permanent disruption of their industry in the crisis at the end of the century, while others, like Lincoln and Winchester, found themselves seriously weakened.[35]

Difficult though times had become for an important sector of the urban cloth-working industry by the early fourteenth century, they would certainly have been worse had it not been for the fortuitous

72 Gildhall, Market Place, Lavenham, first half of the sixteenth century

opening of entirely new markets on the Continent. The Flemish cloth industry, similarly affected by craft insurrections and other troubles, was just then suffering a decline. Not only were the English producers left without serious competition in their homeland, but they were free also to enter important markets in Germany and southern France which the Flemings could no longer supply. The most striking characteristic of England's overseas trade in the fourteenth century is the decline of raw wool exports and the steady climb of the export trade in cloth (Fig. 68). While the one was never fully replaced by the other, there could be no checking the combined effect of heavy export duties on raw wool, of the rise in home consumption and of the progressive out-pricing of the Flemings. Overall, the demand overseas for raw wool was never to recover its earlier level.[36] Nor, in the case of the towns, would it be those which had been most prosperous in the earlier period that would take the lead once again in the later. It is not always easy to arrive at true comparisons, but it would seem clear that at Southampton at any rate, once prospering in the export trade in wool, no burgess fortune of the fifteenth century would compare with that of John of London, of Roger Norman, or of Thomas de Byndon, four or five generations earlier.[37] If, following Dr Bridbury, we are to set the subsidy returns of 1334 against those of 1524, the varying fortunes of the major English towns are significant and very striking. Lincoln, the great cloth centre formerly dominant in the industry, can be shown paying in the ratio 1: 1. Boston, a wool port, exhibits the negative ratio 2: 1. Yet at the new cloth towns, many of which existed primarily to service a rural industry, growth had often been dramatic. Lavenham, in Suffolk, and Totnes, in Devonshire, had both increased their payments in the ratio 1: 18. At Tiverton, another Devonshire cloth-making centre, the increase had been of the order 1: 22.[38]

This changing pattern in the distribution of wealth, vital to every town, has been the theme also of another recent study, again making use of the evidence of the tax assessments to determine the relative wealth, and rates of growth of wealth, of the counties. In the two centuries between the recorded subsidy assessments of 1334 and 1515, as Dr Schofield has shown, the location of wealth in the counties altered appreciably (Fig. 70). The first subsidy accounts, reflecting the importance, at a time of high population, of the wheat-producing regions, show the wealthiest counties to have stretched in a great belt centrally across England, from Gloucestershire, in the west, through Berkshire to Lincolnshire and Norfolk, in the east. Although significant already, the combination of wool and cloth as generators of wealth had not the importance in the fourteenth century that it would acquire before the end of the fifteenth. It was precisely this that the 1515 accounts would illustrate. By that year, wealth had shifted noticeably southwards, to London, in particular, and the Home Counties, and out through Wiltshire and Somerset to the west. These later subsidy accounts, in contrast to the earlier, show Gloucestershire, Wiltshire and Somerset now joined in an island of wealth in the west. To the east, Kent, Surrey, Middlesex, Hertfordshire and Essex drew on the wealth of London. In East Anglia, Suffolk had grown in riches with its cloth. The decline, relatively, of the northern counties may be demonstrated still more strikingly if rates of growth are compared. Against an average threefold increase of wealth, as taken over the country as a whole, the counties north of the Wash had rarely achieved even as much as a twofold advance. Yet in the south-west, the wealth of Devon can be shown to have increased no less than 8·53 times, while Cornwall achieved a growth of 6·60 and Somerset of more than 5. In the London area, the equivalent figure for Middlesex is 8·21; Essex and Surrey were over five times as wealthy, and Surrey and Kent more than four. The cloth

73 Loading a ship at the quayside, Flemish, late-fifteenth-century

industry in Suffolk had increased the wealth of the county by between four and five times.[39]

While the role of the cloth and allied trades in bringing about this new pattern of wealth is undisputed, there were other factors influential too in the growth of individual boroughs, as there were in the decline of many others. At Hull, for example, and at King's Lynn, the worst impact of the recurring late-fourteenth-century trading recessions was avoided as trade through these ports to the Hanseatic towns developed. It was English cloth, of course, which attracted the Hanseatic ships, as it was salt that took them further south to the Bay of Bourgneuf, but they brought with them also valuable cargoes of fish, naval stores and furs from the Baltic, while opening, at least temporarily, new opportunities to English merchants trading to the north in ships of their own.[40] Even so, the Hanseatic trade was subject, as had been that of Flanders before it, to violent fluctuations of fortune. Through the middle decades of the

74 Late-fifteenth-century shops and tenements at Butcher Row, Shrewsbury, as they appeared at the beginning of this century

fifteenth century, political troubles with the Hanse brought about a slump in the trade. It was a decline as drastic as that which, contemporaneously, had gripped the wine trade, broken by the fall of Bordeaux in 1453 and by the severing of its long-standing partnership with England.[41]

There is no way of judging the overall effect of this very general mid-fifteenth-century trading recession on the home-based cloth-making industry. Indeed, the possible compensatory value of an expansion in local demand is still the subject of active debate.[42] However, at York it was precisely this failure of overseas trade, carried out of Hull to the Baltic and to Gascony, that was at least as influential as the mounting competition of rural cloth-working regions in bringing down a once-flourishing local textile industry.[43] And in Devonshire, too, the cloth towns, although likely to make a much quicker recovery than York, were among those petitioning for relief from taxation in the difficult years of the mid-century. The Devonshire re-assessment of 1445, which included the cloth centres at Totnes and Tiverton among the depressed towns, had further significant characteristics. The war and its consequent trading recession had cut back the wealth of the two principal ports at Plymouth and Dartmouth. The smaller market centres, among

75 A fifteenth-century warehouse at Poole, now known as 'Town Cellars'

them Crediton, Okehampton and Modbury, were in a state of obvious decay, while Exeter itself, as dependent as the ports on overseas trade, had suffered a noticeable decline. Yet there were four boroughs that stood out in the record as remaining relatively prosperous, their reductions in the re-assessment being markedly less than the average over the county as a whole. Least affected by the recession had been Torrington, exceptionally favourably situated, with few obvious rivals, as a market centre in north Devon (Fig. 5). Of the three others – Ashburton, Tavistock and Plympton – each was a stannary (or tin-mining) town, closely concerned in a trade whose continued resilience was one of the most remarkable features of England's late-medieval economy.[44]

There are close parallels outside Devonshire to this pattern of prosperity and decay. At Grimsby, the decline of which was attributed locally to the continued misfortunes of war, an active involvement in privateering did little to make up yawning deficiencies in trade.[45] In Cheshire, reversing the experience of the stannary towns, the salt industry of the Wiches had come upon hard times. Bay salt, shipped in from Bourgneuf, frequently retailed at half the price of the better-quality Cheshire white salt, with which it competed from the fourteenth century. It was in that century that the farms of both Middlewich and

Northwich went into a decline.[46] Of particular interest, in the wider context, was the fate of the market towns. In Devonshire, it had been the relative isolation of Torrington that had ensured its continued success as a market centre. Other market towns in the same county, with more competition to face, not only had failed to do as well but had sometimes done very badly. It was not an uncommon sequence. Of the forty-five medieval markets of Staffordshire, it has been observed, some twenty-five had already ceased to function before 1500. Whereas size, of course, had been an important condition of survival, it was not just the smaller settlements which lost their markets, for much depended, too, on location. In the centre and the west of Staffordshire, where market foundations in the boom years had been particularly numerous, many subsequently failed. There were no such failures among the markets bordering Cannock Chase or flanking the southern plateau.[47]

Market failures, a common enough phenomenon in late-medieval England, reflected a rationalization of trading in the boroughs which came close to driving some of the lesser settlements out of business. At the small seigneurial borough of Congleton, in Cheshire, the receipts of the manor began to fall in the fourteenth century, to go into a serious decline after about 1450; fair and market revenues fell appreciably from that date.[48] The same mid-century agricultural recession that brought down the burgesses of Congleton is detectable, too, in the hardships endured in Leicestershire by almost every borough and market town, but it was the townships and hamlets that undoubtedly came off worse and some of these would never recover.[49] Among larger towns, the contrasting development of Warwick and Coventry demonstrates the truth of the maxim that nothing succeeds like success. Warwick, already left behind by the early fourteenth century, was never again in a position to compete. Significantly, among the measures adopted in 1413 to halt the decline of the borough was a change in the date of the traditional Michaelmas fair. As six or seven other fairs were held in the neighbourhood at the same time, it had ceased to bring any profit to the earl.[50] In the same period, Coventry's growth was unchecked. Better situated than its neighbour, at a junction of important ways, it flourished on trading exchanges of all kinds and on the growing demand for its cloth. After 1362, in a gesture of municipal pride, the burgesses of Coventry were to launch a new and costly enterprise, the building of their formidable town wall. Although slow in the making, it came to enclose what was, fittingly, the greatest fortified *enceinte* in the Midlands (Fig. 99).[51]

4 Borough Society

The burgesses whose initiative and enterprise drove forward Coventry's economy would have been, for the most part, of good local Warwickshire stock. Regrettably, the record evidence for burgess origins is markedly defective. In almost every instance, it depends on the identification of topographical surnames, the origins of which might have gone back a very long way. Nevertheless, in a number of separate studies, covering different parts of the country, a similar pattern of recruitment has been revealed, and it can be shown to follow certain unmistakable rules. Understandably, it was the small market centre which drew most heavily on its immediate rural area for manpower. On surname evidence, the survey of Stratford-upon-Avon in 1251–2 would seem to show that as many as ninety per cent of those who had taken up burgage plots at this comparatively new seigneurial borough had been drawn from within a sixteen-mile radius of the bishop of Worcester's foundation. Of these, too, the majority came from a very much smaller local catchment area, perhaps no larger than the six to eight miles in any direction of Stratford's market influence.[1] Similarly, at Market Harborough, another expanding trading centre of about the same vintage as Stratford, those men substantial enough to feature in the subsidy accounts of 1327 had clearly come, where a place of origin is identifiable, from no more than twenty miles away.[2] Of the known Cambridge burgesses of the previous century, few can have been other than Cambridgeshire men,[3] while at Worcester, in the surviving tax return of 1275, over two-thirds of the topographical surnames listed in the return were from Worcestershire or the adjoining counties.[4]

Both Cambridge and Worcester, as county towns, would have recruited from a wider area than either Stratford or Market Harborough, but even at the bigger towns the proportion of local men must always have remained very high. Of the incoming freemen of York, throughout the later Middle Ages, the majority came from the villages and smaller towns of the Vale of York itself.[5] And at Hull, in

the same period, it was men from the East Riding and from northern Lincolnshire who made up the bulk of the burgesses.[6] There might be, of course, special circumstances of growth that would widen, at least temporarily, the circle of recruitment. While York and Hull prospered in the late fourteenth century on the profits of the Hanseatic trade, men were lured there from many parts of England and there were others who came from overseas.[7] Similarly, the continued growth of London, both as commercial and administrative capital, brought men there from far afield, with the consequence that the city became noticeably less dependent for its leadership on men from the Home Counties, attracting to itself the best talents of more distant regions: East Anglia, in particular, and, increasingly, the Midlands.[8] New Winchelsea, strongly backed by the king, its patron, had successfully recruited seafaring men not merely from the other neighbouring Kentish ports, but from Harwich, in Essex, Portsmouth, in Hampshire, and from as far away as Dartmouth.[9] In less favourable conditions, the same tendencies might be exhibited in reverse. A rising total of locally recruited freemen faithfully reflects the sluggish trading situation of mid-fourteenth-century Canterbury. While the recession persisted, some ninety-three per cent of the Canterbury freemen whose place of origin is known were to come from within the county. Before it, between thirty-five and forty per cent of the city's incoming freemen had been drawn from counties other than Kent, or had settled there from overseas.[10]

At Canterbury, as elsewhere, it was from the smaller boroughs and market centres, and not from the rural areas, that the majority of the freemen came. With rare exceptions, that is, the burgess of the average county town would have had a trading or an artisan background. He was neither the child of a serf nor of a nobleman, typically moving from a small trading situation to a larger one, perhaps to move on again in later years to London, where the greatest wealth and opportunities lay. At London itself, the pattern was not so very different. There were extremes, of course, with Simon de Paris, of Norfolk bondman stock, at one end of the scale, and Sir John Pultney, another alderman, of Sussex and Leicestershire gentry extraction, at the other. Yet the majority, even of London's wealthier citizens, were to come to the capital with little inherited property, or with none. Late in the fifteenth century, the admissions records of the London trading companies show that between a third and a half of the total number of apprentices accepted by the

76 A tavern scene, Italian, late-fourteenth-century

77 Illustrations from a
medical treatise,
late-thirteenth-century

companies came from very much the same small-town background as
the Canterbury freemen of two centuries before.[11] They were useful
precisely because of their familiarity with the circumstances of their
chosen trade. Furthermore, although not usually from a wealthy setting,
they were not paupers either. Only Richard Tucker, of the many sixteenth-century mayors of Exeter who were the first of their line in the
city, is said to have been of 'mean parentage', and he, with his background of soldiery, was already an exception among his kind.[12] More
usually, an incoming burgess was required to buy his right to trade,
either by way of a seven-year apprenticeship or by payment of an entry
fine. To qualify, he would need both a skill and social acceptability to
recommend him. Once received, he belonged to a privileged caste.

Such castes, in the nature of things, are self-perpetuating, and at York,
certainly, admissions to the freedom of the city were the subject of
repeated political manipulation.[13] Nevertheless, at York, too, there were
other pressing reasons why the percentage of newcomers among the
city's freemen should have remained consistently high, for even in the
thirteenth century, in a period of population growth, it is unlikely that

the citizenry could have maintained themselves without extensive immigration.[14] One of the reasons for this weakness was a consistent failure of heirs, and it is a noticeable characteristic of English burgess dynasties, wherever these have been examined, that they rarely enjoyed a long life. In the later Middle Ages, although perhaps not so obviously before, a three-generation family span had become exceptional in the towns; nor was it just a decline in business capacity, as William Caxton would have had it for his day,[15] that explained this. Of those same London merchant families about which Caxton wrote, it was rare, through the fourteenth and fifteenth centuries, for the parents to be left with more than two heirs in the direct male line, while with 'sinister uniformity', as Professor Thrupp observed, the average crept closer to one.[16] In effect, it was not just unsuitability of temperament which debarred the English burgess class from the creation of urban patriciates on lines familiar on the Continent. It was reproductive weakness as well.

Undoubtedly, the most convincing explanation for this weakness is the high level of infant mortality in the towns. Average life expectation, for all age groups, was low in the Middle Ages. Although scarcely lower overall than that observed until quite recently in many under-developed countries,[17] where it sank most cruelly in medieval England was in the earliest years of childhood, when resistance to bacteria had not had the opportunity to develop. Direct cemetery evidence of such infant mortality is not easily obtained. Even if the graveyard itself is datable, the bones of children are particularly fragile and their burial in adult cemeteries was not an invariable practice. Nevertheless, in a recent general sample from a village cemetery at Wharram Percy, in Yorkshire, a pattern of high mortality in the early years would seem very clearly to have been established. Of the 174 individuals of all ages examined at Wharram, the overall life expectation *at birth* could be calculated at no more than 18·7 years. In that same rural community, the average lifespan of the adult, once safely beyond the most dangerous years, has been shown to have been 35·3 for the male and 31·3 for the female, the samples being fifty-seven and nineteen skeletons respectively.[18]

There is no means of judging, as yet, the representative value of the Wharram Percy samples, and it could well be that the figure reached at Wharram for life expectation at birth would elsewhere be unacceptably low. But the essential message is clear. While Italian life-tables of 1526 at Florence and 1427 at Pistoia place life expectation at birth much higher, in both cases at nearer thirty, they demonstrate too that the chances of attaining a fair life-span emphatically improved, in Italy as it

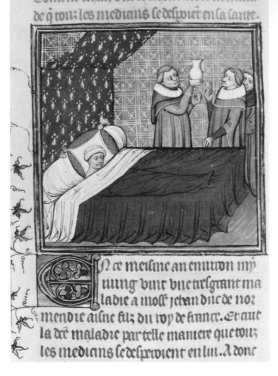

78 Physician and patient, French, end of fourteenth century

must have done in England, from the early adult years. In both cities, a man who reached his twenties could reasonably have looked forward at least another thirty years. Not uncommonly, he might attain a ripe old age.[19]

The young adult's strength protected him, but the building up of immunities in this 'golden age of bacteria'[20] could often have been just as important. Noticeably, it was the children, with little resistance to infection, who were carried off in the greatest numbers by the first two major outbreaks of plague following the Black Death of 1348–9, and though it may be true that plague was not the only, nor perhaps even the most important, obstacle to population recovery in late-medieval England, its threat was continually present.[21] Increasingly an urban phenomenon, the plague was to visit England at least thirty times between 1348 and 1485, on twelve of these occasions as an outbreak on a national scale.[22] With other endemic diseases, including tuberculosis, amoebic dysentery and smallpox,[23] it held down the population of the boroughs, inducing just that condition of nervous strain that Professor Thrupp has seen as a possibly important factor in the reluctance of women to bear children.[24] These were difficult years for young

79 Job feasting with his children, English, early-fifteenth-century

mothers, and they had much, certainly, to worry them. Although more resistant than boys at an early age and likely to outlast the men once past the child-bearing years, it was precisely in those years that women were disproportionately at risk, being exposed to their dangers still further by the practice of early marriage.[25] In striking contrast to what is now the common experience, the medieval cemetery data from Wharram Percy point to a markedly shorter life-span for the female than for the male. Where the appalling dangers of child-birth were well known, and where children themselves were not expected to be long-lived, the discouragements to conception are obvious.

The failure of heirs, although an important factor in the inability of many burgess families to maintain themselves, was not the only cause of the erosion of any strong sense of continuity in their class. It has been calculated that among the families of London's aldermen in the later Middle Ages, barely two-thirds of the aldermen's sons took up their fathers' occupations.[26] Some of those who failed to do so would have entered the Church, others the king's service or professions such as the law. But undoubtedly the most important single incentive to the wealthy to withdraw from trade was the social promise of the countryside. Prominent Londoners, by the end of the fourteenth century, quite commonly thought of themselves as 'gentlemen'; they bore arms like the nobility, and might claim the burial rites of a baron.[27] Increasingly, they sought wives for themselves or for their sons among the daughters of rural landowners of position, and increasingly, too, they were successful in their quest. Richard Cely's marital negotiations, begun at Northleach, Gloucestershire, in the spring of 1482, were not ultimately to be crowned by a match, yet they illustrate, pleasantly enough, the essential preoccupations of his class. Richard had come to the Cotswolds on family business, spending three weeks there in the purchase of a consignment of wool. At the end of his visit, he was introduced, not unwillingly, to a girl who, as he reported it, would have suited him very well. She was a 'genttyll whoman' whose father was the 'gretteste rewlar as rycheste mane in that conttre', and she had been left a substantial fortune by her mother. With such advantages to recommend her, it was known that 'grete genttyllmen' had already sought her hand. As they must have done, Richard Cely, when they spoke together after dinner on Sunday, found her 'whery whellfavyrd and whytty'.[28]

For the Celys and others like them in the towns, the joys and profits of a country life were an ever-present attraction, and it is one of the most obvious characteristics of the English burgess class that, unlike many of its equivalents on the Continent, it built up no tradition of urban loyalty that would override such rural inclinations. Well before Richard Cely's day, it had been common practice for the senior lines of prominent London families to migrate permanently to the countryside, leaving cadet branches only at the capital,[29] while in the provincial towns the security of country estates as investments and the social distinction they conferred, had likewise drawn many of the burgesses from their business interests, if not in the first generation, at least in the second or the third. Rural land-ownership among members of the burgess class has a long history in provincial England. From the late twelfth century, and probably before, Canterbury citizens were holding property in the surrounding countryside, beyond the limits of the common lands of their city. They regarded it, clearly, as a form of investment, for a dozen or more have been shown to hold land within the bounds of a single rural manor.[30] At Cambridge, too, from the thir-

80 Brass (1458) of John Forty, wool merchant, church of St Peter and St Paul, Northleach

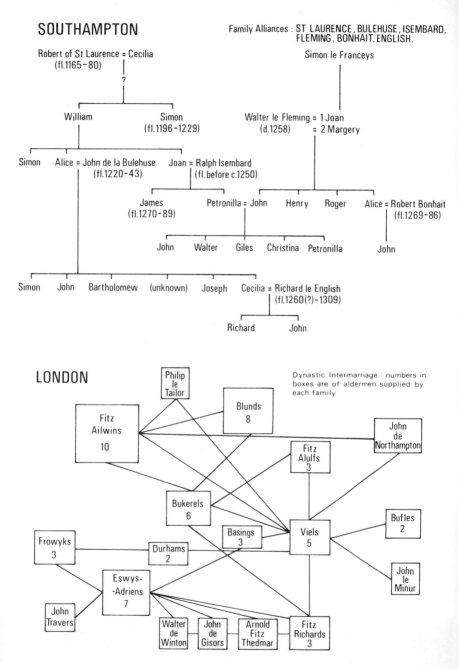

SOUTHAMPTON

Family Alliances : ST LAURENCE, BULEHUSE, ISEMBARD, FLEMING, BONHAIT, ENGLISH.

Robert of St Laurence = Cecilia
(fl. 1165 – 80)

Simon le Franceys

?

William

Simon
(fl. 1196 – 1229)

Walter le Fleming = 1 Joan
(d. 1258)
= 2 Margery

Simon   Alice = John de la Bulehuse   Joan = Ralph Isembard
              (fl. 1220 – 43)   (fl. before c. 1250)

James   Petronilla = John   Henry   Roger   Alice = Robert Bonhait
(fl. 1270 – 89)   (fl. 1269 – 86)

John   Walter   Giles   Christina   Petronilla   John

Simon   John   Bartholomew   (unknown)   Joseph   Cecilia = Richard le English
                                                                 (fl. 1260(?) – 1309)

Richard   John

LONDON

Dynastic Intermarriage : numbers in boxes are of aldermen supplied by each family

Philip le Tailor

Blunds
8

Fitz Ailwins
10

John de Northampton

Fitz Alulfs
3

Bukerels
6

Buffles
2

Frowyks
3

Basings
3

Viels
5

Durhams
2

John le Minur

Eswys-Adriens
7

John Travers

Walter de Winton   John de Gisors   Arnold Fitz Thedmar   Fitz Richards
3

teenth century there were burgesses with important country interests, and they had their equivalents at York.[31] At both, prominent merchant dynasties – the Crouchmans of Cambridge and the Langtons of York – were to convert themselves by the fourteenth century into gentry, and they illustrate a tendency already in being while the towns were still growing and prosperous. In later years, the movement into the country-side would accelerate, as trade itself slowed down. Noticeably, it was only after York's late-fourteenth-century boom that heavy burgess investment in rural estates built up, greatly intensifying the pattern of earlier centuries.[32] In early-modern Southampton it was the receding prospects of the Italian trade, so vital to the prosperity of the port, that prompted many leading burgesses to break their traditional allegiances and to commit themselves to intensive speculation in former monastic lands.[33]

The upward drive into the gentry class was an important motive in the building up of a family's landed interest, to become steadily more so as the concept of gentle status hardened and as less was thought of trade.[34] Nevertheless, the acquisition of property, both rural and urban, by many of the more prominent families in the boroughs may have started with different objectives. In the thirteenth century, the survival of com-paratively long-lasting burgess dynasties was a characteristic of English borough society, and it has been suggested that at York, at least, they owed their stability to just such an endowment in lands.[35] To detect, as some have tried to do,[36] the emergence as early as this of a genuine urban rentier class, would probably be to stretch the evidence beyond what it can bear. However, there is no doubting the continuing associa-tion of propertied families with important office in the boroughs, and it was their wealth that ensured this succession. It is said, for example, of the Chiches of Canterbury that they became, in their time, hereditary aldermen of Burgate ward in the city. Noticed first with Arnold Chich, a goldsmith in late-twelfth-century Canterbury, they were to supply four of the city's bailiffs during the century that followed.[37] At Bristol and at Gloucester, in the thirteenth century, it was the wealthy property-holding families which shared out office between them, and although the association of property and office-holding was not as clear at either Coventry or Worcester, it was there again very obviously at contempor-

81 Family alliances among the ruling class of medieval Southampton and of London (Platt and Williams)

ary Lincoln, and would always be a feature of municipal government at the merchant-dominated port of Southampton.[38] For seventeen years, in thirteenth-century York, there were Selbys in office as mayor, and they were one family alone in a whole galaxy of citizen dynasties, among them the Bolingbrokes and le Specers, the Langtons, the Bonvilles and the Graunts.[39]

Undoubtedly, it was the advancement of individual families such as these that constituted one of the more important driving forces in the economy and the government of the boroughs.[40] Yet at least part of the success of each family, too, would depend on its mating with others. Intermarriage between burgess families was to yield cohesive and powerful alliances: the stuff of which borough government was made. In thirteenth-century Southampton, firm family ties linked the St Laurences with the Bulehuses, the Isembards and the Englishes; a daughter of Joan of St Laurence and Ralph Isembard married John, one of the sons of Walter le Fleming, whose only daughter, Alice, was herself to be married to a Bonhait; a Barbflete was to marry a Fortin, and another, early in the next century, would take Matilda, daughter of John of Holebury, as his wife (Fig. 81).[41] In medieval London, as Professor Williams has shown, the family alliances were as devious and, when it came to government, as compelling. Of the ninety-five aldermen elected before 1263, no fewer than sixty-four belonged to a single complex of interrelated families, among them the ancient lines of the Ailwins, the Viels, the Bukerels and the fitz Alulfs, subsequently linked with the newer fitz Richard family, the fitz Thedmars, Frowyks, Wintons and Gisors. In the same period, a total of sixteen families provided nearly seventy per cent of London's aldermen.[42]

To reinforce the ties of family, there were others of neighbourhood as well. In late-medieval Hull, it was on Hull Street, in particular, that the wealthy elected to live, just as Gosford Street and Earl Street were to become the choice residential areas of medieval Coventry.[43] Exeter, in the sixteenth century, was run for the most part by the wealthy residents of three neighbouring parishes in the northern quarter of the city: St Mary Arches, St Petrock and St Olave.[44] And at Southampton, it was the parish of Holy Rood, on the southern line of English Street adjoining other favoured parishes at St Michael's and St John's (Fig. 105), that would attract a particular gathering of the wealthy from the four-

82 Remains of a spiral staircase in a fourteenth-century tenement, excavated in 1972 at Grimsby Lane, Hull; scales in feet

83 Brass (1401) of
William Grevel, wool
merchant, and his wife
Marion, church of St
James, Chipping Campden

84 (opposite) William
Grevel's house,
Chipping Campden

teenth century, and probably before. Here, it was not merely that the
rich lived in the same parish as each other, but that, successively, they
occupied immediately neighbouring tenements. West of English Street
and south of Broad Lane, a block of no more than half a dozen tenements continued to attract wealthy purchasers, counting among them
some of the most influential burgesses of their time. On the corner itself,
the great house that Walter le Fleming had built before the mid-
thirteenth century was subsequently held by William le Horder, John le
Fleming, Henry de Lym, John atte Barre, the Montagues, Sir John and
Sir Richard, the James family, Peter, William and Henry, William
Justice, and Thomas and Sampson Thomas. Of the houses immediately
to the south, Nicholas de Moundenard, Roger Norman and Thomas de
Byndon were either the owners or the tenants in the second quarter of
the fourteenth century. A century later, when the occupiers of those
same tenements are known again, they included Walter Fetplace 'senior'
and the wealthy William Soper.[45] These men divided the government
and the native, or denizen, trade of the port between them. As partners
in commercial enterprises, contemporaries in municipal office, next-
door neighbours and fellow parishioners, they shared the same interests
and social preoccupations from the cradle right through to the grave.

If there were distinctions of family and of neighbourhood in the boroughs, there were also those, still more obviously, of wealth. Rarely could a provincial fortune have equalled that of a leading London citizen, to whom the accumulated capital of a man like Gilbert Maghfeld, touching £1,500, might have seemed large but certainly far from exceptional.[46] Nevertheless, as has been demonstrated in the case of sixteenth-century Exeter, the income of even a middling merchant at a provincial capital such as this, could have been expected to exceed the average receipts of many among the local country gentry,[47] and in the county towns, industrial centres and greater ports of England, there would always have been at least a handful of really prosperous burgesses whose assets would have placed them on a level with the more considerable nobility. There is no means of estimating in any exact way the wealth of the great merchants of thirteenth- or early-fourteenth-century England, when the towns had reached their prime. But we know of men like William of Doncaster, trading out of Chester in the late thirteenth century,[48] like Walter le Fleming, John of London and Roger Norman in mid-thirteenth- and early-fourteenth-century Southampton,[49] and like the fourteenth-century Salisbury wool merchants, Robert of Knoyle, John Aunger and Robert Woodford,[50] whose assets were

85 The house at Coggeshall built by the heirs of Thomas Paycocke,
clothier, who died in 1461
86 The great door at Thomas Paycocke's house

clearly considerable and whose wealth, in ships, in landed property and
in movable goods, set them apart from their fellows. It would be said of
William Canynges, a great figure in fifteenth-century Bristol, that for
eight years he was employing as many as 800 men to work his ships, and
that he had another hundred, among them carpenters and masons, in his
employ in the town.[51] And the sixteenth-century taxation records in the
towns, which at last enable us to make some contemporary comparisons,
list men if not as wealthy as Canynges, at least of considerable stature.
In 1523, Robert Jannys, grocer and alderman of Norwich, was assessed
for taxation purposes at £1,100; in the same returns, the highest assess-
ment anywhere outside London and the peerage was that of the widow
and daughter of Thomas Spring, the Lavenham clothier, jointly assessed at £1,333 6s 8d.[52] There were other conspicuously wealthy men
in sixteenth-century Coventry, Exeter and Leicester: grocers, drapers
and merchants of the staple. But in the once prosperous port of
Southampton, already touched by a recession in the Mediterranean
trade, fortunes were noticeably more moderate. In 1524, it was a lawyer,

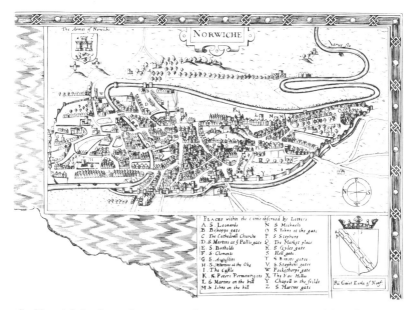

87 Norwich in the early seventeenth century: a great provincial capital (Speed)

Richard Lyster, who was assessed most highly at Southampton, being judged to be worth £250. Henry Huttoft, mayor the following year and the next wealthiest man in the borough, was assessed at only £133 6s 8d.[53]

More striking still than the differences in wealth between one trading centre and another, were the inequalities within each borough society, revealed in the subsidy returns. It was one man, the clothier Thomas Horton, who paid on his own behalf as much as seventy per cent of the entire subsidy of the Wiltshire cloth town, Bradford-on-Avon; while it was the two William Wigstons, of Leicester, who together accounted for a third of the subsidy of their borough.[54] Using the same subsidy records, it has been possible to estimate that some sixty per cent of the wealth of Norwich was in the hands of no more than six per cent of its population; that a mere two per cent, at Coventry, held between them forty-five per cent of the lands and goods of the borough; and that at Lavenham, a small group of wealthy clothiers had engrossed over eighty per cent of the property.[55] Everywhere, such inequalities are repeated.

In the country towns, it has been suggested, it would not have been uncommon for as little as five per cent of the population to control as much as two-fifths of the property; between a third and a half of the assessable resources of each town would have been in the hands of the middle classes, while such wage-earners as had property enough to be assessed at all could rarely have assembled between them as much as a tenth of the community's wealth.[56]

In the distribution of wealth through borough society as a whole, there is little to separate the experience of Leicester, the market centre, from Southampton, the port. If, in each case, the same allowance is made for some thirty per cent of the population too poor to feature in the early-sixteenth-century assessments, then another thirty per cent at Leicester and some thirty-six per cent at Southampton, assessed on wages or goods worth £1, can be identified as the employed working class. A lower middle class, rated at between £2 and £10, made up a further thirty per cent of Leicester's population and twenty-five per cent of Southampton's. With assessments ranging from £10 to £40, the middle class proper constituted no more than a bare seven per cent of the community at Leicester and eight per cent at Southampton. The wealthy, just three per cent at Leicester and two per cent at Southampton, were rated on lands and goods valued, for the most part, far in excess of £40.[57]

Significantly, a regional increase in wealth, the result of an expanding trade, would have more effect at the upper limits of the income range than it ever would at the lower. The prospering provincial capitals at Norwich (Fig. 87) and at Exeter, both with an interest in the cloth trade, could each have shown higher percentages of wealthy citizens than either Southampton or Leicester. At Norwich, nearly six per cent of the taxpayers were assessed at over £40, representing a distinct advance on the Southampton figure even though that was of the population as a whole; at Exeter, the comparable figure was 6·5 per cent. But this wealth had only marginally spread down. Southampton's assessable working class had constituted a full fifty per cent of the taxable population of the borough. The equivalent figures at Norwich and at Exeter were forty per cent and forty-seven per cent respectively.[58]

Although earlier figures are difficult to come by, and there is no evidence at all comparable with that of the sixteenth-century returns, yawning disparities of wealth had perhaps always been a characteristic of the English country town, and still more of the provincial capital. When a tax, or tallage, was levied at York in 1204, as much as £212 of a

ſl e vit onques ſi bele ne de tele faichon
l es cozdes ſont deſoie z doz ſin li paſſon
l ozs deſcent alixands ius del maiſt doignon
o lui les·v·puceles qui li ſont au gieron
s i ſu pozus lindois qui or cuer de lyon

88 A metalworker and a smith, Flemish, mid-fourteenth-century

total of only £373 was found by individually listed contributors in the city, ten of whom paid £10 or more, four between £5 and £10, three between £1 and £5, and fifteen less than £1. If, as seems likely, the remainder was assembled from the multiple contributions of lesser men, the comparative isolation of the rich in York is already very clearly revealed, nor is there much evidence in the tallage figures of a supporting middle class.[59] A century later, the position had scarcely changed. There were some 800 citizens of York listed in the subsidy returns of 1327, but only one of these had assessable goods worth as much as £26; fifty-five citizens were worth £5 or more, the remainder being assessed at anything up to £4, with a great concentration again at the lowest point in the scale.[60]

These early disparities of wealth, which have been noted too in a recent study of the West Midland towns,[61] have also their political significance. Some fifty per cent of the taxpayers in fourteenth-century Southampton were men of little account, worth between £1 and £2, and another thirty per cent were assessed at less than £5. There were twenty men who could reasonably be described as prosperous, and eight who were definitely rich. Of these last, in 1327, Roger Norman, Hugh Sampson, Thomas Nostschilling, Henry de Lym and Nicholas de

befelehel

befelehel

oliab

oliab

Como Befelehel c Oliab fo compagnō lauora el Cancelicro de oro.
Como Befelehel c Oliab fo compagno lauora le colone del tabernaculo.

89 Vestment-makers, Italian, *circa* 1400

Moundenard were the wealthiest, and not one of them would fail to leave his mark in the political history of the borough, having each held high public office. Again two centuries later, in the returns of 1524, it was not only the distribution of wealth in the borough that was recorded, but also the pattern of power. Eleven men stand out among their fellows, with assessments ranging between £40 and £250. Of these, only Richard Lyster, with a career in law outside the borough, never held an office of importance there.[62]

Wealth and rank never fail to leave their mark upon the records, yet on the problems of poverty these are silent. High though we can guess the percentage of poor to have been in any community, we know little or nothing of what kind of person they included, or even of how they lived. In the many surviving late-medieval wills, the pauper features frequently as the recipient of charity. In sermon literature, it is the poor who are called in evidence the better to rebuke the rich, although they, too, might bring the homilist to despair: 'muche peple of this world, as experience proveth, ben dronkenlewe and unclenly. I can not see that Crist dwelleth in hem.'[63] We can perhaps conclude, from the Southampton evidence, that if few of the poor lived within the walls,

90 The Merchant Adventurers' Hall, York

many must have lived outside them, and this would certainly be the
pattern in sixteenth-century Exeter, where it was the extra-mural parishes that held them.[64] Nevertheless, it is by inference only that we
usually proceed to the discussion of the 'submerged 30 per cent' in the
boroughs. In the words of the preacher, 'fodder and a rod and a burden
are for an ass, bread and correction and work for a serf'.[65] None of them
left much of a monument.

It is, perhaps, only with the emergence of the crafts in organized gilds
and charitable associations of their own, that we begin even to approach
a knowledge of the condition of the less well-off in the boroughs. Yet,
even so, the craftsmen themselves were not within the lowest-paid
categories in any English town, and frequently it was only as freemen of
their communities that they were allowed to practise their trade there.
While the craft movement can tell us something of the force of social
pressures in the town, bringing to the fore the aspirations of an important sector of the working and lower middle classes, it usually had
specialist interests of its own to protect and always spoke only for
its members. If a borough proletariat is to be looked for in the crafts, it
will be found there imperfectly represented. In important respects, the
craft movement was itself the client of the existing ruling oligarchy,

91 Undercroft of the Merchant Adventurers' Hall, York

whose supervision it would find it difficult to shake off. Borough governments welcomed the control of standards and even the restraint of trade, for which they could hold the crafts responsible. Wherever possible, they kept a firm grip on their activities.[66]

The craft association, in one guise or another, dates back as far as the early twelfth century, and may well be very much older. In London, there was a gild of weavers from the reign of Henry I; in Oxford, also in the twelfth century, there were gilds of corvesars and of cordwainers; in Canterbury, by 1216 and probably before, there was a gild of smiths.[67] However, the apparent insignificance of the Canterbury body is probably as true of other such early associations elsewhere, for there is little convincing evidence of collective action by the trades before the end of the thirteenth century, and nothing at all that would set them on a level with the contemporary gilds merchant and first socio-religious gilds which had had so much to do, in that century and even before, with the shaping of borough government. In London, the first official recognition of the misteries as self-governing associations dates only to 1327–8, although for some decades already they had been establishing their claim to attention.[68] Not very much later, the craft ordinances of the fishmongers of Bristol date from 1339; those of the weavers, dyers, fullers and tailors from 1346. But it says little for the strength of the Bristol crafts as yet that it was the borough government, not their members, which published these ordinances. Further, although it was to be the crafts that would enforce the regulations and that would police, for the borough, their own trades, it was to the municipality that the bulk of their fines fell due.[69]

It was the power to vet admissions to the freedom of the city, granted to the London crafts by the royal charter of 1319, that confirmed these emergent associations in their place in the civic constitution. The crafts, in fourteenth-century London, were to come to play a dominant role in city politics, and though it remains true that it was only the greater misteries – the fishmongers, the skinners, the corders and others, prospering in the Hanseatic trade – who penetrated the aldermanic class,[70] the organization of craft associations generally spread rapidly downwards through the trades, bringing the possibility of effective collective action for the first time to many who had had no knowledge of it before. In 1328, the twenty-five misteries recognized as self-governing associations had included few of the lesser crafts; for the most part, they were restricted to those wealthy trading and manufacturing misteries that would seek, or had already sought, charters of their own from the king. Through the next decades, however, the range of such formally recognized associations widened, and there were many other specialized trading groups which achieved an individual identity in fraternities of a socio-religious nature. No fewer than fifty-one misteries, including among them many of the lesser crafts, participated in the election of the city's common council in 1377. And when, in 1422, the clerk of the Brewers' Company drew up a memorandum listing the London crafts, 'in case it may in any wise profit the hall and Company of Brewers', he was able to include in it a total of 111 trades, even then overlooking several of the more important misteries which had been represented at the 1377 election.[71]

Very probably, there were many among the lesser London crafts which never registered their ordinances, preferring to continue as informal associations unrecognized by the city authorities. Yet for others, and in particular for the wealthy trades, recognition of independent corporate status became increasingly important as both their responsibilities and their expenses accumulated. As such bodies everywhere would find themselves obliged to do, they sought protection in perpetuity for their rapidly increasing endowments, and it was this gathering together of properties, spreading through all the trades, that did

92 The boy Jesus as an apprentice dyer, English, *circa* 1300

most to stabilize the craft movement as a whole. Of course, associations without property interests would continue to form, dissolve and re-shape themselves throughout the later Middle Ages. But for those that were to be longer-lasting, the holding of property was crucial. In the early history of the Gild of Weavers, Tuckers and Shearmen of Exeter, the year 1471 stands out. It was then that the gild acquired the site in Fore Street on which its chapel was shortly to be built. Later, the chapel would form the body of the gild's secular meeting-place, known as Tuckers Hall.[72]

This quality of the gild as property-holder, theoretically in per-petuity, had long before been recognized by the king, and it was to discover the extent of unlicensed property-holding by the gilds that an enquiry was instituted in 1389. Two years later, the enquiry would result in a reissue of the statute of mortmain that would be important for the towns as well as the gilds (see p. 173), but it elicited too a remarkable series of returns from the trades and religious fraternities, preserved in the public records, which together constitute our best available source for the history of the provincial gild. It was the origin, usages and form of government of each gild that the king required to know, with further details of the frequency and place of its meetings, the titles of its officers, oaths taken and restrictions imposed on admissions. Of the gilds and fraternities of Lynn, he would have discovered that it was the Gild of the Nativity of St John Baptist, founded in 1316, that was the earliest; that gildsmen throughout the town were accustomed to meet solemnly, 'with a good deuocion' and 'faire and honest-liche arayde', on the name day of their saint and on as many as four other occasions through the year; that the gild officers commonly included an alderman, a steward or stewards, a dean and a clerk; that entry fines of as much as five shillings might be exacted; that brethren were expected to contribute to the support of the sick and impoverished in their fellowship; and that it was a solemn obligation on each brother and sister of the gild to attend the funeral rites of an associate.[73] It is not surprising, in view of the purpose of the enquiry, that the king's informants were decidedly less frank when it came to reporting their property. Two out of the eight Cambridge gilds submitting returns in 1389 neglected altogether to answer this particular enquiry, and four reported that they had no property of their own. Of the remaining two which announced their possessions, neither had much to lose. In one, the common fund that year amounted to 12s 8d. Gild property at the other included a chalice worth 10s, an alb with an amice worth 3s, and only 16s in cash.[74]

Where other gild ordinances survive, as they do on occasion elsewhere, it is the purpose of such an association in the restraint of trade that not uncommonly receives most emphasis. The ordinances of the craft of girdlers at York, dated 1307 and an unusually early example of their kind, controlled the admission of outsiders to the craft, limited all purchases of raw materials to suppliers within the city, forbade night work and the farming-out of surplus work to others, restricted master craftsmen to the employment of a single apprentice, and laid down a minimum term of apprenticeship at four years, to be raised a century later to seven.[75] It was seven years again that was the limit of apprenticeship set in the fifteenth-century code of the Shrewsbury weavers, compiled in 1448 and extended the following year. Characteristically, the code mixed social and economic injunctions. If a man of the craft, it was later provided, should be found living in adultery, none of his brethren, whether masters or journeymen, were to have anything to do with him until he should mend his ways. As for trading practice within the borough, 'no manner of foreign men of any foreign shire of England', with certain local exceptions, might sell 'any kind of linen cloth except canvas cloth within the town or franchise of Shrewsbury but only at the time of the fairs of Shrewsbury and that time while the said fairs last'; no master might take more than one apprentice at a time, nor keep him apprentice for less than seven years; no widow might continue the craft of her former weaver husband for longer than the three months deemed sufficient by his associates to work out whatever remained of his stock.[76]

At Shrewsbury, as at other towns, the association between gild and borough was close, being clearly beneficial to them both. Such fines as might become payable on infraction of the weavers' regulations were to be split equally between the bailiffs, the commonalty and the craft; it was the bailiffs, at Shrewsbury gildhall, who witnessed the document and affixed their seal to it; and it was in the borough records that the code of the weavers was enrolled. In return for profits and supervisory rights, the borough's most valuable gift to the craft was protection from the competition of outsiders. It was for just such protection that the tailors, the coopers, the mercers and the drapers were each to petition the borough authorities in fifteenth-century Southampton,[77] and they valued it sufficiently to take on for themselves many of the administrative responsibilities of the town. So important were these mutual services that an experimental abolition of the gilds of Vienna, attempted in 1276, was to last a bare six months,[78] and in the English towns, with similar problems, it is easy to see how a co-operative relationship built up. Above all, quality control, which was to become the responsibility of the searchers of the crafts, was an interest shared by both, but there were other important material ways in which the crafts could assist their borough governments. It was the crafts, for example, in fifteenth-century Salisbury, which were called upon on at least three separate occasions to supply, in lieu of the city, the men and money that the king required to conduct his wars overseas, and it was thirty-eight of the crafts which, in 1440, sent their wardens to a meeting of Salisbury citizens to raise funds to complete the defences.[79] The best evidence surviving for the existence of similar craft associations in medieval

Southampton is a sixteenth-century apportionment of responsibilities for the maintenance of towers along the line of the town wall. Between Arundel Tower, on the north-west angle, and the Bargate, the 'little tower' was to be kept in repair by the shoemakers, the curriers, the cobblers and the saddlers; East Gate Tower and the tower to its north were assigned to the goldsmiths, the blacksmiths, the locksmiths, the pewterers and the tinkers, and on the southern shore, on Porters Lane, the mercers looked after the tower next to the corporation warehouse; along the wall to the west, it was the brewers who cared for St Barbara's Tower and the bakers the Corner Tower, where the wall changed direction towards the north; between the Corner Tower and the West Gate, another tower was allotted to the coopers, and along the next section of the wall, south of Pilgrim's Gate, the three remaining towers south of the castle were assigned to the vintners, the mariners and the lightermen, the weavers, the fullers and the cappers, the butchers, the fishmongers and the chandlers, co-operating in groups of three.[80]

Borough governments had other motives both for seeking the co-operation of the crafts and for maintaining a continuing watch on their activities. Recognition of the crafts had not been achieved without a struggle. In the thirteenth-century boroughs, the motivations of social conflict are usually obscure, for it is rarely possible to determine what interests in the community a dissenting commonalty represented. Nevertheless, it was the craft movement, certainly, which lay behind much of the unrest in London at the turn of the thirteenth and fourteenth centuries, and there is good evidence also in major cloth-working centres throughout the country of the oppressions to which the crafts were exposed. At York, no weaver was admitted to the freedom of the city throughout the reign of Edward I.[81] At Winchester and Marlborough, Oxford and Beverley, both weavers and fullers were 'dependent folk', excluded from the franchise of their boroughs.[82] It was the gild merchant at Leicester that dictated wages and conditions of work to the weavers and fullers of the borough, and it was the borough notables at Norwich, again, who did all they could to halt the first efforts at organization in the trades and to suppress the emergent gilds.[83]

Whether such were the circumstances of the serious ructions in late-thirteenth-century Lincoln, it may never be possible to determine. But there is no doubting the force of social rivalries in the city, nor the tone of class hatred that emerged. Both in 1267 and 1275, charges of oppression and misconduct were to be brought against the ruling elite, to be revived again in 1290 when they provoked the intervention of the king. The contemporary *Provisions* for the government of Lincoln, perhaps a direct consequence of the king's initiative, were firm in their delimitation of mayoral powers and in their restatement of the electoral rights of the commonalty. But they are not as revealing, in the context of class discord, as that astonishing document of the mid-fourteenth-century city, the founding ordinance of the Gild of Corpus Christi, of the parish of St Michael on the Hill:

And whereas this gild was founded by folks of common and middling rank, it is ordained that no one of the rank of mayor or bailiff shall become a brother of the gild, unless he is found of humble good and honest conversation, and is admitted by the choice and common assent of the brethren and sisters of the gild. And none such shall meddle in any matter, unless specially summoned; nor shall such a one take on himself any office in the gild. He shall, on his admission, be sworn before the brethren and sisters to maintain and to keep the ordinances of the gild. And no one shall have any claim to office in this gild on account of the honour and dignity of his personal rank.[84]

At Ipswich, too, the democracy which began so hopefully in the events of the summer and early autumn of the year 1200 (see pp. 157–9), would come under severe strain not much more than a century later. It is in the Ipswich reforming ordinances of December 1320 that some of the causes of grievance can be seen. Bailiffs and other borough officers had ceased to be publicly elected; the borough seal had been misused; admission to the franchise had been granted secretly and irregularly, to the profit of the bailiffs; private transactions with visiting merchants had given the offenders an unfair advantage over their fellows, and there had been forestalling and similar malpractices in the town. In the wake of the ordinances, there were riots at Ipswich in which men of substance were involved on either side, and though it is difficult, as at contemporary Bristol and Southampton, to distinguish the popular element in these disturbances, there is no doubt of its presence or its effect. For a time, certainly, the provisions at Ipswich are likely to have been enforced; the old corrupt magistracy, permanently displaced, made way for a new breed of borough official drawn from a wider social range.[85]

Yet oligarchy, it is possible to argue, was a condition natural to the

93 Central York and its Minster from the air

boroughs, and at Ipswich, as elsewhere, wealth and authority continued to cling together. The popular upheavals of the early fourteenth century, if they released the grip of one governing class, merely opened the way for another. In the later Middle Ages, as had usually been the case before, it was the 'wealthier and discreeter sort' who were held most fit to conduct the affairs of the boroughs: the 'better and more honest burgesses', the 'more honest and discreet', the 'more discreet and fit', the 'wiser and sadder'.[86] It has been one recent view that the 'structure of urban society in the later Middle Ages became, not less flexible, but more so'; admissions to the franchise had come to include the weavers and the fullers, and governing councils were very frequently enlarged.[87] Yet it would be hard to ignore the evidence, everywhere abundant and compelling, of a closing down, rather than a widening, of opportunity. If admissions to the franchise rose in many late-medieval boroughs, it was because the ruling elite could not rightly afford to restrict them, gaining more than it lost from such expansion. Likewise, if a governing council grew in size, the electorate, just as often, might narrow. In borough society at many levels, the same restrictive pressures were felt. Ineluctably, they fenced that society in.

These, indeed, were the circumstances that secured that wealth and commercial success should be the principal conditions for membership of the ruling twenty-four at sixteenth-century Exeter.[88] Nor could there have been anything exceptional in this. In the same century, at the Cornish borough of Liskeard, a distinction was drawn between the nine *capital* burgesses, who were to enjoy superior status for life, and the fifteen others they themselves were to select to assist them in the business of government, drawn from the 'most able and sufficient of the residue burgesses ... which shall henceforth be reputed *inferior* burgesses'.[89] And such divisions, although seldom as forthrightly expressed, had been sharpening for two centuries or more. As much by the neglect of the commonalty as by any ingenuity of their own, the governing bodies of many boroughs were to appropriate to themselves the right of co-option to their number. In 1527 at Nottingham, the Mickletorn jury would be brought to complain of corrupt appointments to the aldermanry, the 'burgesses and commonalty of the said town not being made privy nor thereunto consenting, contrary to the corporation of the same town, and also contrary to the statute of free elections in such case ordained, issued and provided'. Such action, the jurors thought, could be said to threaten the very liberties and franchises of the borough, themselves dependent upon free election.[90]

Already, though, the 'forfeiting and losing' of liberties, of which the men of Nottingham complained, had taken effect elsewhere. From 1421, the twelve aldermen of Cardiff had filled vacancies in their number by nominating replacements from the 'more discreet and fit' of the burgesses. It was they, too, who selected candidates to fill the office of bailiff, and who chose the two serjeants of the borough.[91] At Wilton in the fifteenth century, at Lewes and Lincoln by the sixteenth, the twelve had become self-perpetuating.[92] Where wealth was one criterion of rank, occupation might be another. Of the governing body of York in 1420, no fewer than twenty-two were merchants, two were drapers, and only five had been recruited from the ranks of the manufacturing crafts. And whatever their background, almost all had held office before. Eleven aldermen were listed in 1420, of whom seven had already been mayor of York, one was then serving in that capacity, and another would be mayor the following year. Among the twenty-one councillors of the city, nineteen had already held office as sheriff or bailiff; another, two years previously, had been chamberlain.[93]

Nowhere was the deliberate exclusion of lesser men and of the unenfranchised more rigidly enforced than in fifteenth-century Leicester. Allegedly by the general consent of the mayor, his brethren and all the commons of Leicester, it was provided in 1466 that 'from that time forth no man should presume to enter the gild hall otherwise called the mayor's hall at any common hall held there or to be held but only those and such as are enfranchised, that is to say, men entered into the merchant gild.' The very next year, the terms of the decree were extended. The prohibition, significantly, was to operate 'as well at the day of election of my master the mayor as all other common halls'.[94] Elections, however, continued to cause trouble at Leicester, and in 1489, by authority of Parliament, more drastic remedies were applied. Great discords, it was reported at the time, had arisen at both Leicester and Northampton, 'by reason of the multitude of the inhabitants being of little substance and of no discretion, who exceed in the assemblies the other approved, discreet, and well disposed persons, and by their confederacies, exclamations and headiness have caused great troubles in the elections and in the assessing of lawful charges.' From this time forward, elections to the forty-eight at Leicester were to become the charge of the mayor and the twenty-four brethren of the bench, their choice to be limited to the 'wiser and sadder' of the borough. Both governing bodies were to be concerned in the election of the mayor, but it was the twenty-four alone, already self-perpetuating since 1477, who would choose the

94 Musicians and dancers, Flemish, mid-fourteenth-century

justices of the peace and the parliamentary burgesses of Leicester, and who would appoint to other offices in the borough. Almost immediately, at the next mayoral elections, there was trouble again with the commonalty, but so complete was the victory of the brethren of the bench on that occasion, that their authority was not afterwards seriously threatened.[95]

Of course, control of appointments within the borough, tight and restrictive though it might seem, was also, in some measure, inevitable. To represent adequately his community, a man must have both skill and substance; in conducting its affairs, in one office or another, his effectiveness would increase with experience. Before beginning his first term as mayor of Southampton in 1517, Thomas Lyster had already been steward of the borough in 1509–10, water bailiff in 1511–12, court bailiff in 1512–13, and sheriff in 1514–15. His contemporary, John Mille, town clerk of Southampton for many years, held that office conjointly with the recordership, and would represent his borough at Westminster.[96] Not surprisingly, the parliamentary burgesses of a century before, as studied nationally for the session of 1422, were many of them members of just this administrative class in the boroughs. As Professor Roskell has shown, there were three mayors representing their

146

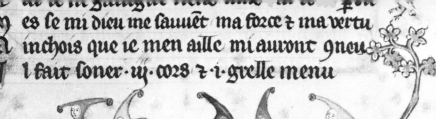

boroughs in 1422, and six others had been mayor during the previous
administrative year; of the twelve representatives returned by the county
boroughs, seven had formerly been sheriff; there were seven bailiffs
present as parliamentary burgesses, with a borough auditor and a treas-
urer. At least forty of these men were merchants in their home community, and there were men of great substance among them.[97]

For better or for worse, the appropriation of office by a single class
spread through the English boroughs. The appointment of parliamentary burgesses by the mayor and council of twelve in fifteenth-century
Wilton,[98] was matched at Stamford and at Grantham, newly incorporated in the mid-century, where it was the same body that came to
elect the borough coroners.[99] Justices of the peace, new to the fifteenth-
century boroughs, from the first were chosen from a very small group.
When, in 1401, the borough of Southampton was empowered to appoint
justices of its own, it was provided that they should be selected from the
aldermen and other 'discreet' men of the community, under the
guidance of the mayor.[100] It was the mayor, similarly, who empanelled
the electors in sixteenth-century Lincoln, when the four justices of the
peace were chosen.[101]

On a very much wider front, effective control of burgess admissions reinforced the mayor and his associates. This might take the form, as was to be the case in the Cinque Ports, of a statutory limitation of numbers.[102] But it was as likely to be employed in a more flexible fashion to manipulate admissions over the years, in tune with the interests of the oligarchy. As early as the mid-fourteenth century, the mayors and stewards of Exeter were to be accused of widening the franchise to suit their own interests, 'against the wishes of the better men of the city, to the disinheritance of the city'.[103] And it is just this characteristic flexibility in freeman admissions that has been noted particularly by Dr Dobson in his recent study of late-medieval York. At York at least, and very probably elsewhere, the city government was not concerned in all circumstances to limit admissions to the freedom, nor could a rise in freeman admissions necessarily have meant progressive emancipation of the craftsmen. Indeed, the manipulation of admissions by the ruling elite was made possible by the weakness of the crafts. In fifteenth-century York, neither right of birth nor the completion of an apprenticeship were the most common avenues for entry to the freedom of the city, and so long as outsiders continued willing to purchase their way into that freedom, the York magistracy, by varying the price of admission continuously over the years, could determine who its freemen should be.[104]

While it might not always have been the case that oligarchy was openly resented, certain aspects of its concentration of office in the hands of the few could not have failed to provoke discontent. The mayor of Doncaster who, after 1467, was both justice of the peace and coroner for his borough,[105] must have had many equivalents elsewhere. Yet where the same man, in the company of his immediate associates, made the by-laws, enforced them, and sat in judgement on offenders, true justice would certainly have been hard to find. In the similar circumstances of contemporary Southampton, complaints of corrupt juries and the power of 'great acquaintance' became commonplace in the fifteenth century. To obtain justice in Southampton's courts, it would be as well to be sure of one's friends. From 1448, when their enemy John Fleming became recorder in the borough, the provost and fellows of Queen's College, Oxford, appropriators of the hospital at God's House, could expect no justice there, for 'no one will gainsay him'. Fleming, of an old and respected Southampton family, had been clerk of recognizances in the borough in 1439 and had already served two terms as mayor; in 1449–50, he would be a parliamentary burgess for Southampton.[106]

Such isolation of power within a small class, and its further concentration, during the period of his office, in the mayor, made of the mayoral elections in many boroughs peculiarly sensitive occasions. Those riots at mayor-making at Northampton and Leicester, complained of in 1489 (see p. 145), were not isolated occurrences. Already in 1460, on just such an occasion, the commons of Southampton had risen to dispute the right of the ruling oligarchy to nominate its candidates for the mayoralty, and had acclaimed successfully their own nomination for the office.[107] Later, they were to riot again on an issue just as fraught: the enclosure of the common lands of the borough.[108] And it was on the matter of rights of common again that Laurence Saunders, one of Coventry's chamberlains in 1480, first set himself up against the oligarchy. In a struggle that lasted sixteen years or more, Saunders disputed the right of powerful men in the borough to run sheep on the Coventry commons in numbers above their entitlement. Although ultimately unsuccessful, it was as the acknowledged champion of the commonalty that Saunders stood out in Coventry for the space of almost two decades, and it was through his own sufferings at the hands of the magistracy that he raised other serious matters of dispute. Already, well before his time, there had been riots at Coventry over the price of bread, during which loaves had been thrown at the mayor. In 1495, the Lammastide verses nailed to St Michael's church door, in complaining of the persecutions of Saunders himself, named further grievances of the commonalty, among them monopolistic restrictions in the cloth trade, oppressive apprenticeship fees, and exclusive limitation of participants in the Lammastide procession. There may, indeed, have been some truth in what Saunders is alleged to have said the previous Lammas Day: 'Sirs, hear me, we shall never have our right till we have struck off three or four of the churls' heads that rule us.'[109]

It was not just class antagonism that fuelled popular resentment at Coventry, for there were tensions, too, between the ruling elite and the crafts, as within the crafts themselves. Some part of these, it is perfectly true, might have been relieved by the small size of the normal manufacturing unit, by rigid apprenticeship regulations which protected as well as restricted the trades, and by the provision of deliberate civic diversions in pageants, mystery plays and regular seasonal festivities. Nevertheless, there can be no doubting the calculating cynicism of the Coventry magistracy in first recognizing and then rebuffing the journeymen gilds in their borough,[110] nor the suspicions that led the rulers of contemporary York to forbid such associations altogether.[111] While it may never be that the great body of the underprivileged urban poor will find an adequate historian,[112] it is not, certainly, of its grievances that we are chiefly ignorant. A reforming mayor of sixteenth-century Southampton would one day speak of the tendency, still on the increase in his town, for all high office to be appropriated by those burgesses, for the most part professional men, 'as do use and occupie sciences and faculties'. They did it, he was sadly to observe, to the exclusion of those 'men of occupacions, artificers and handie crafts men, who seldome or never attaynethe within this towne to that welthe and abilitie to beare the said offices'.[113] In truth, 'pore folkes hath but fewe frendes'.

5 The Borough Constitution

Today's historians are accustomed to make difficulties for themselves in arriving at a definition of a borough: they emphasize the persisting inequalities of privilege among boroughs and stress the inconsistencies of the record. Yet while certainly these inequalities existed, to be recognized and exploited at the time, by the thirteenth century the greater precision of the law and the new demands of government required that, by whatever process, definitions of a kind should be reached, for government without them would have been impossible. When, in that century, the king's justices on circuit came into a county, its sheriff would have to summon representatives to meet them: four men and the reeve from every vill, or minor settlement, a jury of twelve from each borough. And when, later in the same century, the summons to parliament came, he would have to decide again which were the boroughs in his county, before requiring their representatives to attend.[1] On occasion, from one year or from one decade to the next, he might change his mind, and might vary the list of his boroughs. But one thing, at least, is certain; he did not recognize the difficulties that we do. His concern was not to isolate the one privilege or exemption that would fix a settlement's quality as a borough, nor did he, in general, trouble himself with nice distinctions between the economic and the legal characteristics of his 'urban place'. There was always to remain an important technical distinction between the settlement with full borough status and the lesser market town, and this was to become more, rather than less, important in the later Middle Ages. However, in the earlier period, at least, a settlement would come to be rated a borough because it had an appropriate population, because a good proportion of its inhabitants was engaged in industry or trade, because it had a market, because it had a court, because its men held their tenements in free burgage, and could exchange, devise, or sell them as they willed. Among the sheriff's many guides to acceptable borough status, the franchises were important; but they were not alone.

Nobody can say, and this, of course, is one of the difficulties of definition, where many of the already antique borough customs of the twelfth century originated. Nevertheless, by the reign of Henry I, and probably for some generations before, they had begun to take a distinctive shape of their own. To this reign, in particular, there belongs a whole series of early recognitions of gilds merchant, with accompanying exemptions from tolls. And to it, also, relates that very full record of the customs of the borough of Newcastle-upon-Tyne, drawn up in the reign of Henry II but purportedly setting down the practice at the time of his grandfather. As in the case of a contemporary Canterbury document, the Newcastle charter implies that the burgesses had long enjoyed a considerable say in both trading controls and in government. In both charters, the importance of the borough court is made clear, and the rights there of the burgesses are protected: specifically, at Newcastle, to exclude in some causes the intervention of the king's officer, or reeve. Extensive freedoms from tolls, confirmed to the citizens of Canterbury, were to operate 'throughout England and the ports of the sea'. At Newcastle, those vital borough liberties which were so often to be disguised elsewhere in the general 'custom of the city', were spelled out:

Pleas which arise in the borough shall there be held and concluded except those which belong to the king's crown . . . If a burgess have a son in his house and at his table, his son shall have the same liberty as his father. If a villein come to reside in the borough, and shall remain as a burgess in the borough for a year and a day, he shall thereafter always remain there . . . A burgess can give or sell his land as he wishes, and go where he will, freely and quietly unless his claim to the land is challenged.[2]

Arguably, it was the last of these privileges which was also to be the most important, both in the definition of the borough and in the setting in motion of that process which, by separating borough and shire, gave the advantage in growth to the former. To Dr Hemmeon, at least, burgage tenure constituted the unique distinguishing mark of the borough, 'for every borough must have it, and it could not exist outside a borough'.[3] And although this was certainly an exaggeration, rendered less useful by several quite serious exceptions,[4] his point retains much force. In his notoriously laconic recognition of borough status at London, the Conqueror had yet found room for the acknowledgement of special privileges relating to the inheritance of land: 'And I will that every child shall be his father's heir after his father's day.'[5] Nor was this a right confined to London, as the Domesday evidence makes clear,[6] and it came to be valued most particularly in every emergent town.

Heritability of tenements, the right of free sale, the ever more common practice of a fixed money rent: these were the privileges and practices that would rid the towns of oppressive feudal obligations, and would ensure their independence from the landowners. Among the ancient customs of Newcastle-upon-Tyne, a clause had read: 'Any burgess may have his own oven and handmill if he wishes, saving always the rights of the king's oven.'[7] And while the exemption may seem insignificant enough to us, it was yet symptomatic of just that remarkable freedom from feudal obligations that has been noted recently as an outstanding characteristic of tenure in twelfth-century London.[8] Without such freedoms, as it would be easy to demonstrate in the case of some of the less fortunate seigneurial boroughs (see pp. 168–70), the growth of the towns might indeed have been seriously impaired.

That growth, of course, depended in the first instance on economic health. In an early Beverley charter of the reign of Henry I, datable to between 1124 and 1133, there is a particularly significant conjunction. The document is brief and very much to the point. After confirming the men of Beverley in their free burgage, Henry went on immediately to recognize their gild merchant and to warrant their freedom from toll throughout Yorkshire.[9] Merchant gilds, we know, were in existence earlier elsewhere, and some, at least, may have had their roots in pre-Conquest institutions of an essentially similar kind.[10] Nevertheless, what the Beverley document illustrates with exceptional clarity is the bringing together in the king's mind, as well as in that of his subjects, of the one fundamental urban liberty with the economic machinery by which that liberty had been bought and by which privilege, in later years, would certainly be extended. In the generations that post-dated the Conquest and that preceded the grant by John to many of his larger towns of effective independence from the counties, undoubtedly the most important advances achieved by the English boroughs lay in the common recognition within them of free transferability of land, and in the protection, by royal or seigneurial directives, of their trade. Together, as the interference of the local landowners fell away and as conditions grew increasingly favourable to trade, these brought to the towns the social and economic self-sufficiency that would equip them to bargain directly with the king. John's charters, when they came, did not stand in isolation, for the ground had long been prepared. Almost invariably, they included a comprehensive exemption from tolls, but they conferred also an important fiscal privilege: the right to by-pass the sheriff in matters of royal taxation, to hold the town in chief from the king, and to pay its farm, or annual tax, direct into the Exchequer. In the first tentative moves in this direction, frequently unsuccessful though they were, we can trace the emergence in twelfth-century England of a new spirit of independence in the towns.

Professor Tait, in describing the grant by Henry I of the fee farm to London, judged it the 'first great landmark in the development of self-government in the English boroughs'.[11] And though the grant was not itself long-lived, there is no doubt of its essential importance. 'Know,' said Henry, 'that I have granted to my citizens of London that they shall hold Middlesex at farm for 300 pounds by tale for themselves, and their heirs from me and my heirs, so that the citizens shall appoint as sheriff from themselves whomsoever they choose, and shall appoint from among themselves as justice whomsoever they choose to look after the pleas of my crown and the pleadings which arise in connection with them. No other shall be justice over the same men of London.'[12] Within a few years, London was to lose its charter, but important new precedents in self-government had been set, to which the citizens, half a century later, would return. They were precedents which other communities would remember, and which Lincoln, in some measure, had anticipated already in an independent successful proffer for its farm obtained very probably, in fee.[13]

Lincoln was to be more successful than London in retaining control of its farm. It is likely that it was the Lincoln reeve who accounted for his city's farm at the Exchequer throughout the reign of Stephen, and the same would be true again through most of the reign of Stephen's successor. But the transfer of the farm to the sheriff again, early in Henry II's reign, although brief, was nevertheless highly significant. Henry might be prepared to confirm his grandfather's practice of leasing their farms to select boroughs, and indeed would come himself to extend the privilege, beyond the five already so favoured, to Orford, Grimsby, Scarborough and Newbury. But he would never grant a farm in perpetuity.[14] We have no certain means of telling what was on his mind in this, but a reasonable guess might be, as has usually been taken to be the case, that Henry was determined not to allow the contagion of the French sworn commune to spread to his English possessions. Briefly, and abortively, the commune had appeared there already at London, where the citizens, taking swift advantage of the troubled times of Stephen and Matilda, had dared to claim a say in the selection of the king. When it showed itself again in Henry's reign, first at Gloucester and then at York, the movement was summarily crushed.[15]

In northern France, its particular home, the sworn commune had sometimes taken on a revolutionary character, and it was this, no doubt, that appealed to some of the more refractory spirits among its English imitators, as it would certainly have alarmed the king. 'Come what may,' Robert Brand would cry in 1193, 'Londoners shall have no king but their mayor!'[16] However, the significant quality of the English commune, wherever it appeared, was rather its association with an existing ruling class. Even in Robert Brand's London, as Miss Reynolds has recently argued, there is nothing to show that the revolutionary commune of 1191 led to any substantial change in the character of the ruling elite.[17] At Gloucester, in 1169, and at Oxford, following London's lead in 1191, it was the members of the gild merchant who clearly dominated the proceedings.[18] And, indeed, it was precisely in the emergence of the gild itself as an association sworn to protect, among other things, the liberties of the town, that Professor Tait detected the 'active communal principle' in the English twelfth-century borough.[19] Unchecked, and even encouraged, by the king, the gild merchant drew to itself the reins of magistracy. In the thirteenth century, as we shall see, the officers of gild and borough not uncommonly were one and the same. In the twelfth century, while the king's reeve at least nominally retained control of the borough, the organization that would eventually supplant him was growing by his side. In the borough court, the burgesses learnt the techniques of justice. In their gild, it was frequently the same men who discovered the advantages of unity in action, who came to possess and administer property in common, and who developed procedures of common accounting. It was these men who, whenever the king would let them, would assume responsibility for the borough farm. Yet it was not just the exclusion of one royal officer, the sheriff, that they wanted. Both London and Gloucester, it has been pointed out, possessed their farms before the communal movements developed there.[20] Rather, they were ambitious for genuine self-government in economy and law, and it was for this, as the king very probably realized for himself, that they had been preparing themselves throughout the century. Stephen's other anxieties, and Henry's reluctance to be moved on precisely this issue, put back the self-determination of the English boroughs some generations behind many of their French equivalents. Yet one of the results of this prolonged enforced stagnation was to make the towns ready for immediate action just as soon as the king's hand relaxed. The flood of municipal charters that characterized the reigns of Henry's sons has sometimes been seen as the product, chiefly, of the king's pressing financial needs, or of his wish to find allies other than his barons. But the first initiatives in the promotion of the charters came surely from the towns themselves. It is Henry's hostility, far more than any conscious policy of either Richard I or John, that must explain the timing of the charters. What Henry could hold back for his lifetime, they could no longer control.

In the charters of John, as analysed by Adolphus Ballard many years ago, it is easy to follow the new direction that the boroughs of England were taking. They were no longer, that is, concerned primarily with emphasizing the tenurial privileges which had bulked so large in the earlier charters and custumaries of the towns. Burgage tenure, important though it remained, was by now a widely accepted characteristic of borough status, however else that status might be limited and defined. It needed no more specific protection than the general blanket clause which in so many of John's charters conferred on individual towns the customs of an older-established, or more privileged, neighbour. The rights of the borough courts still required definition, and a good proportion of the charters included provisions for the bringing of actions in law before the courts of the boroughs, without recourse to other courts outside. But the real innovations of the charters lay elsewhere. There was to be, as always, a change in emphasis rather than the introduction of policies totally unknown before. Nevertheless, John's very general grant of their fee farms to his burgesses, in towns scattered throughout the country, had no precedent. It was accompanied everywhere by comprehensive exemptions from tolls: a feature of almost every borough charter of the reign.[21]

To the lawyer, these charters were to remain highly unsatisfactory. They spoke of a *communitas*, but did nothing to confer on it a genuine personality in law. Yet it is certain that a new sense of the community of the borough was indeed emerging, and that it was coming to find expression in a number of interesting ways. Among these, there was the holding of property by the borough, a function of the work of the borough court and, still more, of the collection of local tolls.[22] Whereas John's charters commonly conferred a general exemption from tolls, they also sometimes specified the right of individual boroughs to impose such tolls,[23] and the one, certainly, is hardly to be explained without the other. Few towns were to possess much property in lands or in rents before the fourteenth or even the fifteenth centuries, but they all kept money at one time or another in the common chest of the borough, and it was probably in routine transactions relating to this money, even more than by way of the formal charters and other instruments that have come down to us, that they developed that other unambiguous symptom of the emergence of a corporate identity in the community, the common seal of the borough. Of the municipal seals now known to us, it is probable that the Oxford seal of 1191 can be counted the earliest. Nevertheless, York and Winchester, Worcester, Gloucester, Scarborough and London, Exeter, Southampton, Taunton and Ipswich, all were employing seals of their own by the early thirteenth century.[24] And it was at Ipswich that the first use of the seal, in the year 1200, coincided significantly with the grant of a charter by King John, and with the development, uniquely recorded, of an appropriate machinery for self-government.[25]

John's charter to Ipswich was dated 25 May 1200. With the grant of the fee farm, and with the usual exemptions from tolls and protection of burgesses in actions at law outside the borough, it included unusually explicit directions for the election, by the burgesses of Ipswich and *per commune consilium villate sue*, of two bailiffs and four coroners. To effect this, we are told in a further contemporary commentary of exceptional interest, a meeting of the whole town (*tota villata*) was held on the 29 June following, in the churchyard of St Mary Tower (Fig. 95). The elections required by the king were carried out in accordance with his instructions, but on the same occasion the further proposal was made that the men of Ipswich, following a precedent allegedly established already elsewhere in other free boroughs of the realm, should elect for themselves a governing body, or council, of twelve 'capital portmen'. A date was fixed, and an electoral body consisting of four worthy men from each parish met to conduct the election on 2 July. That day also, all the men of the town swore a solemn oath to obey their officers, and to maintain the liberties and free customs of their borough. On 13 July, the newly appointed officers of the town gathered to do business. They established procedures for the collection of tolls, and provided for the setting aside of receipts to meet the farm of the borough; they decided on the appointment of additional town officers to effect attachments and distraints, and to supervise the prison; they suggested the election of a *probus et legalis et idonius* burgess to serve as alderman, or chief executive, of the Ipswich gild merchant, assisted by four of his fellows; they decreed that only men prepared to play their full part in the affairs of the borough might claim exemption from its tolls; and they ordered

95 Ipswich in the early seventeenth century (Speed)

the making of a town seal. It was as if, as has been well said, the community of burgesses at Ipswich had come to feel not only that it was 'passing from a lower to a higher rank among the communities of the land, but that some new degree or even kind of unity has been attained: it must have a seal that is its, for it may now come before the law as pure unit and live as a person among persons.'[26]

On 10 September, in the churchyard again, all the townsmen of Ipswich reassembled to hear and to approve these decisions. They elected new bailiffs and other officers for the coming year, and fixed another meeting for 12 October to complete the business before them. Within the month, the town seal had been fashioned, to be on display at the full meeting of the townsmen in October. Three men were there chosen to look after it, and further selections took place of the gild alderman and his four associates. Before the whole assembly, the best way to maintain the gild was discussed, and suitable rewards were allotted to the alderman and the twelve capital portmen. All the laws and free customs of the borough, it was decided, were to be transcribed onto a roll to be called *le Domesday*, in the charge of the bailiffs for reference. Similarly, the alderman was to preserve in his keeping a full record of the statutes of the gild.[27]

Having come to terms with the king, the burgesses of Ipswich that same year were to decide on their attitude to the Church. Those bishops, abbots and priors, they provided, who might have tenements or other properties in Ipswich, were to continue exempt from custom in the borough on the product of their own lands or on goods bought for their sole use. On anything else, they were to pay the normal tolls. It was to escape such tolls and to avoid discrimination against their goods and those of their servants that, in 1200, the priors of Holy Trinity and St Peter, Ipswich, bought themselves into the franchise.[28]

The Ipswich record is an impressively detailed account of the local initiatives which must everywhere have followed John's charters. But it owes its very special importance to the fact that it is unique. John himself only rarely specified in his charters the election of local officers to replace the royal reeve, and his successors were to be no more explicit. Although John appears to have accepted the existence of mayors in several of the boroughs of his realm, it was only to London that he granted, in 1215, the right to elect to such an office; there was to be no similar royal recognition of the mayoralty in England until Nottingham obtained the same authorization in 1284.[29] In the case of lesser borough officials, the record is only a little more complete. In 1200, contemporaneously with Ipswich, four other boroughs – Northampton, Shrewsbury, Lincoln and Gloucester – were similarly instructed by John to proceed to the election of two bailiffs and four coroners.[30] Occasionally, too, he would authorize elsewhere the election of a reeve or of a head-officer, whatever his title, at a borough. But his concern, in this particular, was clearly erratic, and he seems for the most part to have rested content to leave the sorting out of such details to his burgesses. Quite possibly, he would have done so because the solution in many boroughs had already taken shape. From the Conquest onwards, the reeve had featured in borough documents as a royal official, charged

159

96 The great door of St Mary's Gild, Lincoln, late-twelfth-century

with the collection of the king's dues in the town, and usually having the chief voice there. Yet, by the mid-twelfth century or before, the office had come to be sold not infrequently to speculators, and local men took a part in the bidding. Robert of St Laurence and Gervase of Hampton, successive reeves or *prepositi* of late-twelfth-century Southampton, regarded the borough as their home.[31] At Canterbury similarly, from about 1200, the reeves were changing every year, and were usually, if not always, local men. Briefly, before the autumn of 1216, the men of Canterbury adopted a new and foreign practice, electing a mayor in place of their customary two joint-reeves. But the mayoralty was short-lived and it was the reeves who, on the granting of Canterbury's charter in 1234, were replaced by elected bailiffs.[32]

The Canterbury charter, coming to the city comparatively late in the day, is unlikely to have conferred, in practice, many powers of self-government not already freely enjoyed by the citizens, and elsewhere too, there is reason to suppose, local governing bodies grew up in advance of the charters. When the men of Ipswich, in 1200, had elected their twelve capital portmen, they had done so, allegedly, on good precedents, and though we have only their word for the existence of such councils in boroughs elsewhere in the realm, what they said is not really implausible. It suggests, although it does not establish, that pre-charter associations of some sophistication might have developed in several boroughs, capable of assuming their government, and very probably already concerned in it. Whatever the origins of such councils might have been – and they may, if they existed, have had something to do with continental models, with the borough court, or with the gild merchant – they foreshadowed those councils of twelve or of twenty-four *prudhommes* that commonly began to make their appearance in the records of the thirteenth-century boroughs. At London, a council of twenty-four was elected in 1206, and it is not improbable that the Lincoln council of twenty-four, although first explicitly mentioned only in 1219, was already in being some years before that date.[33] The Northampton council of twelve, elected in 1215, at the king's command, to work in conjunction with the mayor, clearly shows how the responsibilities of such councils would develop. Whereas at Ipswich the twelve capital portmen, an executive council, had included in their number the principal officers of the borough, the role of the Northampton twelve was advisory.[34] Steadily, in later years, the divide would grow, as the power of the executive increased,[35] and there are intimations of this already observable from early in the thirteenth century. In two contemporary Leicester lists, not many years separated in date for many of the same names appear in each, the alderman was first included with the twenty-four and then added to the list as a twenty-fifth.[36] In the first council, his voice might have been one only among many; in the second, he stands out on his own.

It is not just the isolation of the alderman that lends interest to the Leicester record, for the council was the ruling body not of the town but of the gild, and it was of the gild that the alderman was head. By the mid-thirteenth century, a mayor would replace the alderman as head both of the borough and the gild. But contemporary lists of the jurats of the portmanmoot and of the council of the gild show the membership in each case to have been virtually identical, and it is certain that the dominance of the gild merchant at Leicester would have gone back much further than this. When, in 1209, an official at Leicester first appears in the records as a man of the town and not of the earl, he is described as the 'alderman of the gild'. The council of twenty-four gildsmen, first listed in 1225, would have answered also for the borough.[37]

The emergence of the gild merchant at Leicester as the most influential association in the town has been explained as a consequence of the borough's dependence on its earl.[38] At Bury St Edmunds, another seigneurial borough, the gild was to become so prominent in borough affairs that the abbot was driven to abolish it.[39] However, the subordination, in the move towards self-government, of the borough court, or portmanmoot, to the gild, which in Bury was the result of the unpopular activity in that court of the abbot's bailiff, was not to become general. It might have been seen in certain specialized trading communities like Southampton, where wealth and authority continued to centre on those engaged in overseas trade, but elsewhere the gild's function, as the voice of townsmen otherwise unrepresented before the king, came commonly to an end with the charters. The withdrawal of the king's nominees from the borough court, and their replacement by elected bailiffs chosen from among the townspeople themselves, conferred on the court a new representative role.[40] In the twelfth century, the gild's influence had grown as it appeared to offer the only available alternative to otherwise imperfect representation in the borough court. Furthermore, in those exciting past years of communal experiments, the gild had shown itself the most effective independent platform for the expression of revolutionary views. But with the substitution of borough officials for the royal reeve in the portmanmoot, a redistribution of responsibilities almost everywhere took place. In matters of trade, where the authority and the expertise of its members was dominant and unquestioned, the gild continued to speak first. In the policing of the borough and in the formulation of borough custom, the initiatives would lie with the court.

Undoubtedly, it was to be the building-up of the jurisdiction of the borough court that would become the chief objective of the municipal reformers of the period after John's charters. It has been suggested that the greater boroughs had now secured for themselves a satisfactory degree of independence, and certainly it is true that the reigns of Henry III and Edward I were not remarkable for conspicuous progress in the direction of further self-determination for the boroughs. Spread over the two reigns, there were just twelve new grants of boroughs at fee farm, and of these one might only have been a re-grant.[41] Nevertheless, there was to be one unsought advance in the mid-century that would bring to nineteen boroughs, at first unexpectedly, the valuable privilege

97 Bury St Edmunds, with the abbey church (top centre), showing the chess-board planning of the streets

of return of writs. Canterbury and Colchester led the way together in 1252, but the rush of such grants was to occur between three and five years later, when Henry III, under the threat of baronial discontent, set about the cultivation of new friends.[42] For the most part, it was the concern of the burgesses to execute for themselves the precepts of such royal writs as affected them as tax-farmers,[43] but in securing the co-operation of the king in excluding his sheriff from the boroughs they had won the first round in the long battle that would eventually bring to many of the greater boroughs the freedoms of independent county status.

Valuable though it was as a precedent, the privilege of return of writs might have done little in itself to develop the machinery of self-government in the boroughs had there not been other contemporary administrative advances, if not specifically sanctioned by the king, at least not opposed by him either. The free election of coroners is a case in point. In 1200, the right to elect their own coroners had been conferred on five boroughs by the king, as one among many valuable favours. Yet during the following century there would be other boroughs that would simply assume it for themselves. When, late in the thirteenth century, the men of Arundel were taken to task for failing to observe the formalities, they claimed that they had elected a coroner, without the king's writ, from as far back as they could remember. Temporarily compelled to apply for a writ, they would soon return to their former ways, apparently with impunity.[44] In just the same way, whereas the king, by the mid-century, had begun the practice of granting to individual boroughs the right to have a prison of their own, many would assume it for themselves, without troubling to apply for his sanction.[45]

There were other directions too, no specific concern of the king, in which borough administrations throughout England made significant progress in the thirteenth century. In particular, the development of systematic record-keeping in the borough courts, the central theme of much of Professor Martin's recent work, was to be of crucial importance in the shaping of a new spirit of independence in the boroughs. In a contrast sturdily expressed, Professor Martin has set the record of the proceedings in St Mary Tower churchyard, Ipswich, against an inventory of early-fourteenth-century court rolls of the borough, then preserved in two municipal chests. 'There is a world of difference,' in his opinion, 'between the meeting in the churchyard, and the scientific arrangement of the documents in their appropriate chests. Between the

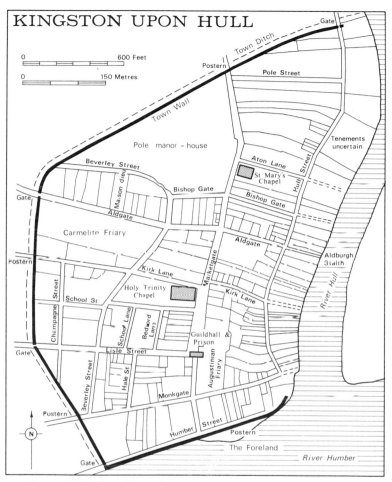

KINGSTON UPON HULL

Gate

Town Ditch

Postern

Pole Street

0 — 600 Feet

0 — 150 Metres

Town Wall

Pole manor – house

Tenements uncertain

Beverley Street

Aton Lane

Hull Street

St Mary's Chapel

Maison dieu

Bishop Gate

Bishop Gate

Gate

Aldgate

Aldgate

Carmelite Friary

Aldburgh Stalth

Postern

Marketgate

Kirk Lane

River Hull

Champagne Street

School St

Holy Trinity Chapel

Kirk Lane

School Lane

Bedford Lane

Guildhall & Prison

Gate

Lisle Street

Augustinian Friary

Beverley Street

Hale St

Monkgate

Postern

N

Humber Street

Postern

The Foreland

Gate

River Humber

98 The probable disposition of tenement plots in medieval Hull, from the evidence of a rental of 1347 (V.C.H.: Stanewell)

two lies a great change in thought and habits, whose course is marked by marginalia and endorsements, by entries collected and then dispersed. These two documents define the birth of the borough of Ipswich as a self-conscious, self-governing community; and in the period between them are laid the foundations of the whole structure of documentary evidence upon which not only the history, but the very growth of the town depends.'[46]

It is characteristic of the continuing concern of all within the towns for the protection and perpetuation of their valuable right to free transferability of lands, that an important part of the work of the borough courts came to be the recognition and the registration of deeds of title. As it developed into the systematic enrolment of deeds, this procedure in the courts was itself to be regarded as an important privilege, of which the burgesses, as they would show in the sixteenth century, would not be lightly deprived. In this, as in so much else, the privileged borough stood apart from the rest of the nation. The rights of the burgess were not those of the ordinary Englishman; in significant particulars, his law was not the ordinary law of the land.[47]

It was through the thirteenth century, then, building on the work of the twelfth, that the mass of borough privilege took shape. Although beset by forbidding technicalities, especially in the definition of the authority of the borough court, its scope, in certain basic principles, was clear. A new town, founded in the thirteenth century, would begin life, as both its lord and its first settlers were agreed, with at least three essential liberties. It would have to be a *liber burgus*, or free borough, in which the new settlers would hold their plots by burgage tenure, enjoying free transferability of lands. Its court would need to be distinct from that of the adjoining manor, and would gain further from independence, so far as this could be achieved, from the sheriff. Without freedom from tolls, on a local and preferably a national level, the new borough might very well fail.[48] Not surprisingly, the charters conferred by their founders on such new and speculative settlements were commonly particularly explicit on the rights and liberties to be enjoyed there. They had to be so. As was noted in the case of the new seigneurial foundations at Salford (*circa* 1230) and Stockport (*circa* 1260), the charters respectively of Randle, earl of Chester, and Robert de Stockport far exceeded in length and in detail the charters that the king himself had earlier granted, even to his greater boroughs.[49] They conferred burgage tenure on the settlers; they granted far-reaching exemptions from the tolls of market and fair; they authorized the election annually of a chief officer in the community; and they defined, in many clauses, the scope and function of the court.[50] These privileges were generous and comprehensive: quite enough to attract new settlement. But they differed in one important respect from those usually enjoyed by the freemen of a typical royal borough. In both towns, the lord's steward continued to preside over the portmanmoot. Although both had burgesses, neither could claim to be a 'borough'. To their loss in some respects, and to their profit in others, they

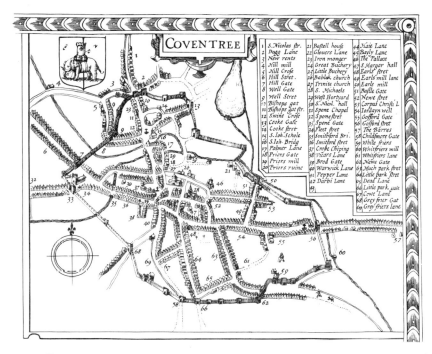

99 Coventry in the early seventeenth century (Speed)

were to remain merely market towns.[51]

Professor Tait has contrasted, to the disadvantage of Manchester and to the favour of nearby Liverpool, the privileges of such a seigneurial market town with those of an established royal borough.[52] And it would certainly be true to say that the town that could expect to benefit most would usually be the one under the lordship of the king. The town of Wyke, later Kingston upon Hull, purchased by Edward I from the abbot of Meaux, offers the classic (if perhaps an extreme) instance of the advantages of continued royal interest. The abbot's foundation at Wyke had not been unsuccessful, for it had grown to a settlement of some sixty households by the time of its acquisition by the king.[53] Yet Edward could clearly offer it much more. Shortly after the purchase of Wyke in 1293, he set about the improvement of the roads leading to the port, to which he had also granted in that year two weekly markets and a fair. Although for some decades under the direction of a royal keeper, Hull was to be granted its borough charter as early as 1299. It acquired

167

the privilege of return of writs; its burgesses were thenceforth to enjoy in perpetuity the protection of their court; they were to be free to dispose of their own property at will; they would elect their own coroner, have their own prison and gallows, and be exempt from tolls wherever they might go in the kingdom. In 1331, the burgesses of Hull bought their freedom from the keeper, with the right to hold the farm of the borough in fee.[54] Already in the 1320s, it was at Hull that William de la Pole had begun to build a great fortune in the wool trade, which would make his family one of the most influential of its age, and which would lead, in due course, to its ennoblement.[55]

At Hull, privilege and growth had accompanied one another, and there is no doubt that to many contemporaries the two would have been considered inseparable. Perhaps, indeed, they commonly exaggerated the economic worth of their liberties, but we shall understand better the force of contemporary demand for privilege in the towns if we see it in the context of the seigneurial boroughs, where the essential liberties were constantly at risk. Certainly, some seigneurial boroughs did well out of the association with their lords. A case for such profitable partnerships has been made out for Warwick,[56] for Grantham,[57] and for Bridgwater,[58] and there were others surely as successful. Nevertheless, for many such boroughs, and particularly for those under monastic lordship, the reverse was frequently as true. Coventry, split in lordship between the earl and the prior, strikingly demonstrated in its early years the economic worth of privilege in an expanding trading community where liberal and conservative policies existed side-by-side. In the 'Earl's Half', a full range of privileges came early to the lord's tenants with the grant, between 1149 and 1153, of free burgage tenure, of a borough court and an elected *justicia*, and of protection and financial incentives to those who would settle in the town. In contrast, progress in the accumulation of the same privileges in the 'Prior's Half' was very much slower, noticeably retarding its economic growth.[59] Discontent with the oppressions of the prior were to reach such a peak that, in 1323, Richard le Latoner and other Coventry associates would turn, in their despair, to sorcery. They promised, it was alleged, a substantial sum to John of Nottingham, reputed a magician, to rid Coventry of its then prior, Henry Irreys, and of others including the king. He was to do this by making wax images, and by stabbing them with the sharpened end of a feather. On the confession of the magician's assistant, the conspirators were brought to trial, but no conviction was obtained.[60]

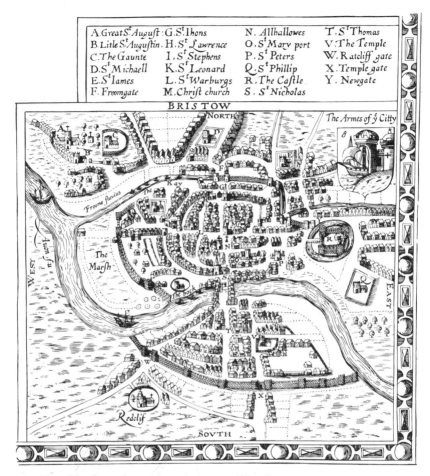

100 Bristol in the early seventeenth century (Speed)

If there are no known parallels to this bizarre incident at Coventry, there are many to the oppressions that provoked it. The abbot of Tavistock, for example, while he remained in most respects a good lord to the borough his predecessor had founded at his gates, continued to supervise it closely. It was he who appointed the portreeve from the list of candidates submitted by the portmen. It was his steward who presided at the Shammel-Moot, or borough court. It was his right to take a percentage on corn ground at the town mill, to collect reliefs on inheritance, and to exact watching and carrying services from his bur-

169

gesses.[61] Only once, in 1258, is there a recorded incident of outright conflict between the abbot and his borough of Tavistock,[62] but in a larger town like Bury St Edmunds, less economically dependent on its abbot, the clashes were to be frequently repeated, and not without good cause. At Bury, the abbey's sacrist and its cellarer enjoyed oppressive rights. It was the sacrist who nominated and who paid the bailiffs, who supervised the town courts, who controlled the market, enforced the assize of weights and measures, and collected tolls.[63] In a commercial community, the claims of the cellarer were peculiarly offensive. As purchaser, he secured precedence over all others in the markets of the borough; as seller, he could charge higher prices for the produce of the abbey's demesnes, exempting his customers from toll.[64]

These were sad oppressions, but they were still not as extreme as those suffered by the would-be burgesses of Cirencester, whose abbot, in defiance of all the evidence, refused even to admit the existence in law of their borough. Originally, Cirencester had been a royal manor, parts of which were granted by Henry I to the new Augustinian foundation that was to grow into one of the greatest houses of the order. Later in the twelfth century, there were burgesses recorded at Cirencester, and it is evident that a town with most, if not all, the attributes of a borough had grown up on what remained of the manor. It was Richard I who sold the manor in perpetuity to the abbot of Cirencester, and it was John, a few years later, who disposed of the right of intervention of his sheriff. By 1225, the burgesses were already complaining of the abbot's uncontrolled exactions. He was to deprive them of their court in 1308, and in 1342, when they took the matter to Chancery with allegations of a deliberate reduction of their privileges, he secured that the proceedings were quashed. The abbot had had to pay heavily for the intervention of the king in the proceedings, but he obtained the promise that he wanted: in future, he was not to be impeached 'touching any borough in Cirencester'.[65] It was to be as if there had never been a borough.

The bitter lesson of the suppression of self-government at Cirencester cannot have failed to be remarked elsewhere. Nor was it altogether a coincidence that the first clear statement of the existence in law of a perpetual borough community should have been framed, in 1345, at the seigneurial borough of Coventry, the direct result of a squabble, finally resolved, between the townspeople and their prior. The Coventry charter was not a charter of incorporation on the later pattern, any more than was the next comparable charter of 1348, conferred on the minor port of Hedon, in the East Riding of Yorkshire, threatened by the growing competition of the king's new borough at Hull. Nevertheless, what both charters confirmed to the burgesses was a shared legal identity, a 'community among themselves', with the power to elect freely, as other towns had done, a mayor and municipal officers.[66] In practice, neither Coventry nor Hedon had achieved for themselves much more than many boroughs had possessed for a matter of five generations, and it was perhaps this, at least as much as the contemporary disruptions of trade depression and plague, that delayed for a quarter of a century the next move in the direction of formal borough incorporation. It would have been difficult, in the first instance, to detect the advantage of incorporation, or to be persuaded of the necessity to seek it. But elevation to separate county status was another matter, for the interference of the sheriff in borough affairs could still be the cause of disquiet. When Bristol, in 1373, was the first to acquire such status, it set an example that others would be glad to follow.

What Bristol successfully contrived was independence from the two counties which had split the borough between them, holding back its administrative development. Confirming the arrangement in letters patent dated 1 September 1373, Edward III re-stated the terms of his charter:

Know that since the 8th of August last past we have conceded to our beloved burgesses of our town of Bristol and to their heirs and successors in perpetuity that the town of Bristol with its suburbs and precincts shall henceforth be separate from the counties of Gloucester and Somerset, and be in all things exempt both by land and sea, and that it should be a county by itself, to be called the county of Bristol in perpetuity, and that the burgesses and their heirs and successors should have in perpetuity within the town of Bristol and its suburbs and precincts certain liberties and exemptions and enjoy them fully and use them as is more fully contained in the said charter.[67]

As befitted its new county status, Bristol was to have now a sheriff of its own. Effectively, too, it had been recognized as a borough incorporate.

What Bristol had secured in 1373, York would acquire for itself in 1396, Newcastle-upon-Tyne in 1400, Norwich in 1404 and Lincoln in 1409.[68] Yet initially what the new county boroughs were anxious to achieve was less a corporate identity in law than a practical independence from the counties, with the exclusion of all royal officials not of their choice or to their liking. While the circumstances existed for the formulation of a full-blown theory of incorporation, it would take another thirty years before the Hull charter of 1440 established a text on which all subsequent charters of the 'classic' age of incorporation would be based. The Hull charter, reciting in full the basic principles without which incorporation, after this date, could not be considered complete, is a very sophisticated document. Its drafting, in 1440, in precisely this form confirms the already long history of the corporation as an idea in the boroughs. Its date suggests the recognition, at just about that time, of the imperative need in many boroughs for sources of revenue other than their depreciated tolls: in effect, for the right to hold property.

Indeed, the quickening interest of the towns in formal incorporation, with the protection that it offered them in the law, could probably be attributed, in the main, to their own growing importance as landowners. For many years already, they had acted each as a community, speaking with a common voice. They had used a municipal seal since the thirteenth century to authenticate documents allegedly the will of the town. They had kept a common chest, and they had collected tolls on behalf of the community to meet its tax obligations and its debts. Persuaded of their corporate identity, they had yet to argue the reality of such an identity in the courts. With property, the position would change. Until the fifteenth century, most boroughs had remained insignificant as landowners, avoiding the worst complications of the law. When borough administrations everywhere turned to property as the most acceptable specific for their ills, they would need to re-define their status.

The problem was not a new one. We can see, if we like, the borough accounts of mid-thirteenth-century Shrewsbury, with their record of communally-held equipment – the wedges, mattocks and picks used in quarrying stone for the defences – as early evidence of property kept by and for the community.[69] And we know that at York, by the late thirteenth century, the citizens had already begun to accumulate some property with a view, very probably, to making up in rents the widening deficiencies of their tolls.[70] But a more important general precedent for the later accumulation of landed property by the boroughs was the recognition, becoming more common in the early fourteenth century, of a borough's right to its waste. If anybody, that is, had questioned the ownership of vacant lots and other waste places in the thirteenth-century town, he would have been told that they belonged to the lord. But, clearly, in a developing community waste lands might become, in due course, a valuable asset, and it was Hull, in precisely this situation in the early fourteenth century, which led the way in 1331 in acquiring from the king the grant of all vacant sites in the town.[71] Four years later, in financial straits, the burgesses of Ipswich, whether or not they were aware of the Hull example, were petitioning for a similar privilege. What they wanted was the right to enclose and develop the waste of their borough, and to turn the income therefrom to their own purposes.[72]

The practice of municipal property-holding, as it came to be recognized throughout the kingdom, led to the inclusion of the towns within the scope of the new mortmain legislation of 1391. The statute of 1391 was designed, chiefly, to check the abuse of unlicensed transfers of land to the many new chantry foundations of the period. But it singled out also two other possible points of evasion of the terms of the original statute of 1279, one of them being the London companies, just then seeking incorporation by royal charter and building up their own endowments in lands, and the other being the towns. In 1279, the statute of mortmain had been directed at those religious houses which, as perpetual institutions, had evaded important feudal incidents on the lands they held, among them wardships, or the profits to be had from holding a minor and his lands in ward, and escheats, the lapsing of property to the lord for want of an heir to succeed to it. In a sweeping gesture of support for those who had lost rights in this way, the statute had prohibited all further gifts of land to the Church, and although the practice soon afterwards developed of issuing licences to alienate lands into mortmain, these could normally only be granted if a local inquisition, set up for the purpose, had found that no existing rights, not already waived, were likely to be infringed. It was not a popular enactment, for the proceedings it initiated were expensive and the results were not always predictable. But it provided a valuable source of additional revenue to the Crown, and attempts to evade a royal licence were blocked wherever possible. By the late fourteenth century, it had become obvious that the towns were everywhere taking on the characteristics of perpetual corporations, identical in many respects to those corporate bodies recognized by the statute of 1279 in the religious houses. In beginning to acquire property of their own, they were proving themselves just as able as the religious houses before them to avoid feudal incidents, for they, too, would never die and would never have heirs to be taken into profitable wardship. To remove the possibility of any such abuses, the statute of 1391 extended the terms of the earlier legislation to cover gilds and fraternities, cities, boroughs and market towns, all of which would now have to seek licences from the Crown to acquire any land for themselves. However, to effect this, an important statement had to be made, certainly of great moment to the towns. They were not to acquire land without licence 'because Mayors, Bailiffs, and Commons of Cities, Boroughs, and other Towns which have a perpetual Commonalty, and others which have Offices perpetual, be as perpetual as People of Religion'.[73] In effect, a full half-century before formal incorporation came generally to be sought by the English boroughs, the existence in reality of perpetual borough corporations had been recognized in the laws of the land.

The statute had been framed because the boroughs were already acquiring property for themselves, but it must also, by making the position of the borough officials clear in law, have encouraged many further acquisitions. That very next year, in 1392, the city of York was granted the right to acquire lands worth £100 annually in rents, to be spent on the maintenance of its bridges.[74] At Winchester, in 1409, the city took charge of its waste and unenclosed lands, and petitioned successfully the following year for a licence to acquire properties worth forty marks in rents.[75] Both had argued the need to accumulate property on behalf of the community to relieve the city finances, and this was to be the common motive everywhere in the country for the building-up of substantial borough endowments. At Southampton, although trade was experiencing a revival in the early fifteenth century, the growing expenses of administration, and in particular of defence, had long made it difficult for the borough authorities to meet the payments due on the farm. Already, before the end of the fourteenth century, the mayor and bailiffs of Southampton had begun to accumulate property in the name of the borough, the first recorded town lease being dated 25 November 1378. But their major purchases of lands and tenements were to follow the grant, in 1415, of a licence to acquire tenements to the value of £100 annually, and within the next two centuries they would gather together an annual revenue from rents worth nearly three times that much.[76]

It was heavy property commitments of this kind that were influential in causing the towns to consider seriously for the first time the devising of a more comprehensive protection for themselves in the law. Already, over many years, the principle of the body corporate had made itself familiar both in the civil and in the canon law. Just recently, it had

101 Two of the gateways of late-medieval York (R. C. H. M.)

YORK
Micklegate Bar

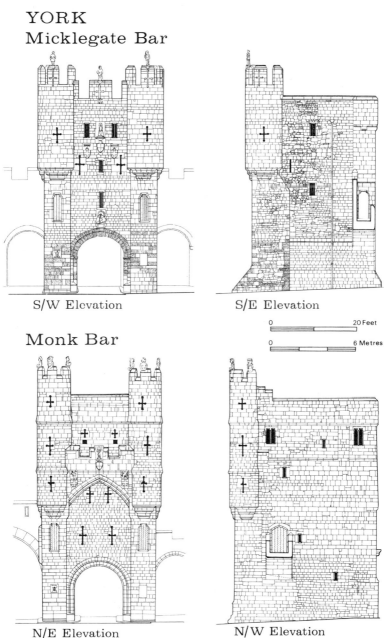

S/W Elevation

S/E Elevation

Monk Bar

0   20 Feet

0   6 Metres

N/E Elevation

N/W Elevation

received a prolonged airing in the public debates that accompanied the Schism, and it had been put to use, in a more practical form, in the first incorporations of the livery companies of London. Certainly, the elaborate and circumspect charter of Kingston upon Hull, granted, as we have seen, in 1440, had not come unheralded, and it would be widely imitated within a very few years because it answered a genuine need. It granted perpetual succession: 'the town of the mayor and burgesses shall be corporate and the mayor and burgesses shall be a perpetually corporate commonalty of the town so incorporated under the name of the mayor and burgesses of that town and shall have perpetual succession.' Disposing of all possibility that the mayor or his officers should be held accountable as individuals for the misdeeds of the community as a whole, it conferred on the new corporation the right to sue and be sued in its own name: '. . . and the mayor and burgesses by that name shall be persons able to pursue and defend all pleas, suits, plaints and demands, and real, personal and mixed actions in any court.' It recognized what was already in practice occurring – the accumulation of property by the authorities: '. . . and the mayor and burgesses shall be persons able and capable in law of acquiring lands, tenements, rents, services and possessions within the said town and its liberty, to be held by them and their successors, notwithstanding the statute of mortmain or any other ordinance or statute to the contrary, saving always to the king the services due.' It acknowledged the validity of the common seal of the borough, and defined the authority, in government and justice, of its officers.[77]

It was by this same charter that Hull was elevated to the status of a county borough, and to contemporaries, undoubtedly, the creation of the new county would have been its most significant innovation. Nevertheless, although formal incorporation, at Hull as elsewhere, was more often the recognition of current realities than the formulation of entirely new doctrine, its practical application in property management was almost immediately put to the test. In 1443, only three years after the recognition of its rights as a property-holder, the new corporation of Hull was granted a licence to accumulate rents to the value of £100, to be assigned to the costs of defence and improvements at the port.[78] In 1435, the comparatively long-standing county borough of Bristol had secured an identical licence, to the same annual value, for the acquisition of lands, tenements, rights of reversion and rents, the proceeds to be spent on repairs to the quays, the walls and the paving of the borough, and on its bridge, worn by the strong tidal flow below it and by the traffic of packhorses and carts.[79]

Essentially, incorporation was as much a response to financial needs as the culmination of a political drive to independence, and these needs were increasing all the time. In the past, the boroughs had been accustomed to rely on the product of their tolls to meet the farm and other administrative expenses. Yet these tolls had everywhere been diminished by exemptions, and could be eroded by a recession in trade. Furthermore, the cost of government itself was mounting. Self-determination in the borough might indeed be a desirable objective, but it was expensive both to achieve and to maintain. If cost had been the only consideration, the elaborate structures of officialdom built up in the late-medieval boroughs must have compared most unfavourably with the simple administrative expedients of the early merchant gild and portmanmoot. Nor had the other charges of government stood still over the centuries. Stone defensive circuits, work on which was to begin at many towns from early in the thirteenth century, would prove a continuous charge, considerably more expensive than the earlier ramparts, ditches and palisades. The paving and proper drainage of the streets, scarcely an issue in the towns before the fourteenth century, would become the urgent concern of late-medieval municipalities. There would be a gildhall to maintain, a weigh-house, prison and other public buildings, municipal water supplies, wharves, cranes, quays, wash-houses and public lavatories. Occasionally, too, the town authorities would engage in business ventures of their own. At Hull, for one, it was the municipality which took charge of the king's tilery and brick manufactory in the borough from as early as 1303. Later in the century, a large part of the product of these kilns was to go into the building of Hull's walls.[80]

In all boroughs, the benefits of more efficient government, continually enlarging its scope, inevitably brought new burdens. The civic establishment of Lincoln, it has been rightly pointed out, was already large by the reign of John: it included the mayor and two bailiffs, four coroners, two city clerks and four beadles.[81] Yet it would grow through the centuries considerably beyond this nucleus, and would come, furthermore, to comprise an increasing proportion of full-time salaried officers, a heavy charge on the revenues of the city. The chief of these, the town clerk, was not, perhaps, generally to come into his own until the fifteenth century or later, but he was making an appearance already in several towns and cities, including Lincoln, in the thirteenth and fourteenth centuries.[82] There were to be recorders in the borough courts from the late fourteenth century, drawing a fee for their services.[83] And one of the consequences of the new propertied status of many fifteenth-century municipalities was the bringing into being of a full-time salaried bureaucracy. It is thought, for example, that the two chamberlains of Salisbury, first appointed in 1408–9, owed their offices to the royal licence of 1406, entitling the city to acquire lands for itself to a rental value of one hundred marks. In 1434, a permanent salaried official, the mayor's serjeant, was engaged to administer these lands.[84]

Everywhere, offices multiplied, and, as civic responsibilities mounted, these would have to be recognized by the voting of commensurate fees. By the end of the fifteenth century, the two constables of Salisbury had become four.[85] A single common serjeant had attended the mayor of Hull in the mid-fourteenth century; by late that same century or early in the next, he had been joined by two other serjeants-at-mace.[86] The growing power of the mayor, recognized by such dignities, had itself to be matched by some reward. In 1364, the citizens of York had thought £20 a sufficient fee for their mayor; yet in 1385 they would raise the sum to £40 and, three years later, to £50.[87] For the first time, in 1420–1, an annual subsidy of £10, to cover his expenses, was assigned to Salisbury's mayor.[88]

Of course, comparatively few borough officers were paid a full wage for their services, and the tradition of amateur participation remained strong in every administration. Nevertheless, at many English boroughs by the later Middle Ages the structure of government had become top-heavy, and the expense of maintaining it was high. Over the whole, the mayor presided, accompanied on all major public occasions by his personal sword-bearer and serjeants-at-mace, bearing the borough regalia. In his judicial and administrative duties, the mayor was assisted from the first by the bailiffs, to be replaced, in the new county boroughs, by the sheriff; for financial help, he could turn to his chamberlains or his steward. At many boroughs, aldermen, assisted by their constables, kept the peace in their separate wards. There might be coroners, a recorder and a town clerk, with a host of lesser officials, some paid and some not, including the beadles, the aletasters, the sealers, searchers, weighers and keepers of the market, the ferrymen and porters, the clock-keepers and criers, the paviours, scavengers and other street-cleaners, the gate-keepers and watchmen of several ranks and kinds. A wealthy borough, in the fifteenth century, might keep two or three minstrels of its own, and few would have been without a chaplain.

6 The Church in the Boroughs

While it was as a public institution, with functions as much social as religious, that the parish church came to prominence in the late-medieval borough, its origins, very often, had been private. In the boroughs, as in the surrounding countryside, the parish system was to develop only exceptionally on the initiative of the bishop, for it was the growth of the community that created the need for a church, and it was the landowner, not the bishop, who built it. Essentially, the pre-Conquest church was both territorial and proprietary: it served the needs of an individual estate and it remained the personal property of its builder. In the twelfth century, as the clergy resumed their own, the whole pattern of church provision and church ownership would change, yet something of the earlier character of the church in the boroughs has been passed down to us in Domesday, and it is there precisely because William's clerks in 1086 saw it as a unit of property.

Such restricted interest must mean, of course, that many existing churches passed unnoticed by the compilers of the survey, and that 'Domesday Book', in consequence, can tell us little of the extent of church provision in the boroughs. Where it is more helpful, though, is in resolving problems of origin. There were, Domesday reveals, significant differences, both geographical and social, in the character of church provision in the kingdom. Broadly, in comparison with the countryside, the boroughs were over-churched, reflecting the partition of lordship that was common there and the supply of a private church, or chapel, to each individual estate. Yet this was more true of the north and east of England, long under pagan influence, than it was of the south or the west, where frequently the grip of a great monastic house had tightened on the parochial organization of the borough in which it was placed. In keeping with the nature of a church in which the proprietary interest was dominant, the town with many lords had many churches; where there was one lord, there might be one church alone, or very few. After the Conquest, the same general tendencies would be observable again,

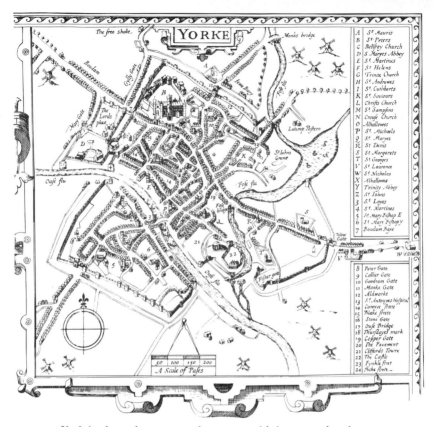

A	St Mauris
B	St Peters
C	Bellfrey Church
D	S Maryes Abbey
E	St Martinus
F	St Helens
G	Trinitie Church
H	St Andrewes
I	St Cuthberts
K	St Saviours
L	Chrifts Church
M	St Sampſons
N	Crouſe Church
O	Alhallowes
P	St Michaels
Q	St Maryes
R	St Denis
S	St Margarets
T	St Georges
V	St Laurence
W	St Nicholas
X	Alhallowes
Y	Trinity Abbey
Z	St Iohns
3	St Loyes
4	St Martines
5	St Mary Bifhop E
6	St Mary Bifhop y
7	Boudam Baxe

8	Peter Gate
9	Collier Gate
10	Goodram Gate
11	Monke Gate
12	Aldwarke
13	St Antonyes Hofpital
14	Comine Strete
15	Blake ſtrete
16	Stone Gate
17	Ouſe Bridge
18	Thurſlayes mark
19	Copper Gate
20	The Pavement
21	Cliffords Towre
22	The Caſtle
23	Fynkle ſtret
24	Picke ſtrete

102 York in the early seventeenth century, with its many churches even after the mergers and closures of the Reformation (Speed)

as new towns developed and others rapidly expanded. Among the relatively late developers, Boston and Grantham were to have only one parish apiece. At Bristol, prosperous and independent already before the arrival of the Normans, the multiplication of parish churches in the twelfth-century borough kept pace with the expansion of its boundaries.[1]

The recognition of the parish church as private property, in both pre- and immediately post-Conquest England, had important consequences in the boroughs. In the first place, churches and private chapels, not always readily distinguishable one from another, might quite often become very numerous; in the second place, they were usually very small. So long as they continued to be regarded as partible, or divisible, inheritances, they were particularly vulnerable to failure, with the result that the life of an individual church might extend no more than a generation, or at least that changes in plan and fabric would be constant. Even in a city as closely studied as medieval Winchester, it is unlikely that we shall ever obtain an adequate picture of church development in the earlier, pre-Conquest years. It is thought, however, that most of the fifty-six parish churches of the city and its suburbs were in existence already before the middle of the twelfth century at latest. Eight of these certainly pre-date the Conquest, and it is very probable that the figure for pre-Conquest foundations will rise substantially as work at Winchester progresses, for already three of the eight are recognizably pre-Conquest in date solely on the archaeological evidence, and there are many still to be tested in this way.[2] Ownership of the Winchester churches would have been divided, as was the case at Norwich, between local landowners, prominent churchmen, and burgesses sometimes acting in concert. In the Norwich Domesday record, Archbishop Stigand is shown to have held two churches, while his brother, Bishop Aethelmaer, had a third; half of one of the Norwich churches belonged to the abbot of Bury St Edmunds; Eadstan, a burgess holding directly from the king, held one-sixth of another church and two more churches of his own; there were fifteen other churches in the hands of Norwich burgesses, and twelve men shared between them the valuable church and glebe of Holy Trinity.[3]

Recent excavations at Winchester and at Norwich have exposed three of these early churches, the most important of which, St Mary Tanner Street, Winchester, is probably also the earliest. The church of St Mary (Fig. 103) is thought to have been a conversion of a small, square, secular building, datable to the ninth century, to which an apsidal chancel was then added. Conversion occurred probably in the tenth century, and would have made the building suitable for use as the private chapel of the large tenement it is known to have adjoined.[4] Both St Pancras, Winchester (Fig. 104), and St Benedict, Norwich (Fig. 107), began life also as simple two-cell structures, to be elaborated greatly in later years.[5] Evidently, they were not built initially to hold large congregations, and they compare closely in this with the diminutive church of St Mary Queningate, Canterbury, the foundations of which were exposed some decades ago.[6] Likewise, it was probably as no more than a family church, at the turn of the tenth and eleventh centuries, that three

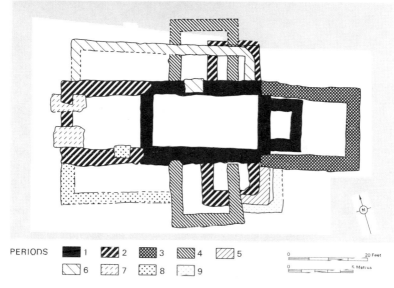

PERIODS ■1 ▨2 ▧3 ▨4 ▨5 ◸6 ▨7 ▨8 ☐9   0   20 Feet   0   6 Metres

103 (Left) Foundations of the church of St Mary, Tanner Street, Winchester, excavated in 1970; an earlier apsidal chancel underlies the later square-ended chancel extension; scale in feet and metres
104 The church of St Pancras, Winchester, progressively enlarged on an early two-cell core (Biddle)

York citizens – Efrard, Grim and Aese – built St Mary Castlegate, York.[7] At Lincoln, before the Domesday survey, Colswein, a speculative builder, had thought it appropriate to supply two churches for the thirty-six houses of his new suburban colony.[8]

With churches both as small and as numerous as these, failures were inevitable, and many of the Domesday churches never reappeared in the records. As early as the mid-eleventh century, it was probably anxiety on this score that prompted Brihtmaer of Gracechurch, alderman of London, to grant away the reversion of his homestead and of the church of All Hallows, with all the endowments that he and his family had bestowed upon it. It was the cathedral priory of Christ Church, Canterbury, that was to have the church and other properties on the death of his wife, Eadgifu, and of his children, Eadmaer and Aethelwine, 'on these terms, that the community shall see to it that the service which belongs to the church neither ceases nor falls off in view of the endowments of the church'.[9]

Brihtmaer, in his own generation, could still feel free to found, endow, and grant away All Hallows as he pleased. Not many years later, a jury at Nottingham was to acknowledge the right of a layman to build a church of his own without licence, and to dispose of its tithes where he wished.[10] But in the Church as a whole, the climate of opinion was turning against lay domination. The debates associated with the Investiture Contest, in exposing the evils of purchased livings and misappropriated dues, were quickly to make it impossible for laymen to retain on the old terms such properties as now arguably belonged only to God. The gift of All Hallows to Christ Church, Canterbury, was only one of a number of similar transactions recorded in a document of about 1100, which listed the priory's London churches. With Brihtmaer's church, these had come to include the valuable 'church of the Blessed Mary with the lands and houses and churches pertaining to it, which Living the priest gave when he became a monk at Canterbury', worth £40 in rents. Another church, probably St Mary le Bow, was given to the cathedral priory by 'Godwine named Bac, the clerk', when he too became a monk there. And there had been similar gifts, also by priests or clerks, of St Pancras, St Michael, St Dunstan and St Alphege, with St Werburga the Virgin, 'which Gumbert possessed with the adjoining house', and 'half the church which is called "Berkinges" which Aelfwine, the son of Farman, gave to the church of Canterbury'.[11]

Of the churches everywhere shed by laymen or simoniacal priests, some went to the bishops, others to long-established monastic communities like Christ Church, Canterbury, and many to the newly founded monastic orders, in particular to the Augustinian canons. Among the earliest and the best recorded of these Augustinian acquisitions were the church and lands of St Botolph without Aldgate, London, granted in 1125 to Holy Trinity Priory, the first London house of the order. The grantors of this exceptionally valuable property were 'certain burgesses of London, descendants of the noble English knights' who, with the assent of King Edgar, had founded the 'Anglisshe cnihtegild' many generations before. A canon of Holy Trinity took charge of the estate and undertook the cure of souls in the parish.[12] Augustinians, again, were to acquire the advowsons of many of the churches at both Ipswich and Southampton,[13] while at Leicester the six churches originally the endowment of a college at the castle were transferred by the earl in 1143 to his new Augustinian foundation in the borough, later to grow into one of the greatest houses of its order, commonly known as the Abbey of St Mary de Pratis, Leicester.[14]

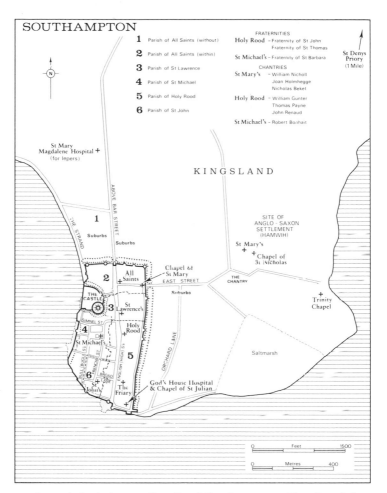

1 Parish of All Saints (without)

2 Parish of All Saints (within)

3 Parish of St Lawrence

4 Parish of St Michael

5 Parish of Holy Rood

6 Parish of St John

FRATERNITIES

Holy Rood – Fraternity of St John
Fraternity of St Thomas

St Michael's – Fraternity of St Barbara

CHANTRIES

St Mary's – William Nicholl
Joan Holmhegge
Nicholas Beket

Holy Rood – William Gunter
Thomas Payne
John Renaud

St Michael's – Robert Boxhart

St Denys Priory (1 Mile)

N

St Mary Magdalene Hospital + (for lepers)

KINGSLAND

ABOVE BAR STREET

THE STRAND

1

Suburbs

Suburbs

SITE OF ANGLO - SAXON SETTLEMENT (HAMWIH)

St Mary's +
+ Chapel of St Nicholas

Chapel of St Mary

All Saints +

2

EAST STREET

THE CHANTRY

THE CASTLE

3 St Lawrence's +

Suburbs

SIMNEL ST

4 St Michael's +

Holy Rood +

ORCHARD LANE

+ Trinity Chapel

BULL (BUGLE) ST

BROAD

ENGLISH HIGH ST

5

Saltmarsh

6 St John's +

The Friary +

God's House Hospital & Chapel of St Julian

+

Feet   1500
0

Metres   400
0

105 An ecclesiastical map of medieval Southampton, with a list of the principal recorded fraternities and chantries in the town

Throughout England, that early 'escalation' of churches which 'shows what happened if the folk were left to develop their cultus according to their own devices',[15] had been checked by the twelfth century, and the churches themselves were coming under the control of appropriate ecclesiastical authorities. Of medieval Stamford's fourteen churches, five were under the patronage of the local Benedictine nunnery, and five more under that of the Norman priory at St-Fromond; two were held by

185

Durham cathedral priory, and one each by the Lincolnshire Benedictine
houses of Belvoir and Crowland.[16] At Lincoln itself, the process may be
followed in the bishop of Lincoln's accumulations, gathering into his
own hands whatever churches he could acquire in the city. Bishop
Robert Bloet, at the beginning of the twelfth century, had secured for
the endowment of his cathedral a formal right to all those churches in
the city held by their priests from the king. It was not stated in the grant
which these churches might be, and successive bishops through the
twelfth century made use of the right to lay claim to each church of
which the ownership came in doubt. In the next century, a local jury
recalled the time when there had been many churches owned by Lincoln
citizens and served by many priests. The king, it was thought, had then
called upon these citizens to answer for the advowsons of their churches,
and it had been neglect of the summons that had brought them into his

106 (opposite) Procession round the church at Le Puy, Auvergne, Flemish, mid-fifteenth-century

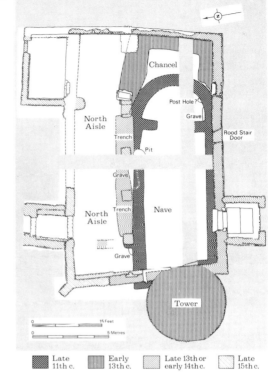

NORWICH St. Benedict

Chancel

Post Hole?

North Aisle

Grave

Trench

Rood Stair Door

Pit

Grave

North Aisle

Trench

Nave

Grave

Tower

0   15 Feet
0   5 Metres

| Late 11th c. | Early 13th c. | Late 13th or early 14th c. | Late 15th c. |

107 The eleventh-century church of St Benedict, Norwich, as later extended and improved (Roberts)

hands. From the king, the churches had come to the bishop, and from the bishop to the precentor, to be held in the name of the cathedral and to its profit.[17]

To the layman, the building of a church or a bridge, or the financing of any public work, might still be the source of spiritual profit, although not of monetary gain. In the words of an early-thirteenth-century penitential, attributed to Robert of Flamesbury:

Concerning remissions which consist in the building of churches or of bridges or in other matters, different men have different opinions as to how much value they have and for whom. But we, whatever is said, commend such remissions to all, especially to those who are burdened and weighed down with sins and penances.[18]

The hesitations were real, but what they did not concern was the ownership of the churches once built.

igans montes a
de fructu opum tuoz

108 A funeral procession of dogs and hares

The church, ceasing to be private property, took on a variety of public roles. With the castle and with the market, it completed the third essential element of medieval settlement, a natural focus for the life of the community. Where an old town grew, the building of new churches and the remodelling of the old characterized each period of expansion, so that at Chester, for example, as many as six of the nine parish churches of the city are likely to have originated in the twelfth century.[19] At York, in the same century, new housing developments at Little Bretgate were provided with two churches;[20] St Mary-le-Port, Bristol, is known to have been substantially enlarged soon after the mid-century;[21] and it cannot have been much later than this that the first major rebuilding occurred of St Benedict's, Norwich, providing the church with a new square-ended chancel and a tower (Fig. 107).[22]

Contemporary new town plantations, although not always successful initially in shaking off the claims of an existing parish church in the vicinity, did what they could to secure full parochial status for themselves. The first church at Rhuddlan, in Flint, recently located in a magnetometer survey of the Norman settlement site, was clearly con-

109 A preaching scene, French, late-fifteenth-century

temporary with the initial planning of the borough, and with the building of its first houses and its castle.[23] More commonly, the dependent
chapel, or chapel-of-ease, at a new settlement gradually earned its separate parochial status, to be recognized, in due course, by the bishop. The
process might be hurried, as it was at Battle on the representations of
the monks, to secure almost immediate recognition.[24] But, in general, it
took rather longer. It was only at the end of the twelfth century that the
burgesses of Tavistock, long served by the chapel of St Matthew, next
to the abbey gates, acquired their new parish church of St Eustace.[25] At
Market Harborough, the cramped siting of the parish church, without a
cemetery of its own, reflects the prolonged dependency of the new
chapel of 'Haverberg' on its nearby mother-church at Great Bowden.
For many years, as Professor Hoskins remarked, the men of
Harborough, when the time came to die, were carried back to Bowden,
'to the rock whence they were hewn'.[26]

There were, of course, other reasons than burial to convince men of
the need for a church. When the men of Ipswich had met, in 1200, to
discuss the implementation of their charter, they had chosen the

189

churchyard of St Mary Tower for their assembly (see pp. 157–9), and it was the size of the parish church and of its annexed open space, making of it the most commodious and best situated public building in the average country town, that continually recommended it for such purposes as this. At Holbeach, in Lincolnshire, it was later recorded, the franchisers 'out of time of remembraunce' had used their church as a forum for the debate of measures to repair or improve the sea defences of the parish, as well as 'any other cause or matter concerning the wealthe of the saide towne'.[27] Churches were employed for council meetings, for the election of mayors, for public audits, inquests, and other court business, and for a variety of strictly commercial purposes, including oath-taking, the ratification of contracts, the payment of fines and of debts, the storage of deeds, valuables, and sometimes even of exceptionally bulky goods for which there might be no other covered space available anywhere else in the town. Quite commonly, a market or a fair might be held in the churchyard, nor was it unknown for stalls to be set up within the body of the church itself.[28] Inevitably, prominent churchmen condemned such uses. Framing, in 1215, what would be published as the nineteenth constitution of the influential Fourth Lateran Council, they affirmed:

We do not wish to leave uncorrected the practice by which certain clerics convert their churches to warehouses for their own and other persons' household goods, so that the churches have the appearance of the houses of lay people rather than the temple of God . . . Therefore, since the zeal of the house of God hath eaten us up, we strictly forbid that household goods be placed in the churches; unless by reason of hostile invasion, sudden fire, or other urgent reasons it should become necessary to store them there.[29]

But the patent lack of success of both this and other similar injunctions may itself be taken as a useful corrective to any view of the medieval Church as an active impediment to trade. Certainly, the canonists had their views, expressed frequently and at length, on the immorality of buying cheap to sell dear; they forbade usury and debated the concept of the 'just price'. Yet in the end, as many of their number concluded, the just price of an article was neither more nor less than what it fetched each day in the market.[30] It was realism of this sort, everywhere the practice of the clergy, that opened the towns to the mission of the Church, and that ensured their mutually profitable co-operation.

Such co-operation was to take many forms, but among its more useful products was the supply of hospitals, almshouses and refuges to the towns. In a unique way, these institutions both captured the loyalty and reflected the constructive piety of the burgesses. Few, perhaps, would ever be as closely linked with the day-by-day business of the town as the Hospital of St John the Baptist, Winchester, with its prestigious associated Fraternity of St John.[31] Nevertheless, the founding initiatives at almost all such hospitals and other charitable institutions were to come from within the urban community, and it was natural for the burgesses themselves to retain a strong interest in their fortunes. The annual audit of the Hospital of St John was presided over by the mayor of Winchester; the community appointed the warden and found his stipend; civic records were kept at the hospital, and the common congregation, or burghmote, met in its hall to elect the mayor and to conduct other general business of the community.[32] In much the same way, the Hospital of St Julian, known as God's House, kept a secure place in the affections of Southampton's leading burgesses for as long as they retained its control. Founded in 1196/7 by Gervase, one of their number, it was unusually richly endowed by his associates and immediate successors, to become the greatest landowner in the town. Southampton men remembered the hospital in their wills; they sent ale, while their gild sat, to cheer the old and the infirm at God's House and to console the lepers at St Mary Magdalene, the only other such institution in the vicinity. Late in the thirteenth century, in the full confidence of a special relationship built up over the years, they claimed for themselves the patronage of both God's House Hospital and the Magdalene, and it was from the failure of their claim in each instance that the decline of burgess interest must have dated.[33]

The Magdalene Hospital at Southampton was one of many lazar houses in the kingdom which disappeared as the menace of leprosy waned,[34] and it was not uncommon in late-medieval England for small hospitals to come under the protection of greater institutions, or to merge with these institutions altogether. At most towns, however, the large and medium-sized hospitals, although always subject to fluctuations of fortune, survived into the sixteenth century, to be joined frequently in the later Middle Ages by a flood of almshouse-type foundations. The earliest known hospital at the new royal borough of Kingston upon Hull was the Maison Dieu, founded in 1344 by a clerk of the king for the benefit of thirteen poor and infirm persons of the town, under the charge of a warden. This was followed, in 1375, by Selby's Hospital, for twelve poor men, by the Charterhouse Hospital of 1394,

Couuent puuciereuteut les freres mmucurs viurcut en la
uille de Walleucieit detouchz lahedixece de burt uouuctre duulle Cai

110 The first
Franciscans arrive in
Flanders, Flemish or
North French,
circa 1500

111 (opposite) Medieval
burials excavated in
1973 below the floor
of the former church
of St Martin and
All Saints, Oxford

for thirteen paupers of each sex, and by several fifteenth-century foundations, all of them quite small, including Bedforth's Hospital (1412),
Gregg's Hospital (before 1438), Trinity House Almshouse (after 1441),
Holy Trinity Maison Dieu (before 1445), Aldwick's Hospital (1448),
and Adryanson's Hospital (*c.* 1485). Compared with these last,
Riplingham's Hospital (1517) was unusually large, having an intake of
twenty paupers, under the direction of two chantry priests.[35]

At York, not many miles from Hull, St Leonard's Hospital had long
been one of the greatest in the land. Founded in 1135, it was to build up
to a full establishment of a master, thirteen chaplain brothers, four
secular chaplains, eight regular sisters, thirty choristers under the care
of two schoolmasters, and sufficient lay-brothers and lay-sisters to look
after the 200 sick. At other centres, Bristol's St Mark Bonhommes kept
twelve poor scholars and provided food daily for a hundred paupers in
the borough; Gloucester's St Bartholomew, in 1333, is known to have
had ninety sick, of both sexes, in its charge; there were sixty poor and
infirm at the Hospital of St John the Baptist, Canterbury, in the care of
a prior and ministers; while at Norwich, at the Hospital of St Giles, a
master, assisted by as many as eight lay-brothers and lay-sisters, tended

the wants of thirteen paupers daily, boarded seven poor scholars, and kept thirty beds for the sick.[36]

For most of these hospitals, large and small, the regular charity of local people was an essential supplement to their endowments. Every year, just after the harvest and on three separate Sundays, alms were collected at Lincoln for the lepers at Holy Innocents, encouraged by appropriate sermons dwelling on the theme of charity.[37] And though Holy Innocents, too, would go the way of other leper hospitals in failing to maintain its independence beyond the mid-fifteenth century,[38] the success it had enjoyed over so many years in attracting the charity of Lincoln citizens, demonstrates very well the high esteem in which it and comparable establishments might be held. It was, of course, direct and continual financial involvement, to be seen as a return for specific services to the community, that kept this relationship in being. Very similar circumstances of mutual profit were to contribute to the popularity of the friars.

Inclination and tradition had united in the twelfth-century town to keep the average regular community outside it, and even the Augustinian canons, dependent though they often were on the revenues of urban churches, had found the requirements of the spiritual life a discouragement to settlement in the towns.[39] In contrast, the mission of the mendicant friars from the very beginning was directed at the towns, and it was there, from the early thirteenth century, that they began to establish their houses. What the friars brought to the towns was the force of their own austere example, with vigorous and effective preaching carried direct to the market-place, an opportunity to be charitable where charity could be seen and felt, and a wide range of spiritual services over which, frequently, they would find themselves in conflict with existing parochial clergy. In England, as elsewhere in western Europe, the success of the new orders was immediate. Within twenty years of 1224, the date of their first landing in England, the Franciscans had established forty houses in the major English towns.[40] Anticipated by the Dominicans, three years before, they set up their third English community at Oxford, in the winter of 1224–25; there would be Carmelites at Oxford from 1256 and Austin friars from 1268, and short-lived communities of Friars of the Sack and Crutched friars were to settle there in 1261–62 and 1342. Norwich, with no academic draw, had yet attracted both Franciscans and Dominicans by 1226, to be followed by Pied friars in 1253, Carmelites in 1256, Friars of the Sack in c. 1258, and Austin friars in c. 1272.[41] In the single county of Lincolnshire, friars were in residence by the end of the century at each of the five major centres of population.[42] There were Franciscans at Lincoln and at Stamford by 1230, at Grimsby by 1240, at Boston by 1268, and at Grantham before 1290. Dominicans had reached Lincoln, Stamford and Boston by 1238, 1241 and 1288, and there were Carmelite houses at the same centres by 1269, 1268 and 1293 respectively. At Lincoln and at Stamford there were Friars of the Sack by 1266 and 1274. The Austin friars, generally rather later in settlement, were to establish themselves at Lincoln in c.1269–70, at Grimsby in 1293, at Boston in 1317–18, and at Stamford by the 1340s.[43]

From their earliest years, the Franciscans at Boston were to demonstrate their usefulness by ministering to the needs of the Easterling community in that port, having many German friars in their number.[44] But the valuable new services that the friars could offer in many towns were not enough to recommend them whole-heartedly to the existing parish clergy, or to their patrons, the monastic impropriators. When the abbot of Reading consented to a Franciscan settlement in the borough in 1233, he did so only reluctantly, making it a condition that the friars should remain truly mendicant, that they should not attempt to extend their property, nor encroach upon the rights of the abbey. Through the thirteenth century, conflict at Reading continued, and there were similar instances of prolonged monastic opposition to the friars at Bury St Edmunds, Durham, Exeter, Winchester and Scarborough.[45] Although the papacy frequently took the lead in defining spheres of interest and in resolving persisting disputes, it was to be mainly at parochial level, by local negotiation and agreement, that compromise eventually was reached. One of the more explicit surviving agreements, dated 1307, was that between the Augustinian canons of Wellow, appropriators of the parish church of St James, at Grimsby, and the community of Austin friars, lately settled in the port. Conflict between the two houses, initially on an issue of rents, had begun within months of the foundation, in 1293, of the friary. Fourteen years later, illuminating the areas of dispute, both this and other problems were resolved in a single comprehensive settlement, broadly to the advantage of the canons. The Austin friars undertook to have nothing more to do with either preaching or other spiritual work on the ships lying at anchor in the port; they promised not to collect dues properly owing to the church of St James, as parish church, nor to preach or hold services of their own while high mass was in course of celebration there; they agreed to abide by their

112 Candlemas procession, French, mid-fourteenth-century

privileges in the hearing of confessions, and not to overstep their acknowledged rights in this or in similar matters; and they allowed that,
although burials might take place in the cemetery of their friary, masses
for the dead and funeral offerings would go, as before, to the rector and
his assignees at St James.[46]

Later, there would be disputes of another sort at Grimsby, between
the friars and the men of the town, but neither at Grimsby nor elsewhere in the English towns can there be any doubt of the continuing
popularity of the friars as a religious movement, right through until the
sixteenth-century suppression of their communities. From the beginning, a special relationship had grown up in many towns between the
friaries and the governing elite. It had, for example, been the ruling
bodies at Lincoln, Oxford, Cambridge, Bridgwater and London that
had found sites for the first Franciscan houses, and it was common
thereafter for borough authorities to hold such properties in trust for the
friars, who might enjoy but who were not allowed to own them.[47] Not
unnaturally, in disputes with ecclesiastical rivals, townsmen took the
part of their protégés. In the long history of burgess partiality to the
Franciscans settled at Southampton, one incident especially stands out.

The rector of St Mary's, early in the fifteenth century, had begun to insist on his right to conduct at Southampton's mother church the first mass for the dead, and to have all bodies carried there expressly for this purpose, even when burial was later to take place at the friary. The right was disputed by the Franciscans and their allies in the town, burgesses and friars uniting in 1425 in an appeal to Rome which followed an earlier decision in the rector's favour. That same year, the abbot of Abingdon was appointed by Martin V to examine the case, with the particular instruction to respect the 'ancient custom' of the friars to bury all who might have stated this to be their wish. If he found in their favour, he was to license the friary for burial as before, without regard to the claims of the rector.[48]

Many at Southampton had taken advantage of this custom already, and others would continue to do so through the fifteenth and early sixteenth centuries, so long as the friary remained in being. They showed their preference for the friars, too, in other unequivocal ways. In the wills of Southampton burgesses throughout the later Middle Ages, the needs of the friary and of the parish churches continued to be remembered, even while bequests to the hospital at God's House and the neighbouring priory at St Denys fell away sharply. Of the chantry and obit foundations, commonly established under the care of the Franciscans and of the parish priests, God's House and St Denys in this later period were lucky to receive one apiece.[49]

It was not just the growing unpopularity of the two other religious institutions in the town that had encouraged in Southampton men a growing preference for the parish churches and the friary, for the altering balance of their own affections reflected a national trend. The parish fraternity, with its equivalent associations in the crafts, had multiplied swiftly in the late-medieval boroughs, concentrating loyalties in a new way in support of the neighbourhood church. When the Franciscans of Grantham took their place at the head of the solemn procession of the borough's Corpus Christi gild,[50] they were accepting a role in a popular religious movement which had already, by the late fourteenth century, taken a firm hold in the towns. Not uncommonly, this evolution of the religious fraternity marched with the emergence of the crafts, for the first time, as significant social and political groupings. At Exeter, the bakers, the tailors and the clothworkers were also to be known as the fraternities, respectively, of St Clement, St John the Baptist, and the Assumption of the Blessed Virgin Mary.[51] It is likely, too, that craft associa-

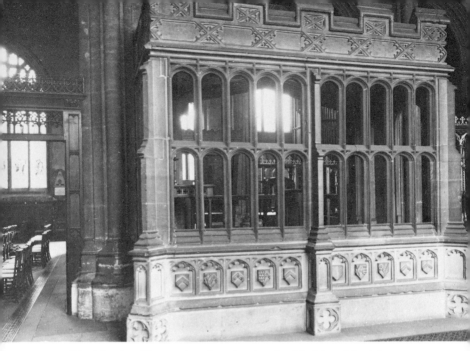

113 The Meyring Chantry (1500) at the church of St Mary Magdalene, Newark

tions frequently found it convenient to meet, at least in their early stages, under the cover of some charitable disguise. In fourteenth-century Hull, for example, there is no record of craft associations, yet it was the tailors who later supported the gild of St John the Baptist, and it was the merchants and the shipmen who founded the gilds of Corpus Christi and Holy Trinity.[52] However, to see the parish fraternities as clandestine political organizations, and nothing more, would be seriously to misjudge their role. Even where the association of a craft and of a religious fraternity was close, there was no necessary coincidence of interests, nor even perhaps of membership. The carpenters of York, while supporting a religious brotherhood of their own, did not require every member of their craft to belong to it,[53] and it is likely that the London painters' fraternity of St Luke came into being at the church of St Giles Cripplegate as much because many of the painters actually lived in the parish as because the craft needed separate religious representation of its own.[54]

Indeed, it was just this neighbourhood quality of the fraternity, with less regard for distinctions either of craft or of class, that remained its most important characteristic. York, it has been said, was 'honey-combed' with parish fraternities,[55] and even at the small town of Bodmin, in Cornwall, with a population of barely 2,000, there would be forty gilds by the early sixteenth century, the great majority founded for a religious or a charitable purpose, and only five securely associated with a craft.[56] Everywhere, parish gilds multiplied, particularly in the late fourteenth and the fifteenth centuries, but the history of the religious fraternity goes back much further than this, and it was some of the earliest fraternities in the towns that came also to be the most powerful. Already, something has been said (see p. 191) of the important political role in thirteenth-century Winchester of the Fraternity of St John the Baptist, and it was not, even then, unique. The Gild of St Mary, at Cambridge, although not to last as long, attracted during its compar-atively short life an influential membership, in which few of the more powerful burgesses of the late-thirteenth- and early-fourteenth-century town failed to be represented.[57] At Coventry and at Salisbury, the wealthy and politically dominant gilds of Holy Trinity and St George grew on the backs of the gilds merchant.[58]

Among later fraternities, the objectives were usually more limited. Many, required to publish their constitutions in the returns of 1389, announced their first purpose to be the keeping of a candle burning at some selected altar at the local parish church. They went on frequently to elaborate on this, with an account of membership dues, feast days and processions, benefits to destitute members, and the obligations of all brothers and sisters of the gild to attend the burials of their fellows.[59] Yet there is no reason to believe that the majority of these associations ever grew beyond a modest size, or that they started with any clear ambition to do so. At Great Yarmouth, the Fraternity of St Peter, founded in 1379 by its own account, brought together initially only four men and their wives in the town, associated in the purchase of a candle to burn daily during mass at St Nicholas, the parish church. Two of the parish gilds of Spalding, in Lincolnshire, had been founded originally to provide, and subsequently to care for, items of church furniture,[60] while in striking contrast to the declared objectives of many of its more am-bitious fellows, the London fraternity of St Katherine claimed only to maintain a chaplain, supported by four annual collections, to pray daily for the poor of the parish at an altar in the church of St Sepulchre; the gild required its members to contribute each one equally to the collec-tions, but admitted no other rules than this and had accumulated no property of its own.[61]

114 John Greenaway's chapel (1517) at the church of St Peter, Tiverton
115 (opposite) A late-fifteenth-century Doom, or Last Judgement scene,
over the chancel arch at the church of St Thomas, Salisbury

Where a gild did gather property, and where the size of the accumulated endowment came to allow it, it not uncommonly assumed the
functions of a benefit society, or distributed charity outside its ranks.
The gild, in a variety of ways, might help its members find work when
unemployed; it might support the destitute with small donations from
the common fund; and it could even be responsible for founding and
endowing, as did the Fraternity of Our Lord and the Virgin, at York, a
hospital or an almshouse of its own.[62] Yet these, in general, were the
occasional by-products of an association designed for something else,
and it was the role of the religious fraternity as 'co-operative chantry'
that did most to give it a continuing purpose.[63] As a chantry, too, it was
most obviously a creature of its times.

In popular belief, the memorial mass had peculiar strength in lifting the
soul beyond Purgatory: 'amongst other means of restoring fallen
humanity, the solemn celebration of Masses . . . is to be judged highest
in merit and of most power to draw down the mercy of God.'[64] And this

being so, the endowment of an adequate number of memorial masses became the ambition of all who felt they could afford them. In the late-medieval town, a wealthy individual might found a chantry, with a full-time priest of its own, to keep in remembrance his soul and those of his family and his friends, with all the faithful departed. Lesser men might endow an obit, or anniversary mass, for a term of years or sometimes in perpetuity, or might have to be content with the purchase of a stated number of masses, to be said or sung in the name of the deceased as soon as might be after death. It was for those who, as individuals, could afford not even the least of these provisions, that the smaller fraternities were founded, and what they offered, above all, was a full range of spiritual services – memorial masses, mourners at funerals, the keeping and the management of obits – at comparatively low shared costs. Few townsmen, in the later Middle Ages, would choose to face death alone. In a special sense, as had already been the case with the hospitals and the friaries before them, both the chantries and the priests who served them came to be the concern of the municipal authorities. In the opinion of a contemporary mayor of York, 'the priests of this city and suburbs having chantries, and others, stipendiaries, who have not such chantries, are the special orators of the citizens their patrons and masters, from whom they have had and have their chantries and stipends from which they live.'[65]

A guide to this concern, and one of the chief reasons for it, was the number of chantry and obit foundations which came to be managed by the corporations in the towns. Borough records everywhere preserve copies of the original deeds of gift, and the expenses incurred at anniversaries may feature in borough accounts. In the Southampton corporation terrier of 1495/6, one such list of expenses relates to the joint obit, celebrated at Holy Rood Church, of William Nicholl, Richard Thomas and Thomas Payne, each of whom, in their day, had been prominent burgesses in the town. On 25 April, the record runs, the steward of Southampton had paid twenty pence to the vicar of Holy Rood, and twopence to his clerk; he had given eightpence each to the other curates in the town and sixpence to their clerks; he had bought ale for the poor and wine for their betters, including the priests and borough officials, who had attended the memorial mass; he had laid in a stock of 400 white buns and 300 spiced buns for distribution after the ceremony, and had made other purchases of saffron, butter and cheese. For their pains in managing and attending the obit, the steward and the mayor each received two shillings; the bedeman was rewarded with twopence.[66]

116 A celebration of mass, with street scenes, Flemish, *circa* 1500

Prominent among the deeds and memoranda preserved in the so-called *Black Book* of Southampton, are the elaborate funerary precautions of William Soper, for long a notable figure in the fifteenth-century town, of which he had himself been steward, twice mayor, and many times parliamentary representative. Dying childless, he was able to lay out a large part of his wealth towards the future security of his soul, beginning to make his dispositions at least six years before he was overtaken by his final illness. It was his wish to be buried at the friary, to which he had been a good neighbour and benefactor for many years, and already, in 1452, he was making his first arrangements for the setting up and the endowment of an anniversary mass, to be held in the Franciscan church. Six years later, when he came to draw up his will, a tomb of fine marble, probably in the Italian fashion, had been built to his order in the south aisle of the church. At the altar next to it, he specified, there were to be thirty days of 'solemn services and requiem masses' immediately following his death. He had set aside his country estates at Eling, Dibden and Fawley in 1452 to support the original obit, and he now added to these the rents of his English Street properties, near the friary and among the most important in the town. From the receipts, a penny should be given each day in Soper's name to the collection at morning mass in the friary; an anniversary mass would be maintained in perpetuity, and distributions of pennies made annually to the needy to mark the occasion of the obit. Every year, in the 'customary places', the Southampton crier was to proclaim the approach of Soper's anniversary; the assembly bell was to be rung by the parish clerk of Holy Rood on the eve and the day of the obit; the town clerk, after celebration of the requiem mass which he himself attended, was to read aloud in public the terms of Soper's will.[67]

William Soper, with his long record of public service in the town, could rely on his friends and successors in the Southampton corporation to carry out his wishes as he stated them. Others, seeking similar security, preferred to put their faith in their associates of fraternity or gild. At Boston, in Lincolnshire, it was the wish of John Nuttyng that his brethren of the Corpus Christi gild should keep his anniversary in proper style on 9 September, the morrow of the feast of the Nativity of the Blessed Virgin Mary. The gild was a rich one, with a wide and wealthy membership extending beyond the town, and its nine permanent chaplains could well handle commissions of this sort. On the Saturday previous to his anniversary, Nuttyng provided, the bellman of Boston was to announce the obit, 'as is usual with other obits', throughout the town, and the day itself was to be kept with 'full solemnity of wax and cloth'. All the gild chaplains were to participate in the principal memorial mass, and two at least of their number were to conduct additional services for the dead in the gild chapel on the Saturday before and the Sunday after the anniversary. 'All this is to be done without music.'[68]

It might be thought, and both Chaucer and Langland are commonly invoked to support just such a view,[69] that the chantry priests and others of their kind, upon whom John Nuttyng and his contemporaries relied, were underworked, idle, inclined to the abuse of pluralism, and frequently of scandalous deportment. Nevertheless, although it is surely true that the shrinking real value of clerical stipends was to put clergy of all kinds to the test, it is now more generally considered that they came out of this reasonably well.[70] Clearly, those laymen who held the patronage of chantries, often themselves experienced administrators with a deep-seated knowledge of the town, had no cause to make unsuitable appointments to such offices. Nor is there much evidence that they did so. It was, rather, by due election that the successful candidate was chosen in 1520 from the four 'honest priests' who 'laboured' for it, to be chaplain of St Thomas the Martyr, in Lincoln.[71] And elsewhere it was common for the founders of chantries to insist on at least some basic qualifications in their chaplains, and to lay down a procedure for appointments. Joan Holmhegge, a rich Southampton widow who had buried three husbands in her time, provided in 1462 that the chaplain of her chantry at St Mary's should be admitted by the precentor of that church, 'provided always that the said chaplain be examined by the said precentor and his successors as to learning and character, and that he be admitted if he be altogether capable; and if incapable, be rejected'. Once appointed, he was not to be let off lightly. He was to celebrate mass every day at St Mary's; he was to be present on 'every Sunday and feast day at prime, vespers, matins, high mass and second vespers, and other canonical hours of the day from the beginning to the end'; once a week, he was to 'say services and commemorations for my soul, etc., and in like manner a requiem mass on the day following with a special collect, mentioning my name, to wit, Joan, in the same collect'.[72] There were still more explicit directions to the chaplain, dictating the form of service to be followed on each day of the week, in the foundation document of Robert Parys's chantry at Chester. On Sundays, Parys provided, his chaplain was to celebrate a mass of the Trinity; on Mondays, a mass of St Mary; on Tuesdays, a requiem mass; on Wednesdays, a mass of the Holy Spirit; on Thursdays, another requiem mass; on Fridays, a mass of the Cross; and on Saturdays, another mass of St Mary. There were special instructions for feast days.[73]

The stipend of Joan Holmhegge's Southampton chaplain had been set at £6 13s 4d; in the same town, thirty years later, William Gunter assigned his chantry priest the sum of £6 a year. And while it is true that these sums compared favourably enough with the common lot of the gild and chantry priests of Chester, drawing £5 or less at the beginning of the sixteenth century,[74] it is nevertheless worth remarking that they showed no change over the next decades of galloping inflation, remaining precisely the same as they always had been, on the day that the chantries were suppressed.[75] This was not a problem confined to the lesser clergy and stipendiaries, for the beneficed clergy, although usually better off overall, had incomes in the later Middle Ages rarely exceeding an upper limit of £10 at most, commonly drawing rather less.[76] Inevitably, in conditions such as these, where supplementary revenues became vital, clergy of all ranks drifted to the towns, including some even of the beneficed clergy among them.[77] They came, for example, to a town like Boston, with its openings for gild priests and for personal or chantry chaplains,[78] and everywhere they deserted the rural deaneries.

Well before the Reformation, the problems of shrinking endowments

COVENTRY St Michael

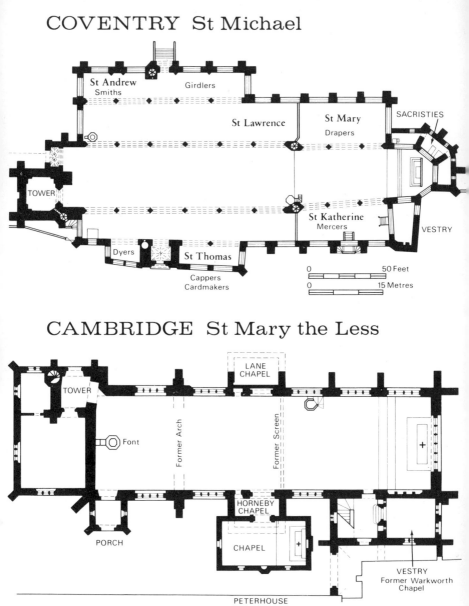

St Andrew
Smiths

Girdlers

St Lawrence

St Mary
Drapers

SACRISTIES

TOWER

St Katherine
Mercers

VESTRY

Dyers

St Thomas

Cappers
Cardmakers

0   50 Feet
0   15 Metres

CAMBRIDGE St Mary the Less

LANE
CHAPEL

TOWER

Font

Former Arch

Former Screen

+

HORNEBY
CHAPEL

PORCH

CHAPEL

+

VESTRY
Former Warkworth
Chapel

PETERHOUSE

0   50 Feet
0   15 Metres

206

and diminishing profits had had to be met by the amalgamation of lesser chantries, and by the closing down of such of the smaller churches as could not sustain clergy of their own. In an action that was certainly an influential precedent elsewhere, Robert Braybrooke, bishop of London, agreed before the end of the fourteenth century to a rationalization of the chantries at St Paul's, uniting the incomes of two or more foundations to support a single cantarist between them.[79] And the closing of churches and the reorganization of parishes were to go on throughout the later Middle Ages. Already, in early-thirteenth-century Canterbury, the small parish of St Helen was to be incorporated in the adjoining parish of All Saints.[80] At Stamford, in 1308, the churches of St Michael Cornstall and St George were united.[81] The general rationalization of the churches of Wilton, which occurred in 1435, brought the two surplus churches of St Nicholas and St Mary, in West Street, into union with the priory of St John, while the church of St Nicholas in Atrio was merged with St Michael, Kingsbury.[82]

The depression of clerical revenues, so harmful to the morale of the clergy as a whole, showed itself in other ways. In a recent study of the churches of Lincoln diocese, it has been shown that many of the parish churches were in poor condition by the end of the Middle Ages, and that it was the chancels, in particular, that had suffered.[83] The singling out of the chancels for this melancholy distinction is significant. They had remained the financial charge of the incumbent, and it was he, or the monastic institution he served, that had come upon bad times. Further, the contrasting condition of the chancel and the main body of the church, the responsibility respectively of the priest and his parishioners, has much to tell us of what the parish church, as institution, had become. Where respect for the clergy had receded, checked by their poverty and diminished by the stirrings of heresy and unbelief, affection for their churches had advanced, to take the form of a powerful social habit. Townsmen in the later Middle Ages were generous to their churches in a way they had never been before. They spent money lavishly on their enlargement, embellishment and furnishing, and took a pride in exhibitions of charity. Among Englishmen, a Venetian would note, there were many with 'various opinions concerning religion', yet 'they all attend Mass every day, and say many Paternosters in public'. It was their practice, too, always to 'hear mass on Sunday in their parish church, and give liberal alms'.[84]

117 Gild and chantry chapels at churches in Coventry and Cambridge (V.C.H. and R.C.H.M.)

It was, of course, the exceptional profits of the cloth trade that built the great churches of East Anglia and the West Country, but it was not there alone that wealth, in the fifteenth century, flowed liberally into programmes of church improvement. Although the best days of Chester's economy were long past by the fifteenth century, it was then, and particularly in the last decades of the century, that the majority of the parish churches were extensively reconstructed, in campaigns of work headed, on at least one occasion, by the mayor of Chester himself.[85] The archaeology of quite minor churches in Winchester and Norwich (Figs. 104 and 107) has pointed to considerable alterations and extensions in the fifteenth century, or not very much before.[86] And it was in that century again, when York's recently prospering cloth trade was already in decline, that at least seven of its parish churches were rebuilt.[87] In London, the collecting point of wealth, fifty or more parish churches were notably altered and extended in the century and a half after 1300.[88]

Broadly, it was not the object of these programmes of improvement to give greater space for the congregation. Few urban parishes, after the onset of plague, were as crowded as they had been before. Rather, they more commonly took the form of the provision of additional chapels, giving altar-space to the chantries and the gilds. Such chapels might make use of an existing or an extended aisle, as was the case at St Michael's church, Southampton, where it was the north aisle that became, traditionally, the Corporation Chapel, to be used in the swearing-in of mayors.[89] Or they could, as at the same church, be attached externally to the existing fabric: the chapel, now demolished, that adjoined the south chancel aisle at St Michael's having once, perhaps, served the needs of the fraternity of St Barbara. In a great urban church like the Holy and Undivided Trinity at Hull, additional altars and the chapels of chantries and gilds packed every available space. Among the chantry chapels identified, there were those of Hanby, Haynson, Ravenser, Alcock, Eland and Rotenhering, along the south side of the church. The recorded dedications of some of the altars in the church to Corpus Christi, St John the Baptist, St Katherine, St Anne and St Eloy, link each with the religious fraternity of that name.[90]

The parishioners of Holy Trinity, Hull, active in the improvement of the fabric of their church, were generous also with its furnishings. At one with a tradition which everywhere led to great accumulations of church goods in the parishes, they gave Holy Trinity the images, pictures, vestments, coverlets, altar cloths and frontals for which they hoped to be remembered in future time.[91] At St Ewen's, Bristol, it was John

Pembroke and Richard Batyn, wealthy parishioners, who furnished the altar of St Katherine, and John Nancothan who equipped the altar of St Margaret. Richard Batyn again, a goldsmith by trade, had given a chalice to St Ewen's, as had Gillam Sampson and John Wotton, the latter having had his name inscribed upon the base. Other parishioners contributed altar cloths and vestments, and some made gifts of books.[92] In another fifteenth-century inventory of church furniture, at the London church of St Mary at Hill, the names of the individual donors were carefully recorded against the gifts they had made. With many others, John Smarte (grocer), John Mongeham (fishmonger), and William Baker (pewterer) had contributed, often very generously, to the 'Appareyle ffor the hyghe Aulter' at St Mary's. Of the five great bells of the church, the fourth was 'clere of the gyfte of John Duklyng, ffysshmonger, as is graved uppon the bell'. Mistress Juliana Roche had given the church a fine corporal (a cloth for the consecrated elements) in a case of needlework and purple velvet, and had contributed also a sacring bell, silver 'parcell gylt'; Mistress Jentyll had donated two plain linen tablecloths for the high altar; Mother Jenet had given a towel.[93] Amongst the objects collected by another London church, St Margaret's in New Fish Street, were some truly remarkable relics. They included pieces of the burning bush and of Moses's rod, the comb of St Dunstan, and one of the teeth of St Bridget.[94]

Relics and images, costly furnishings, elaborate ceremonial and processions, were all to find their critics before the Reformation. But although Lollards, we know, held the purchased mass in contempt, and there were others who disapproved of images, who rejected relics, and who held pilgrimages in low esteem, there is nothing to suggest that the towns, as a body, found themselves ill-suited by the religious institutions which had grown up within them, and which they had had a hand in shaping for themselves. It was not popular demand which brought the reforming Observant friars to England in the last years of the fifteenth century, but the king's personal convictions and the peril of his soul.[95] Nor was there to be much support in the towns for the fundamentalism of the more radical Reformation divines. When the Reformation came, it overturned many cherished local institutions. Burgesses everywhere had invested heavily in the fabric and the furnishings of their churches; they had relatives as priests; and they had themselves grown up in full acceptance of the ancient and traditional practices of the Church. On the Continent, heresy had grown where the towns were set most thickly. It had flourished along the lines of major routes, in particular at those crucial meetings of the ways that brought men of differing convictions and experience together. But in England – isolated, strongly governed and only lightly urbanized – heresy was at best a feeble plant, reflecting no more than faintly contemporary experience on the Continent. It was at Stamford, on the road to the North, that there were reports in the fifteenth century of heretical friars,[96] yet over the diocese of Lincoln as a whole, the record of heresy is sparse.[97] While there were Lollard groups at Leicester and at the immediately neighbouring village of Wigston, such sentiments in the surrounding countryside would always have been hard to find.[98] Lollards met, where they could, at the great centres of population: at London, at Bristol, or at Coventry. They seldom risked the almost certain exposure of a smaller borough society.

Where religious experiment was rare and the mood of the Church unexciting, men came increasingly to view the parish as a civic as much as a religious institution. It was at the parish church that each neighbourhood found a point of focus, and it was upon parish officials that civic responsibility inevitably devolved. In the post-Reformation towns, it was to the church-wardens that many new tasks in local government were delegated, in particular in the care of the poor. But this essentially matter-of-fact view of the parish church and of its functions had already been long in preparation. 'As the people,' the proverb would run, 'so the priest.' It was both the strength and the weakness of the Church.

7 The Early-Modern Borough: Continuity and Change

Severe inflation at any time is a wearisome burden to bear, but its impact in sixteenth-century England was the crueller for having followed a period of prolonged stability of prices. Foodstuff prices, leading those of manufactured goods, rose sharply in the 1520s, more than doubling by the 1550s; they had doubled again before the end of the century, and in the 1630s stood at six times their 1500 level.[1] Accompanying this inflation and, in the view of many modern commentators, explaining it, there was a significant increase in population. It is by no means certain when this increase began, but, on a recent theory, it need have been no earlier than the 1520s, after which the population of England would rise by almost a quarter before 1545; by the mid-seventeenth century, it had doubled (Fig. 118).[2] Not all classes in the towns were affected equally by these developments, and it was perhaps only the landless labourer, in town and country alike, who suffered a measurable decline in living standards throughout the century. Nevertheless, few could have remained completely untouched by them, in attitude if not in material well-being. One obvious pointer to this is the rapacity with which the already propertied classes fell upon the lands of the former monastic houses and of the hospitals, chantries and other religious institutions that went with them. In a period of mounting financial uncertainty, beyond the ability of the state to control, the possession of landed wealth offered one of the few obvious hedges against inflation. In the towns only slightly less so than in the countryside, a wholesale redistribution of lands was to characterize the sixteenth-century economy.

Inflation, population growth and the sudden availability of land for investment were all to have a major impact on the towns, but they were not alone in bringing changes to them. During the time it had taken the national population to double, and while population growth in some provincial centres such as Norwich remained sluggish,[3] London was to expand on its 1500 figure by a factor of seven or eight; from some two

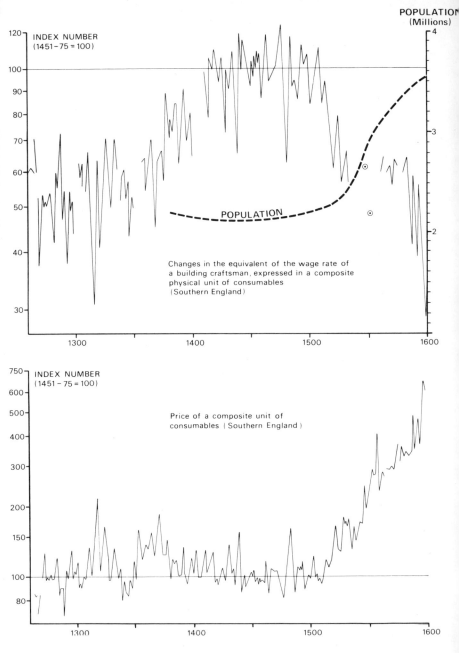

POPULATION
(Millions)

INDEX NUMBER
(1451–75 = 100)

POPULATION

Changes in the equivalent of the wage rate of
a building craftsman, expressed in a composite
physical unit of consumables
(Southern England)

INDEX NUMBER
(1451 – 75 = 100)

Price of a composite unit of
consumables (Southern England)

and a half per cent of the total population of England and Wales together, London's share rose to as much as eight.[4] We have been warned recently in several quarters of the dangers of over-stressing London's role in the Tudor economy, and it is certainly true that London's domination of the cloth trade, which was such an important element in its early-sixteenth-century growth, fell back with the decline of Antwerp, its natural trading partner, in the last decades of that century.[5] But London's continued draw as the administrative and social, as well as the economic, capital of the realm has never been in doubt,[6] and there were some provincial centres, in particular the ports, that never fully recovered from London's prolonged cornering of their trade. In Grimsby as in the very much larger Southampton, both blighted in this way, the reaction of the townsmen was very much the same. While they deplored London's dominance and never quite lost hope of recovering their own former overseas trades, they also turned more realistically to the exploitation of the booming local exchanges, and to the encouragement and regulation, for this purpose, of their markets.[7] It was, as they surely realized for themselves, to the trade of the immediate region that both population growth and rising prices promised, at least in the short term, their best prospect of good profits.

It was precisely these circumstances of growth that ensured that, however pernicious the influence of London might be, a provincial town of standing would never suffer in the sixteenth century too drastic a decline. Norwich, while probably the best example of its kind, was yet only one of a number of provincial capitals, among them York, Bristol, Salisbury and Exeter, that thrived on growing demand within the region and on the requirements of a newly affluent gentry. Those Worcestershire county families which, after the mid–century, had neglected their own county town to shop for luxuries in London, were to become, not so very much later, patrons of those same trades in Bristol.[8] And where the higher aristocracy might continue to find both its pleasure and its profit in London, in the shadow of the court, the lesser gentry, formidable spenders in their own right, sought the same at their provincial capitals. At Norwich, in the early sixteenth century, it was the textile trades that still overshadowed all the rest, in line with the ancient tradition. Yet by 1575 the luxury trades were already gathering strength. Many of the country gentry, if they had not done so already, would buy

118 Population, wages and prices in late-medieval and early-modern England (Cornwall [revised]; Phelps Brown and Hopkins)

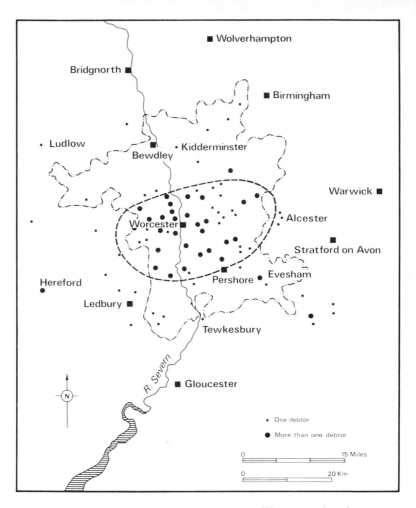

119 The market region of sixteenth-century Worcester, based on recorded debts to Worcester tradesmen (Dyer)

themselves town houses at Norwich, to reside there during the season. Many more came to Norwich to make their purchases at the drapers and the haberdashers in the city, to stock up on groceries, to buy jewellery, furniture or weapons, and to get their business correspondence written.[9]

To an appreciable extent, the continuing attraction of the provincial towns, against all the competition of London, was owed to changing patterns both of trade and manufacture. The development of England's inland trade, in the late sixteenth and in the early seventeenth centuries, has rightly been seen as 'one of the most potent forces of economic and social change' in the period.[10] It was furthered by wayfaring traders, operating usually from the inns in the towns, whose numbers are known greatly to have increased.[11] Bringing new business to the provincial capitals, these traders had nothing to do with London, and were to be at least partially instrumental in reversing those trends which, in the later Middle Ages, had promoted a centralization of trade. Contemporaneously, the sources of important trading commodities had themselves begun to change, as the new home-based industries gathered momentum. Glass and iron, brasswares, alum and copperas, gunpowder and paper had come, by the late sixteenth century, to be the products of English industries. Salt came again into common production as coal, more intensively mined, offered an economical fuel. It was in the sixteenth century that the first sugar was refined in England.[12]

For all these products, and for much more besides, the home market proved exceptionally strong. Local demand, for example, was sufficient in the last decades of the sixteenth century to absorb almost the whole production of English worsteds, known as the 'New Draperies' and very much the fashion in the trade.[13] Yet in this trade, as in others, exportable surpluses were becoming available, frequently before 1600. In a port like Chester, the export trade to Ireland can be shown, late in the sixteenth century, to have undergone a significant change. It carried now an increasing proportion of manufactured goods: iron and other metal objects, soap, glass, tablewares of wood or of pottery, paper, furniture, building materials and books.[14]

While, evidently, in a growing economy the long-term prospects were good, there were few contemporary observers who could easily have seen them so. To all, the 'great debasement' of 1544–51, aggravating an already dangerous inflationary situation, came as an unpleasant shock. The stability of the coinage was broken, and there was no way, seemingly, to restore it. Monopolies and trading companies, although frequently encouraged by the Tudors, were no convincing remedy for economic ills. Indeed, their overall influence would appear to have been very slight. And where the government achieved its only remarkable economic coup was not in the promotion of trade or of industry, but in a religious settlement.

Perhaps, had the economy looked better, the events of the

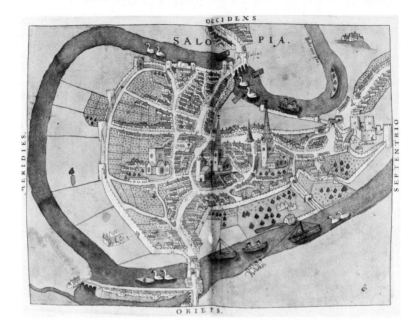

120 Shrewsbury in the late sixteenth century

Reformation in England might have taken another turn. But the financial insecurity of both rulers and ruled gave them the courage to plunder the Church, in a series of raids on ecclesiastical property that, once started, was impossible to check. One thing led to another, with the result that the towns which had consented to the suppression of the monastic houses, with which they had little sympathy, found themselves condoning the confiscation of chantry and fraternity lands, the appropriation of church goods, and the closing of many of their hospitals. Certainly, they found occasion to object, and it was the parliamentary burgesses of Coventry and King's Lynn who led the attack on the re-grant of gild and chantry lands to Edward VI, recently secured for himself by Henry VIII in the autumn session of 1545.[15] Nevertheless, there are indications everywhere of an unsentimental realism in the disposal of church property, as much on the part of the municipal corporations as on that of the king and his divines. Their problems, of course, were identical. Inflation everywhere had drastically reduced the real value of all fixed municipal receipts, to the extent that few town

216

authorities could meet their farms, and all cast around wherever they could for alternative sources of revenue. When, in April 1536, the corporation of York secured, by act of parliament, the suppression of seven chantries and three obits maintained by itself, it did so specifically to use their endowments to make good a growing financial deficit.[16] The costs of paving at Hull were met, that same year, by a sale of church ornaments and plate, and it was a man of Hull who urged similar action on Grimsby.[17] Anticipating the final royal confiscations by several years, the greater part of Southampton's church plate was to be put to various purposes in the town. At St Lawrence, for example, a small central parish, the king's commissioners found only a single silver-gilt chalice and paten, three copes, a black pall, two altar cloths and three surplices. Just a few years before, a sale of ornaments and plate at St Lawrence, for the purposes of the town, had realized the considerable sum of £41 14s 1d. The money had been spent on a 'piece of brass', to supplement the borough's artillery.[18]

It was, undoubtedly, this second phase in the confiscations, a part of the so-called 'Edwardian Reformation' of the mid-century, that had the most immediate impact on the towns. For it cut directly at cherished local institutions, among them the religious fraternities, the hospitals and the parish churches themselves, and upset traditional beliefs, such as that in the value of the memorial mass in reducing the term of Purgatory, in which the burgesses and their ancestors had made substantial investment. But 'Edwardian Reformation' and 'great debasement' coincided almost exactly, and the one problem was quickly submerged in the other. What came, in point of fact, to be the most significant immediate product of the Reformation in the English towns was not a radical re-thinking of religion, in which the burgesses were always slow to change their views, but a massive re-apportionment of lands: a tenurial revolution the effects of which are still imperfectly understood. It was during these decades that as many as two-thirds of the citizens of York acquired new landlords, to become the tenants of laymen;[19] while over the country as a whole between twenty-five and thirty per cent of the total land stock, formerly the property of religious institutions, came up for public sale.[20] It may well be that, in individual cases, such changes might have been for the better; for others, it was certainly for the worse. Overall, the sudden and frequently ill-organized transfer of lands in the towns to lay ownership could not have been without profound social consequences of its own, touching landlord and tenant alike.

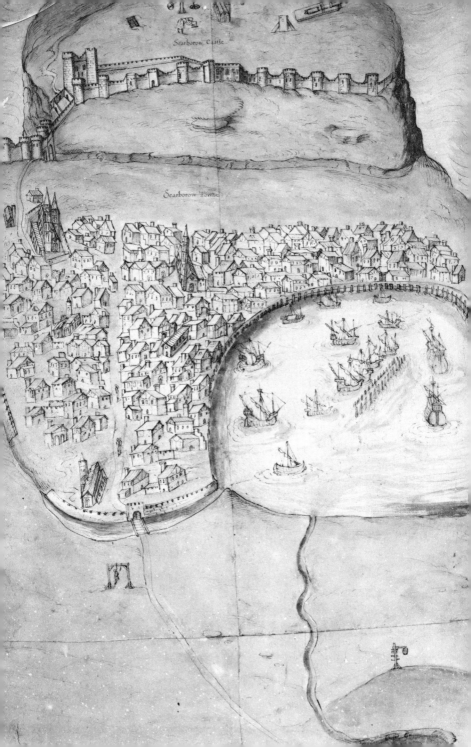

Searborow Castle.

Searborow Towne.

Of these consequences, perhaps individually the most important was the promotion, for the first time in the English towns, of something approaching a genuine *rentier* class. Such a category of urban landholder, living exclusively off rents, had long been familiar on the Continent, and in England, although rare, was not unknown. Rents, we have reason to believe, comprised an important part of the income of at least some twelfth-century Londoners, and there were Londoners again in the fourteenth century with considerable rent-rolls to sustain them.[21] In thirteenth-century York, it has been suggested, some burgess dynasties were to live off rents, at least in their later generations,[22] while it would be difficult to explain the persistence of the long-lived Barbflete clan in thirteenth- and fourteenth-century Southampton without invoking land-ownership to do so.[23] Nevertheless, a man like John Barbflete (d.1412), the last of his line and living, in all probability, on his rents, is not easy to find in many English towns, for while it is true that most considerable merchants invested at least some part of their surplus in urban property as well as, more commonly, in rural estates, there is nothing to suggest that they were in the habit of viewing these investments as permanent endowments for their families.[24] Not uncommonly, as has been shown at both Winchester and Southampton, they would build up their urban properties in convenient groupings, where these could best serve their enterprises,[25] but the intention of their heirs to keep such consolidated holdings intact is very much harder to establish. Clearly, whereas property in the towns might be gathered in burgess ownership for its convenience – to house a workforce, to yield a supplementary income, or to serve as a safe repository for surplus cash – its worth as permanent investment was not considered high. It is not difficult to see why this was so.

Chiefly, the reason was competition. Before the Dissolution, the Church had been the principal landowner in many towns; in others, that position might be held by a great local aristocrat or by the king. In each case, a common characteristic shared by them all was a strictly limited concern to make the best economic use of the investment. The clergy, in particular, were notoriously soft landlords. They had usually held the property so long that they were content to accept rents at levels undercutting the economic rate. Similarly, if a gild held tenements, considerations of charity might be allowed to determine the rents, just as the king and his greater lords might think more of patronage than of maximizing,

121 Scarborough in the early sixteenth century

in each instance, their returns.[26] In these conditions, burgess investment in town property, while not wholly stifled at any time, was obviously restricted in scope. It was further discouraged by the very general collapse of rents in the fifteenth-century boroughs, itself in part the product of the inflexibility of institutional landlords, but affecting all property-owners alike. By the early sixteenth century, as declining receipts had forced many landowners to neglect their properties, there were tenements ruined and vacant in boroughs all over the country. The religious houses had acquired a reputation, for which they were not wholly to blame, as 'evil repairers of their lands', and it was in 1540, immediately following their suppression, that the government took action to 're-edify', by injunction, many of the principal county towns, where 'divers and many beautiful houses of habitation . . . now are fallen down, decayed, and at this day remain unrecdified, and do lie as desolate and vacant grounds . . . and some houses be feeble and very like to fall down.'[27]

It is doubtful whether such government exhortations to repair town properties would have had much effect by themselves, but the timing of the statute was clearly important, and already much former ecclesiastical property was finding its way into private hands. The weak tradition of property-holding in the boroughs may have been one of the reasons why the burgesses commonly reacted rather slower than most to the opportunities presented by the Dissolution. But whatever their motive for holding back initially, they were to come, within a generation, to share between them, and with their corporations, the best part of the former religious lands.[28] Simultaneously, as population pressure mounted in the towns and as inflation everywhere gathered pace, rents rose sharply, and the incentives to invest in urban property increased. Already, in the 1540s, complaints of rack-renting had become common.[29] However, it was probably rather later than this that the combined effects of population increases and wholesale changes in land-ownership fully reached the towns. In the mid-century, reversing earlier policy, many former crown leases were converted to outright sales, while both in the towns and in the country, as earlier leases expired, harsher terms were introduced. In a sequence that cannot have been untypical, a substantial portion of the St Denys Priory estates, adjoining Southampton, had been granted initially to Sir Francis Dawtrey, son of a former royal customs collector at the port. When Sir Francis died, in 1568, his lease

122 A sixteenth-century house in Tudor Street, Exeter

was taken up within a few months by William Bettes, of another Southampton family with interests in the St Denys estates. Sir Francis, it was reported at the time, had done little to improve the St Denys lands, already sadly decayed before the Dissolution; probably his own local prestige and conservative inclinations had tempted him to be lenient to his tenants. Bettes was made of sterner stuff. Faced with the many expenses he must meet in improving the neglected priory estates, he set about immediately the re-negotiation of agreements and the raising of existing rents. It was against this that his copyholders united, complaining of rack-renting in a joint appeal to the Court of Requests.[30]

Effectively, then, the quickening of burgess interest in urban property, noted by Professor Hoskins as characteristic of the later sixteenth century,[31] was the product of improved investment yields. Among landowners, competition was now drastically reduced. Church holdings were minimal; for the queen and her aristocracy, growing financial pressures forced a greater attention to yields. In the circumstances, there were many considerable men in the towns who, for the first time, could consider property as more than a personal hedge against inflation. As many urban communities doubled in size through the century, there would be no shortage of tenants. Furthermore, rents were at last sufficient to put money back into repairs. The change came none too soon in the towns, for it followed generations of institutional neglect. Along with the availability of new materials, in particular brick and glass, and with changes in taste and in standards of domestic comfort, it brought the so-called 'Great Rebuilding' to the towns.

The wave of building activity, affecting all regions of England in the late sixteenth and early seventeenth centuries, was first observed in the rebuilding of many yeoman farmsteads and in an unprecedented boom in country-house construction to meet the demand of the gentry.[32] But it took place just as clearly in the towns. At Norwich, where the use of brick in building was becoming increasingly common, the peak period of building activity has been dated to the fourteen years between 1576 and 1590.[33] Elsewhere, it might very well have begun somewhat earlier. Both at King's Lynn and at Worcester, for example, there was extensive rebuilding of tenements from the first years of Elizabeth's reign.[34] This was to be followed by an expansion of the built-up areas: at Worcester in the 1570s, at Plymouth perhaps a decade later.[35] Among other indica-

123 14 Trinity Street, Cambridge, *circa* 1600

tions of a similar building boom in progress in contemporary Leicester was a noticeable increase in the number of glaziers admitted to the freedom of the borough, taking effect particularly in the last three decades of the sixteenth century and coinciding with widespread improvements both in the housing within the borough and in its public amenities.[36] Late in the same century, William Harrison was to note the 'curious' building of his compatriots, their growing use of glass in the windows of houses of every condition, and the multiplication everywhere of chimneys. He had much to say also of luxurious tastes and of a transformation of domestic standards which had touched both the houses themselves and their fittings.[37] Critical himself of this new attention to luxury, Harrison was joined by others in attributing to self-indulgence at least some of the ills of the period. When, in 1582, an anonymous critic wrote of the decay of the once-flourishing port of Southampton, he laid the blame squarely on his co-burgesses, guilty of heedless extravagance. Shortly before, in the third quarter of the sixteenth century, Southampton had undergone a brief commercial revival, the product of new contacts with Spain:

Then beganne costly apparell: then downe with old howses, and newe sett in their places: for the howses where the fathers dwelt could not content their children. Then must everie man of good calling be furnished with change of plate, with great store fyne lynnen, rich tapistrie, and all other things which make shewe of braverie. And who then but Hampton for fyne dyett and great cheare.[38]

A total rebuilding of the medieval tenements, from the ground up, was perhaps less common than the Southampton critic made out. Nevertheless, in almost all houses of large or medium size, the new taste for privacy was reflected in a multiplication of apartments, to be achieved in many cases by subdivision. Most commonly, in the older adapted tenement, this would take the form of the insertion of a new ceiling in the former two-storey hall, thus creating another chamber above it. To furnish access to this and other upper apartments, a new staircase might have to be provided, its importance increasing as more use was made of the upper chambers as the private quarters of the owner. Where the medieval house had had to make do with a cramped newel stair (Fig. 82), built into the thickness of a wall, with simple flying staircases to the galleries of the hall, and with loft-ladders of various kinds to serve the uppermost storeys, a majestic framed principal staircase was given increasing prominence in houses of the late sixteenth century. A mid-century example, at 46 High Street, Exeter, illustrates

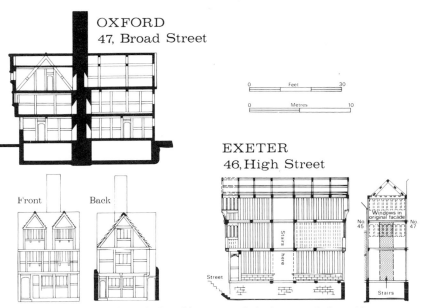

OXFORD
47, Broad Street

Feet 0 30

Metres 0 10

EXETER
46, High Street

Front   Back

124 The central stair and the chimney stack in houses of the mid-sixteenth and the early seventeenth centuries at Exeter and Oxford (Portman and Pantin)

just this feature. Within it, the stair was of considerable importance, mounting, in the original design, to the full height of the building (Fig. 124).[39]

If a staircase had become necessary to give fitting access to more intensively used upper chambers, it was the possibility of heating these chambers that had made them initially more attractive. In most medieval houses, only the hall had been heated, with the result that this one apartment had had to combine the functions of sitting-room and dining-chamber, and frequently of kitchen and bed-chamber in addition. As fuel, especially coal, became more plentiful, and as brick was introduced for chimney-building, this emphasis on the hall could slacken. One good chimney-stack could serve six apartments, or more, and the room with a specialized part-time function, like the dining-room or the study, was at last to become a practical possibility. Typically, the staircase and great chimney of 47 Broad Street, Oxford, centrally sited in the tenement (Fig. 124), brought together in a single structure two of the most significant architectural innovations of the period.[40] It was a period characterized also by the multiplication of living-rooms and bed-chambers, and by the decline into insignificance of the hall.

The modernizations of the 'Great Rebuilding', the concern of the well-to-do, owed their comprehensive quality at least in part to the changes that were beginning to occur within the property-owning class. When Richard Carew, in the 1580s, wrote of the Cornish towns, he remarked on the growth of Truro, but noted too that, in buildings at least, Truro compared ill with Launceston, the county town, where a 'new increase of wealth expresseth itself in the inhabitants' late repaired and enlarged buildings', and 'where there is more use and profit of fair lodgings, through the county assizes'.[41] Far more than the ports and other industrial centres, the county towns of sixteenth-century England were coming into a new prominence of their own. It was not just economic circumstances that contrived this, for there was a social revolution at work as well, bringing the professional classes and the gentry into ever closer contact with the burgesses.

Even before the sixteenth century, the flirtation of the burgess class with the legal profession had had a long and useful life. The appointment, becoming common in the fifteenth-century boroughs, of recorders and professionally qualified town clerks, with the new responsibilities of many borough officers as justices of the peace, had long since confirmed the place of the lawyer in borough administrations. In the first parliament of Henry VI, it has been noted, a good proportion of the serving parliamentary burgesses were lawyers;[42] while in London, during the fifteenth century, old-established city families were beginning to choose the law as a profession for their sons, in preference to an apprenticeship in trade.[43] Not uncommonly, in contemporary borough societies, lawyers sought admission to the freedom, as they were doing in increasing numbers in fifteenth-century York, along with physicians, scriveners and other professional men.[44] But their real penetration of the English boroughs occurred rather later, when the special conditions of the sixteenth century brought about a boom in their profession.

In particular, the great dispersal of ecclesiastical lands was to be the cause of exceptional activity on the property market during this period, but it was to be made more active still by the breakdown of medieval entails and by the increasing ease of alienation of lands once such restrictions had been lifted.[45] Dealings upon credit, rapidly expanding in the period 1570–1640,[46] further required legal services, and these were just the circumstances to bring burgess families increasingly in touch with the law. In Exeter, for example, the Bridgeman family, the Hakewills and the Martins were all to produce lawyers in their time, as were the Barklays and the Wildes of Worcester.[47] And everywhere it was the well-to-do burgess families that fed the stream of would-be lawyers, pushing up calls to the bar at the Inns of Court by as much as forty per cent between the 1590s and the 1630s.[48] Lawyers, from the sixteenth century, played an increasingly important role in borough government, and it was in their hands, too, that much of the new wealth accumulated. By far the wealthiest man in early-sixteenth-century Southampton was Richard Lyster − a lawyer, not a merchant − who in 1524 was living in one of the most handsome, up-to-date houses in the town.[49] Of the total wealth of Northampton in the later sixteenth century, the share of the professions was still minimal; during the immediately pre-Civil War decades, it rose to as much as ten per cent.[50]

As striking as the growth of the professions in the towns, and as deeply rooted in their history, was the mounting concern there of the gentry. From the mid-fifteenth century, and perhaps before, gentry shared with the lawyers the role of parliamentary burgesses at all but the major centres.[51] There were protests locally, at some of the larger towns, at what was seen as an invasion of rights: at Nottingham in 1437, at Salisbury in 1448, at Cambridge in 1459, and at Ipswich in 1474.[52] But for many of the smaller boroughs, representation at Westminster was to become a luxury they felt they could ill afford, nor was there much to be lost by the recruitment of more powerful spokesmen. Already in 1422, only one of the twelve parliamentary burgesses of the Cornish boroughs had been identifiably a merchant,[53] and even in a town as careful of its rights as fifteenth-century Worcester, there would be experiments, in the decade after 1467, with the sharing of representation with the gentry.[54] Grimsby, in Lincolnshire, notoriously exposed to the meddling of its local aristocracy, found itself driven, in 1491, to draw up a new constitution specifically to exclude them. If necessary, the constitution provided, the burgesses were to rally to their mayor with armed force; they were to have, as mayor or bailiff, only such as would be profitable to the town, duly elected by themselves; should there be internal dissensions, they were to submit to arbitration without seeking the support of outsiders in their quarrels; they were to report immediately, for action by their mayor, any offences committed by John Missenden 'or by any other gentleman or yeoman'.[55] Grimsby's mayor and burgesses of the previous generation had been approached in 1470 by Ralph Nevill, earl of Westmorland, concerning an arrangement he thought must be to their mutual advantage. Professing concern at the high costs the burgesses would have to meet if they sent representatives of their own choosing to Parliament, he urged them immediately to send

125 The Feathers Hotel, Ludlow, early-seventeenth-century

him the writ requiring such an election, 'wheche I shall cause to be substauncially retourned and appoynt ij of my Counsale to be Burgessis for youre seid towne, who shall not only regarde and set forward the welle of the same in suche causis, if ye have any, as ye shall advertise me and theym upon, but also dymynysshe yor chargis of olde tyme conswete and used for the sustentacioune of these seid costes.' They were not to fail in this, the earl felt called upon to add, 'as ye intend to have my goode wylle and favor in lyke maner shewed accordingly'.[56]

Ralph Nevill knew his burgesses, and the patronage he threatened to withdraw was clearly of some value to them. It was not a one-sided relationship, and many towns in sixteenth-century England would go out of their way to welcome aristocratic involvement in their affairs. Grimsby's own mayoralty, over that century, was held on at least thirty-six occasions by a 'gentleman' or an 'esquire'.[57] while at Bury St Edmunds, Southampton and elsewhere, important municipal office is known frequently to have come the way of the gentry.[58] Their influence as officers could be important, and it could be bought in other ways. The practice of conferring honorary freedoms on powerful men in the vicinity, although still relatively undeveloped, was already known in fifteenth-century York.[59] In Southampton, throughout the next century, the device was in frequent use to attach the interest of powerful men and to ensure their advocacy in the counsels of the region and the realm. Among the more prominent patrons of the borough, Thomas Wriothesley, later given the title of earl of Southampton, was admitted to a free burgess-ship in 1538. Subsequently, he and his successors maintained a fine town house in Southampton, and regularly lent their voice to its concerns. Sir John Worsley, granted a similar burgess-ship the year before, had earned this honour 'for divers considerations by him done touching the liberties of the town'. Other free burgesses of Southampton, later in the century, were to include Sir Thomas Leighton, Sir Humphrey Gilbert, Sir Henry Carey and Sir Walter Raleigh.[60]

While it was certainly exceptional for an honorary burgess of this rank to reside in the town that had adopted him, the practice of gentry settling in the towns, if only for the length of the season, was undoubtedly growing in the sixteenth century, promoting those interchanges between gentry and burgesses that were to become so common in the society of the English counties. In sixteenth-century Exeter, as for many comparable county towns, the flow of gentry into the city could be compared for the first time with that outward tide of wealthy burgesses which had characterized medieval borough society even in its most independent years.[61] In a contemporary tract on the respective virtues of the *Cyvile and Uncyvile Life* (1579), we can find some of the reasons that brought them. Vincent and Valentine, gentlemen advocates of the rural and the urban life styles, debate in a lengthy dialogue the merits of their chosen abodes. To Vincent, the advantages of the countryside lay in its wholesomeness and its offer of the joys of the chase, but he had, after all, to concede that the town was indeed the place 'fittest for a Gentleman'. Among Valentine's strongest points had been those urging the comforts of residence in the suburbs:

The manner of the most Gentlemen and Noble men also, is to house them selves (if possible they may) in the Subburbes of the Cittie, because moste commonly, the ayre there beeinge somewhat at large, the place is healthy, and through the distaunce from the bodye of the Towne, the noyse not much: and so consequently quiet. Also for the commoditie wee finde many lodginges, both spacious and roomethy, with Gardaines and Orchardes very delectable. So as with good government, wee have as litle cause to feare infection there, as in the verye Countrey: our water is excellente, and much better then you have anye, our ground and feeldes most pleasaunte, our fier equall with yours.[62]

In the great houses of the gentry and professional classes, spaced out elegantly along the immediate approaches to many of our country towns, we can still see some of the products of such thinking.

The return of the gentry to the towns, so much a characteristic of early-modern England, might have been more important politically had not its members retained their country interests as well. Nevertheless, it marked a weakening of the already fragile English urban spirit, and a retreat on the standards of independence set up in many towns as much as four centuries before. Almost everywhere, from the sixteenth century and sometimes before, the burgess and tradesman bowed to the nod of the gentry. The grip of the ruling oligarchy tightened, and its composition too had altered, to include the gentleman, the lawyer and the doctor, loyally supported by the priest.

These changes were noticed and were sometimes lamented by contemporaries. But it is not at all clear that the majority could have found in them much to regret. The spectacular growth of urban institutions in twelfth- and thirteenth-century England had been followed by years of debilitating stagnation and neglect. Many towns had grown with the wool and cloth trades, and over-dependence upon them had ended by pulling them down. At others, it was frequently a foreigner, or an individual native entrepreneur, who appropriated the bulk of the profits. There were those, of course, who might still look back with nostalgia to an age during which town air had indeed made a man free: when borough right stood out as a covetable privilege, beyond the ordinary law of the land. Yet this had been the product of a rich overseas trade, and of the interest of the king in maintaining it. And there must have been others, too, who welcomed the new equilibrium which a quickening local industry and a reduced dependence on the outsider, whether as supplier or customer, had brought to borough finances.

Every community is different, and there is little point in laying down maxims for them all. Yet it could be said, with some justice, that the fine spirit of independence and self-pride which had breathed through the resolutions of the men of Ipswich in the summer and autumn of the year 1200 (see pp. 157–9) is much harder to find amongst their sixteenth-century successors. Too often, that is, such rejection of outside interference as we have seen, for example, at fifteenth-century Worcester and at Grimsby, takes on the aspect of a rearguard action in a retreat that had already become irreversible. The struggle for greater administrative efficiency in the towns had not been won without cost. Undoubtedly, the typical early-modern country town was a pleasant enough place in which to live. It was Valentine's opinion, as we have seen, that a gentleman was better off living in the suburbs. Yet by his generation what he called the 'bodye of the Towne' was usually adequately paved and well-watered; street-lighting was not uncommon; fire control and building regulations had been accepted; policing and poor-relief had been provided for; the noisy and the malodorous trades had been banished from heavily built-up areas; there were public lavatories and wash-houses within the walls, and municipal plague-houses well beyond them. But, of course, the price of good government, as we all have cause to know, is more of it. 'After the starry night, the grey morrow.'

Notes

Chapter 1   Urban Origins

1   Lawrence Stone, 'Social mobility in England, 1500–1700', *Past and Present*, 33 (1966), p. 20.

2   R. H. Hilton, *A Medieval Society. The West Midlands at the End of the Thirteenth Century*, 1966, pp. 167–8.

3   Julian Cornwall, 'English country towns in the fifteen twenties', *Ec.H.R.*, 2nd series, 15 (1962–3), p. 61.

4   James Tait, *The Medieval English Borough*, 1936, pp. 70–3, 114–17; see also William Urry, *Canterbury under the Angevin Kings*, 1967, pp. 105–6; for York, see *V.C.H. City of York*, p. 498.

5   *V.C.H. Warwick*, 8: 483; W. G. Hoskins, 'An Elizabethan provincial town: Leicester', in *Studies in Social History: a tribute to G. M. Trevelyan*, ed. J. H. Plumb, 1955, pp. 40–1; R. H. Hilton, op. cit., p. 185.

6   R. A. Pelham, 'The urban population of Sussex in 1340', *Sussex Archaeological Collections*, 78 (1937), p. 217.

7   W. B. Stephens (ed.), *History of Congleton*, 1970, pp. 53–4; Julian Cornwall, op. cit., p. 67.

8   C. A. Sneyd (ed.), *A Relation, or rather a True Account, of the Island of England . . . about the Year 1500*, Camden Society, 37 (1847), pp. 31, 41.

9   *Cal. State Papers Venetian 1621–1623*, p. 430.

10 R. B. Dobson, 'Admissions to the freedom of the city of York in the Later Middle Ages', *Ec.H.R.*, 2nd series, 26 (1973), p. 15.

11 Edward Gillett, *A History of Grimsby*, 1970, p. 63.

12 For the Later Middle Ages, see A. R. Bridbury, *Economic Growth: England in the Later Middle Ages*, 1962, pp. 79, 111.

13 K. M. E. Murray, *The Constitutional History of the Cinque Ports*, 1935, p. 29.

14 A. R. Bridbury, 'The Dark Ages', *Ec.H.R.*, 2nd series, 22 (1969), pp. 526–37.

15 For recent discussions of archaeological and other work at these centres, see H. H. van Regteren Altena, 'The origins and development of Dutch towns', *World Archaeology*, 2 (1970–1), pp. 130–2, and Peter Foote and David M. Wilson, *The Viking Achievement*, 1970, pp. 191–231.

16 Martin Biddle, 'Archaeology and the beginnings of English society', in *England before the Conquest. Studies in Primary Sources presented to Dorothy Whitelock*, eds Peter Clemoes and Kathleen Hughes, 1971, pp. 395–7.

17 P. V. Addyman and D. H. Hill, 'Saxon Southampton: a review of the evidence', parts 1 and 2, *Proceedings of the Hampshire Field Club and Archaeological Society*, 25 (1968), pp. 61–93, and 26 (1969), pp. 61–96.

18 For the view that the alternatives to trade in the Dark Ages were more important than trade itself, see Philip Grierson, 'Commerce in the Dark Ages: a critique of the evidence', *T.R.H.S.*, 5th series, 9 (1959), pp. 123–40. There is a recent, more balanced, discussion of that trade in Georges Duby's *The Early Growth of the European Economy*, 1974, in particular pp. 97–111.

19 Henry Loyn, 'Towns in late Anglo-Saxon England: the evidence and some possible lines of enquiry', in *England before the Conquest*, eds Peter Clemoes and Kathleen Hughes, 1971, p. 116.

20 Ibid., pp. 117–19.

21 James Tait, op. cit., p. 20.

22 Hilary L. Turner, *Town Defences in England and Wales*, 1971, pp. 52–3; for useful recent discussions of Hereford defences, see Ron Shoesmith, 'Hereford', *Current Archaeology*, 33 (1972), pp. 256–8, and M. D. Lobel, 'Hereford', pp. 3–4, in the same author's *Historic Towns*, 1969.

23 Martin Biddle and David Hill, 'Late Saxon planned towns', *Antiquaries Journal*, 51 (1971), pp. 76–8.

24 Martin Biddle, op. cit., p. 396.

25 Henry Loyn, op. cit., pp. 121–2.

26 Ibid., pp. 123–4.

27 Carl Stephenson, *Borough and Town. A Study of Urban Origins in England*, 1933.

28 Ralph A. Griffiths, 'The medieval boroughs of Glamorgan and medieval Swansea', in *The Middle Ages: Glamorgan County History 3*, ed. T. B. Pugh, 1971, pp. 334–5.

29 The point is made by Henry Loyn, *The Norman Conquest*, 1967, p. 173.

30 A. R. Bridbury, 'The Dark Ages', *Ec.H.R.*, 2nd series, 22 (1969), pp. 536–7.

31 Alan Rogers (ed.), *The Making of Stamford*, 1965, pp. 32–3.

32 *V.C.H. City of Leicester*, p. 31.

33 *V.C.H. Warwick*, 8: 480; H. A. Cronne, *The Borough of Warwick in the Middle Ages*, Dugdale Society Occasional Papers, 10 (1951), p. 10.

34 H. A. Cronne, op. cit., p. 11.

35 M. D. Lobel and J. Tann, 'Gloucester', p. 4, in *Historic Towns*, ed. M. D. Lobel, 1969.

36 Helen M. Cam, *Liberties and Communities in Medieval England*, 1944, pp. 23–4.

37 William Urry, op. cit., p. 172.

38 Colin Platt, *Medieval Southampton: the Port and Trading Community, A.D. 1000–1600*, 1973, p. 235.

39 Helen Cam, op. cit., p. 24.

40 W. G. Hoskins and H. P. R. Finberg, *Devonshire Studies*, 1952, p. 172.

41 Maurice Beresford, *New Towns of the Middle Ages: Town Plantation in England, Wales and Gascony*, 1967, p. 327.

42 Ibid., pp. 328–31, 338.

43 Ibid., pp. 334–7.

44 R. H. Hilton, op. cit., pp. 192–3.

45 Ibid., pp. 189–91.

46 Bryan E. Coates, 'The origin and distribution of markets and fairs in medieval Derbyshire', *Derbyshire Archaeological Journal*, 85 (1965), pp. 99, 102.

47 D. M. Palliser and A. C. Pinnock, 'The markets of medieval Staffordshire', *North Staffordshire Journal of Field Studies*, 11 (1971), p. 52.

48 Bryan E. Coates, op. cit., p. 96.

Chapter 2   The Urban Landscape

1 For the market-based town, see Maurice Beresford, *New Towns of the Middle Ages*, 1967, p. 153.

2 M. D. Lobel (ed.), *Historic Towns*, 1969, p. 3 (Hereford).

3 Ibid., pp. 2–3 (Salisbury).

4 Ibid., p. 3 (Nottingham).

5 M. R. G. Conzen, *Alnwick, Northumberland, a Study in Town Plan Analysis*, 1960, p. 29 and fig. 5.

6 W. G. Hoskins, *Provincial England*, 1963, pp. 57–8.

7 Martin Biddle and David Hill, 'Late Saxon planned towns', *Antiquaries Journal*, 51 (1971), pp. 70–3, 81; Henry Hurst, 'Excavations at Gloucester, 1968–1971: first interim report', *Antiquaries Journal*, 52 (1972), p. 67; William Urry, *Canterbury under the Angevin Kings*, 1967, p. 185.

8 M. V. Taylor (ed.), *Liber Luciani de Laude Cestrie*, Lancashire and Cheshire Record Society, 64 (1912), pp. 46–7.

9 Martin Biddle and David Hill, op. cit., pp. 84–5. For a possibly even earlier eighth-century grid at North Elmham, Norfolk, see Peter Wade-Martins, 'North Elmham', *Current Archaeology*, 36 (1973), pp. 22–5.

10 Maurice Beresford, op. cit., pp. 147, 154.

11 See, for example, H. M. Colvin, 'Domestic architecture and town-planning', in *Medieval England*, ed. A. L. Poole, 1958, 1: 59.

12 M. R. G. Conzen, 'The use of town plans in the study of urban history', in *The Study of Urban History*, ed. H. J. Dyos, 1968, pp. 124–6.

13 H. M. Colvin, op. cit., p. 56 and fig. 18.

14 Martin Biddle and David Hill, op. cit., p. 82; Colin Platt and Richard Coleman-Smith, *Excavations in Medieval Southampton, 1953–1969*, 1975, 1: 132–4.

15 William Urry, op. cit., pp. 190–1.

16 Vanessa Parker, *The Making of King's Lynn*, 1971, pp. 21–2.

17 H. A. Cronne (ed.), *Bristol Charters, 1378–1499*, Bristol Record Society, 11 (1946), pp. 31–6.

18 M. D. Lobel, op. cit., passim. A. G. Little has argued that this extra-mural siting was usually a late development, following the expansion of established houses which then required more space for their buildings

(*Fratris Thomae, vulgo dicti de Eccleston, tractatus De adventu fratrum minorum in Angliam*, 1951, p. xxx).

19   F. W. Maitland and M. Bateson (eds), *The Charters of the Borough of Cambridge*, 1901, p. xxx.

20   W. G. Hoskins, *Two Thousand Years in Exeter*, 1960, p. 48.

21   Marjory Honeybourne, 'The leper hospitals of the London area', *Transactions of the London and Middlesex Archaeological Society*, 21 (1967), p. 5.

22   G. H. Martin, 'Church life in medieval Leicester', in *The Growth of Leicester*, ed. A. E. Brown, 1970, pp. 33–4.

23   M. D. Lobel, op. cit., p. 6 (Gloucester).

24   Edward Gillett, *A History of Grimsby*, 1970, p. 80.

25   Alan Rogers (ed.), *The Making of Stamford*, 1965, p. 55.

26   William Urry, op. cit., pp. 185–6, 189–90.

27   *V.C.H. Warwick*, 8: 487; H. A. Cronne, *The Borough of Warwick in the Middle Ages*, Dugdale Society Occasional Papers, 10 (1951), p. 18.

28   *V.C.H. Warwick*, loc. cit.

29   D. J. Keene, *Some Aspects of the History, Topography and Archaeology . . . of Winchester*, Oxford D.Phil., 1972, p. 80.

30   W. G. Hoskins, 'An Elizabethan provincial town: Leicester', in *Studies in Social History: a tribute to G. M. Trevelyan*, ed. J. H. Plumb, 1955, pp. 40, 43.

31   Colin Platt, op. cit., pp. 264–6.

32   Hilary L. Turner, *Town Defences in England and Wales*, 1971, p. 92; for the Oxford seal, see R. H. C. Davis, 'An Oxford charter of 1191 and the beginnings of municipal freedom', *Oxoniensia*, 33 (1968), p. 55.

33   Hilary L. Turner, op. cit., pp. 13, 16, 91.

34   Eileen Gooder, *Coventry's Town Wall*, 1971, passim.

35   Hilary L. Turner, op. cit., p. 89.

36   John Bartlett, 'The medieval walls of Hull', *Bulletin of the Kingston upon Hull Museums*, 3–4 (1969–70, revised 1971), pp. 6–13, 21.

37   S. E. West, 'Excavations at Cox Lane (1958) and at the town defences, Shire Hall yard, Ipswich (1959)', *Proceedings of the Suffolk Institute of Archaeology*, 29 (1961–3), pp. 291–7, 301–2.

38   Terence Paul Smith, 'The medieval town defences of King's Lynn', *Journal of the British Archaeological Association*, 3rd series, 33 (1970), pp. 57, 73, 86.

39   Colin Platt and Richard Coleman-Smith, op. cit., 1: 36–7; Eileen Gooder, op. cit., pp. 48, 50; M. W. Barley, 'Medieval town wall, Park Row, Nottingham', *Medieval Archaeology*, 9 (1965), pp. 164–7; and see also the three papers on medieval Norwich in *Norfolk Archaeology*, 30 (1952), pp. 295–8, 31 (1955), pp. 12–13, 33 (1963), pp. 139–40.

40   Ron Shoesmith, 'Hereford', *Current Archaeology*, 33 (1972), pp. 256–8.

41   F. L. Ganshof, *Étude sur le Développement des Villes entre Loire et Rhin au Moyen Âge*, 1943, in particular pp. 53–9.

42   Hilary L. Turner, op. cit., p. 56; Colin Platt, op. cit., p. 36.

43   *Cal. State Papers Venetian 1621–1623*, p. 430.

44 Hilary L. Turner, op. cit., p. 82.

45 Ibid., p. 50.

46 Colin Platt and Richard Coleman-Smith, op. cit., 1: 37–8; Colin Platt, op. cit., pp. 122–4.

47 M. R. G. Conzen, *Alnwick, Northumberland, a Study in Town Plan Analysis*, 1960, pp. 40–1.

48 D. J. Keene, op. cit., pp. 38, 40.

49 Colin Platt and Richard Coleman-Smith, op. cit., 1: 32.

50 Terence Paul Smith, op. cit., p. 60.

51 M. D. Lobel, op. cit., p. 5 (Salisbury).

52 E. M. Carus-Wilson, 'The first half-century of the borough of Stratford-upon-Avon', *Ec.H.R.*, 2nd series, 18 (1965), p. 62.

53 G. H. Martin, *The Borough and the Merchant Community of Ipswich, 1317–1422*, Oxford D.Phil., 1955, p. 165.

54 D. C. Douglas and G. W. Greenaway (eds), *English Historical Documents 1042–1189*, 1953, p. 958.

55 H. E. Salter, *Medieval Oxford*, 1936, pp. 84–5.

56 Elspeth M Veale, *The English Fur Trade in the Later Middle Ages*, 1966, pp. 44–5.

57 Charlotte Augusta Sneyd (ed.), *A Relation, or rather a True Account, of the Island of England . . . about the year 1500*, Camden Society, 37 (1847), pp. 42–3.

58 *V.C.H. Wiltshire*, 6: 133.

59 D. J. Keene, op. cit., p. 167, Martin Biddle, 'Excavations at Winchester, 1970. Ninth interim report', *Antiquaries Journal*, 52 (1972), pp. 107–9, 111.

60 E. M. Carus-Wilson, op. cit., p. 61; Vanessa Parker, op. cit., p. 36; M. R. G. Conzen, op. cit., pp. 41–3.

61 A. Carter and J. P. Roberts, 'Excavations in Norwich – 1972. The Norwich Survey – second interim report', *Norfolk Archaeology*, 35 (1973), pp. 457–62, 464–7.

62 Vanessa Parker, op. cit., pp. 33, 37.

63 Colin Platt, op. cit., p. 52 (note 40).

64 *V.C.H. City of York*, p. 89; *V.C.H. City of Kingston upon Hull*, p. 57.

65 *Current Archaeology*, 27 (1971), p. 112; Alec Down and Margaret Rule, *Chichester Excavations I*, 1971, p. 157 and Fig. 9.1.

66 Colin Platt, op. cit., p. 171.

67 *Cal. P.R. 1281–1292*, p. 260.

68 T. G. Hassall, 'Excavations at Oxford 1970: third interim report', *Oxoniensia*, 36 (1971), p. 8.

69 D. J. Keene, op. cit., p. 44.

70 Ernest L. Sabine, 'City cleaning in mediaeval London', *Speculum*, 12 (1937), pp. 21–5.

71 C. H. Williams (ed.), *English Historical Documents 1485–1558*, 1967, p. 189.

72 Colin Platt, op. cit., p. 171.

73 C. H. Williams, op. cit., p. 974.

74 E. M. Carus-Wilson, op. cit., pp. 60–1.
75 Maurice Beresford, op. cit., p. 162.
76 Colin Platt, op. cit., pp. 222–3 and passim.
77 James Dallaway, *Antiquities of Bristow in the Middle Centuries,* 1834, passim; for comments on the street patterns of Southampton and Winchester, see Colin Platt, op. cit., pp. 43–8, and D. J. Keene, op. cit., pp. 35–45.
78 D. J. Keene, op. cit., p. 37.
79 M. R. G. Conzen, op. cit., p. 31.
80 Adolphus Ballard (ed.), *British Borough Charters 1042–1216,* 1913, p. 47.
81 D. J. Keene, op. cit., pp. 96–7; William Urry, op. cit., p. 194.
82 E. M. Carus-Wilson, op. cit., p. 57; Adolphus Ballard, op. cit., p. 51; R. H. Hilton, *A Medieval Society,* 1966, p. 185.
83 M. D. Lobel, op. cit., p. 3 (Banbury).
84 E. M. Carus-Wilson, op. cit., p. 59.
85 W. A. Pantin, 'Medieval English town-house plans', *Medieval Archaeology,* 6–7 (1962–3), p. 203.
86 Alan Rogers, *The Medieval Buildings of Stamford,* 1970, p. 10.
87 Martin Biddle, op. cit., pp. 110–11.
88 Alan Carter (Norwich Survey), pers. comm.; *Medieval Archaeology,* 9 (1965), p. 196; Colin Platt and Richard Coleman-Smith, op. cit., 1: 234, 238–9.
89 Colin Platt and Richard Coleman-Smith, op. cit., 1: 33.
90 Ibid., 1: 78–9.
91 V. D. Lipman, *The Jews of Medieval Norwich,* 1967, pp. 27–32; Margaret Wood, *The English Mediaeval House,* 1965, p. 5.
92 William Urry, op. cit., p. 193.
93 Colin Platt, op. cit., pp. 39–40.
94 Henry Thomas Riley (ed.), *Munimenta Gildhallae Londoniensis,* 1859, 1: 328–9.
95 A. G. Little, op. cit., p. 79.
96 Martin Biddle, 'Excavations at Winchester, 1969. Eighth interim report', *Antiquaries Journal,* 50 (1970), pp. 307–9; K. J. Barton, 'Excavations at Back Hall, Bristol, 1958', *Transactions of the Bristol and Gloucestershire Archaeological Society,* 79 (1960), p. 256; and notes in *Medieval Archaeology,* 11 (1967), p. 293, and 14 (1970), pp. 183–4.
97 Maurice Beresford and John G. Hurst (eds), *Deserted Medieval Villages,* 1971, p. 93.
98 Colin Platt and Richard Coleman-Smith, op. cit., 1: 104–7.
99 William Urry, op. cit., p. 194.
100 Helen Bonney, ' "Balle's Place", Salisbury: a 14th-century merchant's house', *Wiltshire Archaeological and Natural History Magazine,* 56 (1964), pp. 159–60; D. J. Keene, op. cit., pp. 107–8; Vanessa Parker, op. cit., p. 69.
101 G. H. Martin, *The Borough and the Merchant Community of Ipswich, 1317–1422,* Oxford D.Phil., 1955, pp. 194–5.
102 T. B. Pugh (ed.), *The Middle Ages: Glamorgan County History 3,* 1971, p. 372.

103 W. A. Pantin, op. cit., pp. 203–5.

104 Patrick Faulkner, 'The surviving medieval buildings', in *Excavations in Medieval Southampton, 1953–1969*, Colin Platt and Richard Coleman-Smith, 1975, 1: 104–7.

105 Ibid., 1: 94–6.

106 Robert Douch, *Visitors' Descriptions of Southampton, 1540–1956*, 1961, p. 9.

107 Vanessa Parker, op. cit., pp. 56–62; for a very full description of the buildings at Hampton Court, see W. A. Pantin, 'Some medieval English town houses: a study in adaptation', in *Culture and Environment. Essays in Honour of Sir Cyril Fox*, eds I. Ll. Foster and L. Alcock, 1963, pp. 447–55.

108 D. J. Keene, op. cit., p. 111.

109 P. A. Faulkner, 'Medieval undercrofts and town houses', *Archaeological Journal*, 123 (1966), pp. 128–30.

110 W. A. Pantin, 'The development of domestic architecture in Oxford', *Antiquaries Journal*, 27 (1947), p. 127 and figs 2–4.

111 Helen Bonney, op. cit., pp. 162–4.

112 W. A. Pantin, 'Medieval English town-house plans', *Medieval Archaeology*, 6–7 (1962–3), pp. 224–6.

113 L. F. Salzman, *Building in England down to 1540. A Documentary History*, 1967 (2nd edition), pp. 483–5, 554–6, 598.

114 Vanessa Parker, op. cit., pp. 63–4 and figs 12 and 34.

115 D. Portman, *Exeter Houses 1400–1700*, 1966, pp. 4, 73–4, 91.

116 Angelo Raine, *Medieval York*, 1955, p. 47; *Cal. P.R. 1313–17*, pp. 476–7.

117 Angelo Raine, op. cit., p. 151; L. F. Salzman, op. cit., pp. 430–2.

118 Vanessa Parker, op. cit., p. 66.

119 D. J. Keene, op. cit., 113–14.

120 S. R. Jones and J. T. Smith, 'The Wealden houses of Warwickshire and their significance', *Transactions and Proceedings of the Birmingham Archaeological Society*, 79 (1960–1), pp. 24–30.

121 Martin Biddle, 'Excavations at Winchester, 1967. Sixth interim report', *Antiquaries Journal*, 48 (1968), pp. 265–6. Other small houses, set in what might have been a terrace of three, have been identified in an early-fourteenth-century context at Hull, but these were probably two-chamber houses, considerably more spacious than the Winchester cottages (John Bartlett, 'Medieval Hull. Excavations in High St. 1971', *Bulletin of the Kingston upon Hull Museums*, 7 (1971), pp. 5–7). For some evidence of small rectangular thirteenth-century cottages at Rhuddlan, in North Wales, see Henrietta Miles, 'Rhuddlan', *Current Archaeology*, 32 (1972), p. 246.

122 Ernest L. Sabine, 'Latrines and cesspools of mediaeval London', *Speculum*, 9 (1934), pp. 306–9; Mary Bateson (ed.), *Records of the Borough of Leicester*, 1901, 2: 60–1; D. J. Keene, op. cit., p. 117; *V.C.H. City of Kingston upon Hull*, p. 75; Colin Platt, op. cit., p. 171; W. G. Hoskins, *Two Thousand Years in Exeter*, 1960, p. 47.

123 A. R. Myers, *London in the Age of Chaucer*, 1972, pp. 62–5; D. Portman, op. cit., p. 16, and Aileen Fox, 'The underground conduits in Exeter,

exposed during reconstructions in 1950', *Reports and Transactions of the Devonshire Association*, 83 (1951), pp. 172–8; Colin Platt, op. cit., pp. 96, 144; H. A. Cronne (ed.), *Bristol Charters 1378–1499*, Bristol Record Society, 11 (1946), pp. 188–91; M. D. Lobel, op. cit., p. 11 (Gloucester); *V.C.H. City of Kingston upon Hull*, pp. 74–5.

124 *Cal. C. R. 1330–1333*, p. 610.

125 G. G. Coulton, *Social Life in Britain from the Conquest to the Reformation*, 1918, pp. 330–1.

126 Colin Platt and Richard Coleman-Smith, op. cit., 1: 273–5, 293; K. J. Barton, op. cit., pp. 260, 262.

127 Colin Platt and Richard Coleman-Smith, op. cit., 1: 34.

128 L. F. Salzman, op. cit., pp. 432–3, 443–4.

129 D. Portman, op. cit., pp. 15–16, 63–4, 82–3, and figs vii and x: l.

130 Colin Platt and Richard Coleman-Smith, op. cit., 1: 34–5; see also D. J. Keene, op. cit., p. 117.

131 Henry Thomas Riley, op. cit., l: xxxi.

132 William Brenchley Rye (ed.), *England as Seen by Foreigners in the Days of Elizabeth and James the First*, 1865, pp. 78–9.

133 Frederick J. Furnivall (ed.), *Harrison's Description of England in Shakspere's Youth*, 1877, p. 238.

134 A. R. Myers (ed.), *English Historical Documents 1327–1485*, 1969, pp. 1145–6.

135 Ibid., pp. 1068–72.

136 Sylvia L. Thrupp, *The Merchant Class of Medieval London*, 1948, p. 140.

137 Colin Platt and Richard Coleman-Smith, op. cit., 1: 32.

Chapter 3 The Borough Economy: Growth and Decline

1 Quoted by Bryan E. Coates, 'The origin and distribution of markets and fairs in medieval Derbyshire', *Derbyshire Archaeological Journal*, 85 (1965), p. 105, and again by D. M. Palliser and A. C. Pinnock, 'The markets of medieval Staffordshire', *North Staffordshire Journal of Field Studies*, 11 (1971), p. 54.

2 For recent comments, see Constance M. Fraser, 'The pattern of trade in the north-east of England, 1265–1350', *Northern History*, 4 (1969), p. 46, and R. H. Hilton, *A Medieval Society*, 1966, pp. 180–1.

3 E. M. Carus-Wilson, 'The first half-century of the borough of Stratford-upon-Avon', *Ec.H.R.*, 2nd series, 18 (1965), pp. 55–6.

4 *V.C.H. Warwick*, 8: 153.

5 Elspeth M. Veale, 'Craftsmen and the economy of London in the fourteenth century', in *Studies in London History*, eds A. Hollaender and W. Kellaway, 1969, p. 139.

6 Colin Platt, *Medieval Southampton*, 1973, pp. 160–1.

7 Constance M. Fraser, op. cit., p. 45.

8 *V.C.H. City of York*, p. 97.

9 Ibid., pp. 69, 98.

10 *V.C.H. City of Kingston upon Hull*, pp. 54–5. For an early survey of road

and bridge maintenance in late-medieval England, see J. J. Jusserand's still unreplaced *English Wayfaring Life in the Middle Ages*, first published in 1889.

11 F. M. Stenton, 'The road system of medieval England', *Ec.H.R.*, 7 (1936), p. 21.

12 For a useful discussion of the probable development of a medieval road system in the Midlands, see W. G. Hoskins, *Provincial England*, 1963, pp. 61–3.

13 The map is discussed by Professor Stenton, op. cit., pp. 7–13.

14 Constance M. Fraser, op. cit., p. 48.

15 *V.C.H. City of Leicester*, p. 48.

16 Bryan E. Coates, op. cit., p. 99.

17 D. J. Keene, *Some Aspects of the History, Topography and Archaeology . . . of Winchester*, Oxford D.Phil., 1972, pp. 65–6.

18 Charles Gross (ed.), *Select Cases Concerning the Law Merchant, A.D. 1270–1638*, Publications of the Selden Society, 23 (1908), p. xvii.

19 Colin Platt, op. cit., p. 168 and note 10.

20 F. W. Maitland and M. Bateson (eds), *The Charters of the Borough of Cambridge*, 1901, pp. xxx–xxxi.

21 C. Verlinden, 'Markets and fairs', in *The Cambridge Economic History of Europe*, vol. 3, eds M. M. Postan, E. F. Rich and Edward Miller, 1965, p. 151. Professor Verlinden is at pains to emphasize throughout his chapter the continuing importance of the fair in medieval and early-modern Europe.

22 Paul Studer (ed.), *The Oak Book of Southampton of c. A.D. 1300*, 1911, 2: 18–27.

23 *Cal. State Papers Venetian 1621–1623*, p. 431.

24 For recent discussions of these points, see M. M. Postan, *The Medieval Economy and Society*, 1972, pp. 191–2, and T. H. Lloyd, *The Movement of Wool Prices in Medieval England*, 1973, pp. 13–15.

25 T. H. Lloyd, op. cit., pp. 17–18.

26 P. H. Sawyer, 'The wealth of England in the eleventh century', *T.R.H.S.*, 5th series, 15 (1965), pp. 145–64.

27 D. C. Douglas and G. W. Greenaway (eds), *English Historical Documents 1042–1189*, 1953, p. 970.

28 Edward Miller, 'The fortunes of the English textile industry during the thirteenth century', *Ec.H.R.*, 2nd series, 18 (1965), p. 67.

29 Eileen Power, *The Wool Trade in English Medieval History*, 1941, pp. 51–5.

30 D. J. Keene, op. cit., p. 169; Colin Platt, op. cit., pp. 72–3; Eileen Power, op. cit., pp. 59–60.

31 E. M. Carus-Wilson, *Medieval Merchant Venturers*, 1967 (2nd edition), pp. 213–14.

32 Edward Miller, op. cit., p. 76.

33 Ibid., p. 73; E. M. Carus-Wilson, op. cit., pp. 222–38.

34 R. H. Hilton, op. cit., pp. 209–13; E. M. Carus-Wilson, 'An industrial revolution of the thirteenth century', *Ec.H.R.*, 11 (1941), pp. 39–60.

35   Edward Miller, op. cit., p. 79; D. J. Keene, op. cit., p. 169.
36   T. H. Lloyd, op. cit., p. 28.
37   Colin Platt, op. cit., pp. 236, 248, 253.
38   A. R. Bridbury, *Economic Growth: England in the Later Middle Ages*, 1962, pp. 112–13.
39   R. S. Schofield, 'The geographical distribution of wealth in England, 1334–1649', *Ec.H.R.*, 2nd series, 18 (1965), pp. 506–9.
40   Eleanora Carus-Wilson, 'The medieval trade of the ports of the Wash', *Medieval Archaeology*, 6–7, (1962–3), pp. 196–8; M. M. Postan, op. cit., pp. 194–5; Elspeth M. Veale, *The English Fur Trade in the Later Middle Ages*, 1966, pp. 68–70.
41   *V.C.H. City of Kingston upon Hull*, pp. 61–4; Margery Kirkbride James, *Studies in the Medieval Wine Trade*, 1971, pp. 42–7.
42   M. M. Postan, op. cit., pp. 196–7, 203–5.
43   J. N. Bartlett, 'The expansion and decline of York in the later Middle Ages', *Ec.H.R.*, 2nd series, 12 (1959–60), pp. 27–30.
44   W. G. Hoskins and H. P. R. Finberg, *Devonshire Studies*, 1952, pp. 229–31. For the tin trade, see A. R. Bridbury, op. cit., pp. 24–5.
45   Edward Gillett, *A History of Grimsby*, 1970, p. 50.
46   A. R. Bridbury, *England and the Salt Trade in the Later Middle Ages*, 1955, pp. 94–5, 107–9; H. J. Hewitt, *Medieval Cheshire. An Economic and Social History of Cheshire in the Reigns of the Three Edwards*, Chetham Society, new series, 88 (1929), pp. 118–21.
47   D. M. Palliser and A. C. Pinnock, op. cit., p. 58.
48   W. B. Stephens (ed.), *History of Congleton*, 1970, p. 36.
49   W. G. Hoskins, *Provincial England*, 1963, pp. 65–6.
50   *V.C.H. Warwick*, 8: 480–1.
51   Ibid., p. 209.

Chapter 4   Borough Society

1   E. M. Carus-Wilson, 'The first half-century of the borough of Stratford-upon-Avon', *Ec.H.R.*, 2nd series, 18 (1965), p. 54.
2   W. G. Hoskins, *Provincial England*, 1963, pp. 60–1.
3   Helen M. Cam, *Liberties and Communities in Medieval England*, 1944, p. 22.
4   R. H. Hilton, *A Medieval Society*, 1966, p. 184.
5   *V.C.H. City of York*, pp. 40, 108.
6   *V.C.H. City of Kingston upon Hull*, pp. 20, 80.
7   Ibid., p. 80; *V.C.H. City of York*, pp. 85–6.
8   Sylvia L. Thrupp, *The Merchant Class of Medieval London*, 1948, pp. 208–10.
9   Maurice Beresford, *New Towns of the Middle Ages*, 1967, p. 194.
10   Sylvia L. Thrupp and Harold B. Johnson, 'The earliest Canterbury freemen's rolls 1298–1363', *Kent Record Society*, 18 (1964), pp. 175–6.
11   Sylvia L. Thrupp, op. cit., pp. 211, 213, 217.
12   W. G. Hoskins, 'English provincial towns in the early sixteenth century',

T.R.H.S., 5th series, 6 (1956), pp. 8–9; Wallace T. MacCaffrey, *Exeter, 1540–1640. The Growth of an English County Town*, 1958, p. 258.

13 R. B. Dobson, 'Admissions to the freedom of the city of York in the later Middle Ages', *Ec.H.R.* 2nd series, 26 (1973), pp. 1–21.

14 *V.C.H. City of York*, p. 41.

15 Quoted by Sylvia L. Thrupp, op. cit., p. 191.

16 Ibid., pp. 199–200.

17 J. C. Russell, 'Population in Europe 500–1500', in *The Fontana Economic History of Europe. The Middle Ages*, ed. Carlo M. Cipolla, 1972, p. 46.

18 Don Brothwell, 'Palaeodemography and earlier British populations', *World Archaeology*, 4 (1972), pp. 83, 86.

19 Richard C. Trexler, 'Une table florentine d'espérance de vie', *Annales: Économies, Sociétés, Civilisations*, 26 (1971), p. 137; David Herlihy, *Medieval and Renaissance Pistoia. The Social History of an Italian Town, 1200–1430*, 1967, pp. 79–83, 283–8. For recent comments on the incidence of old age at London and Southampton, see Gerald A. J. Hodgett, *The Cartulary of Holy Trinity Aldgate*, London Record Society Publications, 7 (1971), p. xx, and Colin Platt, *Medieval Southampton*, 1973, p. 263.

20 Sylvia L. Thrupp, 'The problem of replacement-rates in late medieval English population', *Ec.H.R.*, 2nd series, 18 (1965–6), p. 118. Professor Thrupp describes in this fashion the period from the Black Death through to the 1470s.

21 J. M. W. Bean, 'Plague, population and economic decline in England in the later Middle Ages', *Ec.H.R.*, 2nd series, 15 (1962–3), p. 432.

22 Ibid., pp. 428–30.

23 J. C. Russell, op. cit., pp. 53–4.

24 Sylvia L. Thrupp, 'Plague effects in medieval Europe', *Comparative Studies in Society and History*, 8 (1965–6), p. 478.

25 Sylvia L. Thrupp, *The Merchant Class of Medieval London*, 1948, p. 196.

26 Ibid., p. 205.

27 A. R. Myers, *London in the Age of Chaucer*, 1972, pp. 177–8.

28 Henry Elliott Malden (ed.), *The Cely Papers*, Camden Society, 3rd series, 1 (1900), pp. 102–3. Professor Myers (op. cit., p. 179) observes that a quarter of the wives of the fourteenth-century London aldermen, where their origin is known, were the daughters of country landowners; in the fifteenth century, the number had risen to a third.

29 Sylvia L. Thrupp, *The Merchant Class of Medieval London*, 1948, p. 230.

30 William Urry, *Canterbury under the Angevin Kings*, 1967, pp. 177–9.

31 Helen M. Cam, op. cit., pp. 21–2; *V.C.H. City of York*, p. 45.

32 *V.C.H. City of York*, p. 113.

33 Colin Platt, op. cit., chapters 16–17

34 For a comment on the later developments, see Lawrence Stone, 'Social mobility in England, 1500–1700', *Past and Present*, 33 (1966), pp. 18–19.

35 *V.C.H. City of York*, p. 46.

36 A. B. Hibbert, 'The origins of the medieval town patriciate', *Past and Present*, 3 (1953), pp. 20–1; Gwyn A. Williams, *Medieval London*, 1963, p.

55. For some cautions on this point, see Susan Reynolds, 'The rulers of London in the twelfth century', *History*, 57 (1972), p. 346.

37   William Urry, op. cit., p. 176.

38   R. H. Hilton, op. cit., pp. 203–5; J. W. F. Hill, *Medieval Lincoln*, 1948, pp. 295–6; Colin Platt, op. cit., passim.

39   *V.C.H. City of York*, pp. 34, 46.

40   This point was made some years ago, in a rather different context, by Sylvia Thrupp, 'Social control in the medieval town', *Journal of Economic History*, 1: supplement (1941), pp. 47–8.

41   Colin Platt, op. cit., pp. 14, 261 and figure 10.

42   Gwyn A. Williams, op. cit., pp. 75, 318 and table d.

43   *V.C.H. City of Kingston upon Hull*, p. 73; *V.C.H. Warwick*, 8: 209.

44   Wallace T. MacCaffrey, op. cit., pp. 250–1.

45   Colin Platt, 'Southampton, 1000–1600 A.D.: wealth and settlement patterns in a major medieval seaport', *Hansische Geschichtsblätter*, 91 (1973), pp. 17–19. In medieval Winchester, there is a parallel to the Southampton evidence in the continued use by the wealthy of a group of tenements in the Brooks area, between Wongar Street and Tanner Street (D. J. Keene, *Some Aspects of the History, Topography and Archaeology ... of Winchester*, Oxford D.Phil., 1972, p. 192).

46   Margery Kirkbride James, *Studies in the Medieval Wine Trade*, 1971, p. 212; for a table showing the value of some London estates, see Sylvia L. Thrupp, *The Merchant Class of Medieval London*, 1948, p. 110.

47   Wallace T. MacCaffrey, op. cit., p. 265.

48   H. J. Hewitt, *Medieval Cheshire*, Chetham Society, new series, 88 (1929), pp. 129–30.

49   Colin Platt, *Medieval Southampton*, pp. 240, 248, 253.

50   *V.C.H. Wiltshire*, 6: 124.

51   James Dallaway, *Antiquities of Bristow in the Middle Centuries*, 1834, p. 114; see also E. M. Carus-Wilson, *Medieval Merchant Venturers*, 1967, pp. 86–7.

52   J. F. Pound, 'The social and trade structure of Norwich 1525–1575', *Past and Present*, 34 (1966), p. 51; W. G. Hoskins, 'English provincial towns in the early sixteenth century', *T.R.H.S.*, 5th series, 6 (1956), p. 7.

53   Colin Platt, op. cit., p. 265.

54   W. G. Hoskins, op. cit., pp. 6–7.

55   J. F. Pound, op. cit., p. 50.

56   Julian Cornwall, 'English country towns in the fifteen twenties', *Ec.H.R.*, 2nd series, 15 (1962–3), pp. 63–4.

57   W. G. Hoskins, 'An Elizabethan provincial town: Leicester', in *Studies in Social History: a tribute to G. M. Trevelyan*, ed. J. H. Plumb, 1955, pp. 44–5; Colin Platt, op. cit., p. 264.

58   J. F. Pound, op. cit., pp. 50–1; Wallace T. MacCaffrey, op. cit., pp. 248–9.

59   *V.C.H. City of York*, p. 44.

60   Ibid., p. 109.

61   R. H. Hilton, op. cit., pp. 200–201.

62 Colin Platt, op. cit., pp. 264–5.

63 Quoted by G. R. Owst, *Literature and Pulpit in Medieval England*, 1933, p. 362.

64 Colin Platt, op. cit., pp. 265–6; Wallace T. MacCaffrey, op. cit., p. 251.

65 G. R. Owst, op. cit., p. 361.

66 For a comment on the Exeter evidence, see Joyce Youings, *Tuckers Hall, Exeter*, 1968, pp. 10–11.

67 D. C. Douglas and G. W. Greenaway (eds), *English Historical Documents 1042–1189*, 1953, pp. 947–8, 973; William Urry, op. cit., pp. 131–2.

68 Elspeth M. Veale, *The English Fur Trade in the Later Middle Ages*, 1966, p. 52.

69 R. H. Hilton, op. cit., p. 207.

70 Gwyn A. Williams, op. cit., pp. 282, 309.

71 George Unwin, *The Gilds and Companies of London*, 1963 (4th edition), pp. 87–8; Elspeth M. Veale, 'Craftsmen and the economy of London in the fourteenth century', in *Studies in London History*, eds A. Hollaender and W. Kellaway, 1969, pp. 139–40.

72 Joyce Youings, op. cit., p. 15.

73 Toulmin Smith, *English Gilds*, Early English Text Society, 1870, pp. 45–109.

74 Mary Bateson (ed.), *Cambridge Gild Records*, Publications of the Cambridge Antiquarian Society, 39 (1903), p. xxxv.

75 *V.C.H. City of York*, pp. 92–3.

76 A. R. Myers (ed.), *English Historical Documents 1327–1485*, 1969, pp. 1094–5.

77 Colin Platt, op. cit., pp. 162–3.

78 Sylvia L. Thrupp, 'The gilds', in *The Cambridge Economic History of Europe*, volume 3, eds M. M. Postan, E. E. Rich and Edward Miller, 1965, p. 245.

79 *V.C.H. Wiltshire*, 6: 133.

80 Colin Platt, op. cit., p. 173.

81 R. B. Dobson, op. cit., p. 14.

82 *V.C.H. Wiltshire*, 4: 118.

83 Edward Miller, 'The fortunes of the English textile industry during the thirteenth century', *Ec.H.R.*, 2nd series, 18 (1965), p. 73; E. M. Carus-Wilson, *Medieval Merchant Venturers*, 1967 (2nd edition), p. 230.

84 J. W. F. Hill, op. cit., pp. 211–13, 298, 300–1, 402–5.

85 G. H. Martin, *The Borough and the Merchant Community of Ipswich, 1317–1422*, Oxford D.Phil., 1955, pp. 59–73; for almost exactly contemporary disturbances at Bristol and at Southampton, see R. H. Hilton, op. cit., pp. 202–3, and Colin Platt, op. cit., pp. 92–3.

86 Julian Cornwall, 'English country towns in the fifteen twenties', *Ec.H.R.*, 2nd series, 15 (1962–3), p. 56; A. L. Rowse, *Tudor Cornwall*, 1941, p. 90; T. B. Pugh (ed.), *The Middle Ages: Glamorgan County History 3*, 1971, p. 347; *V.C.H. City of Leicester*, p. 29.

87 A. R. Bridbury, *Economic Growth: England in the Later Middle Ages*, 1962, p. 58.

88 Wallace T. MacCaffrey, op. cit., pp. 251–2.

89 A. L.Rowse, op. cit., p. 90.

90 C. H. Williams (ed.), *English Historical Documents 1485–1558*, 1967, p. 973.

91 T. B. Pugh, op. cit., p. 347.

92 *V.C.H. Wiltshire*, 6: 11; Julian Cornwall, op. cit., p. 56; J. W. F. Hill, op. cit., p. 302.

93 *V.C.H. City of York*, pp. 78–9.

94 A. R. Myers, op. cit., p. 575.

95 *V.C.H. City of Leicester*, pp. 29–30.

96 Colin Platt, op. cit., pp. 249, 251.

97 J. S. Roskell, 'The social composition of the Commons in a fifteenth-century parliament', *Bulletin of the Institute of Historical Research*, 24 (1951), pp. 156–8; elaborated further in the same author's *The Commons in the Parliament of 1422*, 1954, pp. 50–3.

98 *V.C.H. Wiltshire*, 6: 11.

99 R. F. Hunnisett, *The Medieval Coroner*, 1961, p. 160.

100 Colin Platt, op. cit., p. 165.

101 J. W. F. Hill, op. cit., p. 302.

102 K. M. E. Murray, *The Constitutional History of the Cinque Ports*, 1935, p. 224.

103 Margery M. Rowe and Andrew M. Jackson (eds), *Exeter Freemen 1266–1967*, Devon and Cornwall Record Society, extra series, 1 (1973), p. xvi.

104 R. B. Dobson, op. cit., pp. 18–19.

105 R. F. Hunnisett, op. cit., p. 161.

106 Colin Platt, op. cit., pp. 176, 240.

107 Ibid., pp. 175–6; Alwyn Ruddock, *Italian Merchants and Shipping in Southampton, 1270–1600*, 1951, pp. 176–7.

108 Colin Platt, op. cit., pp. 205, 218.

109 *V.C.H. Warwick*, 8: 210; A. R. Myers, op. cit., pp. 1109–14.

110 *V.C.H. Warwick*, loc. cit.

111 *V.C.H. City of York*, p. 95.

112 For a recent encouraging attempt at this, emphasizing the oppressions of the Paris journeymen, see Bronislaw Geremek, *Le Salariat dans l'Artisanat Parisien aux xiiie–xve siècles*, 1968, in particular pp. 45–66.

113 Colin Platt, op. cit., p. 179 (note 55).

Chapter 5   The Borough Constitution

1 F. Pollock and F. W. Maitland, *The History of English Law before the Time of Edward I*, 1898 (re-issued 1968), pp. 634–5.

2 D. C. Douglas and G. W. Greenaway (eds), *English Historical Documents 1042–1189*, 1953, pp. 970–1; for the text of the Canterbury charter, see William Urry, *Canterbury under the Angevin Kings*, 1967, pp. 80–1.

3 Morley de Wolf Hemmeon, *Burgage Tenure in Mediaeval England*, 1914, p. 157.

4 Adolphus Ballard and James Tait (eds), *British Borough Charters 1216–*

1307, 1923, pp. l–li.

5 D. C. Douglas and G. W. Greenaway, op. cit., p. 945.

6 James Tait, *The Medieval English Borough*, 1936, pp. 101–2.

7 D. C. Douglas and G. W. Greenaway, op. cit., p. 971.

8 Gerald A. J. Hodgett, *The Cartulary of Holy Trinity, Aldgate*, London Record Society Publications, 7 (1971), pp. xviii–xix.

9 D. C. Douglas and G. W. Greenaway, op. cit., p. 963.

10 Ibid., p. 965 (Burford), 968 (Leicester); William Urry, op. cit., pp. 124–8; for the origins of gilds in general, stressing the element of continuity, see Emile Coornaert, 'Les ghildes médiévales (v^e–xive siècles)', *Revue Historique*, 199 (1948), pp. 22–55, 208–43.

11 James Tait, op. cit., p. 157.

12 D. C. Douglas and G. W. Greenaway, op. cit., p. 945.

13 James Tait, op. cit., pp. 157–8.

14 Ibid., pp. 162–3, 169–70.

15 Ibid., pp. 176–7.

16 Quoted as the opening sentence in Gwyn Williams, *Medieval London: from Commune to Capital*, 1963.

17 Susan Reynolds, 'The rulers of London in the twelfth century', *History*, 57 (1972), p. 349.

18 M. D. Lobel and J. Tann, 'Gloucester', p. 5, in *Historic Towns*, ed. M. D. Lobel, 1969; R. H. C. Davis, 'An Oxford charter of 1191 and the beginnings of municipal freedom', *Oxoniensia*, 33 (1968), p. 63.

19 James Tait, op. cit., p. 230.

20 Ibid., p. 183.

21 A. Ballard, 'The English boroughs in the reign of John', *E.H.R.*, 14 (1899), pp. 93–104.

22 F. Pollock and F. W. Maitland, op. cit., p. 685.

23 Adolphus Ballard (ed.), *British Borough Charters 1042–1216*, 1913, p. lxviii.

24 R. H. C. Davis, op. cit., pp. 54–6.

25 For a discussion of the circumstances of the grant and subsequent action, see G. H. Martin, *The Early Court Rolls of the Borough of Ipswich*, 1954.

26 F. Pollock and F. W. Maitland, op. cit., p. 684.

27 Charles Gross, *The Gild Merchant: a Contribution to British Municipal History*, 1890, 2: 114–23; these events are summarized by G. H. Martin, op. cit., pp. 8–9.

28 Charles Gross, op. cit., 2: 123.

29 Adolphus Ballard and James Tait, op. cit., pp. lvi–lvii.

30 Adolphus Ballard, op. cit., pp. 244–7.

31 Colin Platt, *Medieval Southampton*, 1973, pp. 14–15.

32 William Urry, op. cit., pp. 86–8.

33 J. W. F. Hill, *Medieval Lincoln*, 1948, p. 294.

34 James Tait, op. cit., pp. 272–3.

35 See, for example, *V.C.H. City of Leicester*, pp. 26–7; *Wiltshire*, 6: 97; *City of York*, pp. 70–1; *City of Kingston upon Hull*, pp. 30–1.

36 James Tait, op. cit., p. 274.

37 *V.C.H. City of Leicester*, p. 37.

38 G. H. Martin, 'The English borough in the thirteenth century', *T.R.H.S.*, 5th series, 13 (1963), p. 133.

39 M. D. Lobel, *The Borough of Bury St Edmunds*, 1935, p. 74.

40 James Tait, op. cit., p. 234.

41 Adolphus Ballard and James Tait, op. cit., pp. xviii, lvi.

42 Ibid., p. lxi. I am grateful to Dr M. T. Clanchy for drawing my attention, since the first publication |of this book, to his valuable revisionary paper 'The franchise of return of writs' (T.R.H.S., 5th series, 17 (1967), pp. 59–82) in which he argues for a different origin for the privilege in the conflict between the king and his magnates, the towns being able to turn this to their profit only much later in the following reign.

43 Ibid., p. lxiii.

44 R. F. Hunnisett, *The Medieval Coroner*, 1961, p. 156.

45 Ralph B. Pugh, *Imprisonment in Medieval England*, 1968, pp. 97–8.

46 G. H. Martin, *The Early Court Rolls of the Borough of Ipswich*, 1954, p. 38; similarly, in his doctoral thesis, Dr Martin was to see, in the elaboration of the records, evidence for a 'corporate purpose', which was 'fully as important a contribution to the doctrine of fictitious personality as was the recognition of any of its formal attributes', *The Borough and the Merchant Community of Ipswich, 1317–1422*, Oxford D.Phil., 1955, p. iv; and see also the conclusion of his 'The English borough in the thirteenth century', *T.R.H.S.*, 5th series, 13 (1963), p. 144.

47 G. H. Martin, 'The registration of deeds of title in the medieval borough', in *The Study of Medieval Records. Essays in Honour of Kathleen Major*, eds D. A. Bullough and R. L. Storey, 1971, pp. 151–73; see also D. J. Keene, *Some Aspects of the History, Topography and Archaeology ... of Winchester*, Oxford D.Phil., 1972, pp. 4–9.

48 Maurice Beresford, *New Towns of the Middle Ages*, 1967, pp. 206–19.

49 James Tait, *Mediaeval Manchester and the Beginnings of Lancashire*, 1904, p. 47.

50 Ibid., pp. 47–51.

51 Ibid., pp. 52–5.

52 Ibid., p. 55.

53 *V.C.H. City of Kingston upon Hull*, p. 20.

54 Ibid., pp. 19–21, 28, 55.

55 Ibid., pp. 66, 81–2, 85; for tables showing wool and cloth exports from Hull in the Later Middle Ages, see E. M. Carus-Wilson and Olive Coleman, *England's Export Trade, 1275–1547*, 1963, pp. 128–9, 146–7.

56 H. A. Cronne, *The Borough of Warwick in the Middle Ages*, 1951, pp. 5–6, 21.

57 G. H. Martin (ed.), *The Royal Charters of Grantham, 1463–1688*, 1963, p. 11.

58 Sir William Savage, 'Somerset towns. I. Origins and early government', *Proceedings of the Somersetshire Archaeological and Natural History Society*, 99–100 (1954–5), pp. 56–7, 73.

59 *V.C.H. Warwick*, 8: 151.

60 Ibid., 2: 56.
61 W. G. Hoskins and H. P. R. Finberg, *Devonshire Studies*, 1952, pp. 183–4, 187–8.
62 Ibid., p. 189.
63 M. D. Lobel, op. cit., pp. 33–7, 47–51.
64 Ibid., p. 25.
65 H. P. R. Finberg (ed.), *Gloucestershire Studies*, 1957, pp. 74–7; for a very full discussion of the monastic borough, dwelling at length on the conflicts between lord and tenant, see N. M. Trenholme, *The English Monastic Borough. A Study in Medieval History*, 1927.
66 Martin Weinbaum, *The Incorporation of Boroughs*, 1937, pp. 47–54.
67 A. R. Myers (ed.), *English Historical Documents 1327–1485*, 1969, p. 560.
68 Martin Weinbaum, op. cit., pp. 58–9.
69 G. H. Martin, 'The English borough in the thirteenth century', *T.R.H.S.*, 5th series, 13 (1963), pp. 136–7.
70 *V.C.H. City of York*, p. 35. There is evidence of similar property-holding at Leicester in the mid-thirteenth century, although it remained on a very small scale (*V.C.H. City of Leicester*, p. 20).
71 *V.C.H. City of Kingston upon Hull*, p. 28.
72 G. H. Martin, *The Early Court Rolls of the Borough of Ipswich*, 1954, p. 35. For a general discussion of borough rights in waste, see F. Pollock and F. W. Maitland, op. cit., pp. 652–4.
73 *Statutes of the Realm*, 2: 80; see also Helena M. Chew, 'Mortmain in medieval London', *E.H.R.*, 60 (1945), p. 14
74 *V.C.H. City of York*, p. 69.
75 D. J. Keene, op. cit., p. 147.
76 Colin Platt, op. cit., pp. 169–70.
77 Martin Weinbaum, op. cit., pp. 65–8, 93–6; A. R. Myers, op. cit., pp. 570–3.
78 *V.C.H. City of Kingston upon Hull*, p. 29
79 H. A. Cronne (ed.), *Bristol Charters 1378–1499*, Bristol Record Society, 11 (1946), pp. 121–2.
80 *V.C.H. City of Kingston upon Hull*, p. 57; John Bartlett, 'The medieval walls of Hull', *Bulletin of the Kingston upon Hull Museums*, 3–4 (1969–70, revised 1971).
81 J. W. F. Hill, op. cit., p. 299.
82 Betty R. Masters, 'The town clerk', *The Guildhall Miscellany*, 3 (1969), p. 55.
83 The York recordership dates from 1385 (*V.C.H. City of York*, p. 74), but the office usually came into existence rather later at most boroughs, following on the enlarged judicial responsibilities of the mayor and his associates as justices of the peace.
84 *V.C.H. Wiltshire*, 6: 98.
85 Ibid., loc. cit.
86 *V.C.H. City of Kingston upon Hull*, p. 30.
87 *V.C.H. City of York*, p. 70.
88 *V.C.H. Wiltshire*, 6: 98.

Chapter 6   The Church in the Boroughs

1   David Walker, *Bristol in the Early Middle Ages*, 1971, pp. 18–19.
2   D. J. Keene, *Some Aspects of the History, Topography and Archaeology . . . of Winchester*, Oxford D.Phil., 1972, p. 54.
3   Frank Barlow, *The English Church 1000–1066*, 1963, p. 192.
4   Martin Biddle, 'Excavations at Winchester, 1970. Ninth interim report', *Antiquaries Journal*, 52 (1972), pp. 104–7.
5   Ibid., pp. 111–15; A. Carter and J. P. Roberts, 'Excavations in Norwich – 1972. The Norwich Survey – second interim report', *Norfolk Archaeology*, 35 (1973), pp. 455–7.
6   William Urry, *Canterbury under the Angevin Kings*, 1967, p. 209.
7   G. W. O. Addleshaw, *The Development of the Parochial System from Charlemagne (768–814) to Urban II (1088–1099)*, 1970 (2nd edition), p. 13; John Godfrey, *The Church in Anglo-Saxon England*, 1962, p. 324.
8   J. W. F. Hill, *Medieval Lincoln*, 1948, pp. 133–4.
9   D. C. Douglas and G. W. Greenaway (eds), *English Historical Documents 1042–1189*, 1953, pp. 953–4.
10 Frank Barlow, op. cit., p. 192.
11 D. C. Douglas and G. W. Greenaway, op. cit., pp. 954–6; for the Latin text and identifications of the churches mentioned, see B. W. Kissan, 'An early list of London properties', *Transactions of the London and Middlesex Archaeological Society*, new series, 8 (1938), pp. 57–69.
12 Gerald A. J. Hodgett, *The Cartulary of Holy Trinity, Aldgate*, London Record Society Publications, 7 (1971), pp. 167–9.
13 G. H. Martin, *The Borough and the Merchant Community of Ipswich, 1317–1422*, Oxford D.Phil., 1955, p. 156; Colin Platt, *Medieval Southampton*, 1973, p. 26.
14 G. H. Martin, 'Church life in medieval Leicester', in *The Growth of Leicester*, ed. A. E. Brown, 1970, pp. 29, 31–2.
15 C. N. L. Brooke, 'The missionary at home: the church in the towns, 1000–1250', in *The Mission of the Church and the Propagation of the Faith*, ed. G. J. Cuming, 1970, p. 83.
16 Alan Rogers (ed.), *The Making of Stamford*, 1965, p. 53.
17 J. W. F. Hill, op. cit., pp. 144–5.
18 John T. McNeill and Helena M. Gamer, *Medieval Handbooks of Penance*, 1938 (reprinted 1965), p. 354.
19 Douglas Jones, *The Church in Chester, 1300–1540*, Chetham Society, 3rd series, 7 (1957), p. 6.
20 *V.C.H. City of York*, pp. 52–3.
21 David Walker, op. cit., p. 19.
22 A. Carter and J. P. Roberts, op. et loc. cit.
23 Henrietta Miles, 'Rhuddlan', *Current Archaeology*, 32 (1972), p. 246.
24 Maurice Beresford, *New Towns of the Middle Ages*, 1967, p. 170.
25 W. G. Hoskins and H. P. R. Finberg, *Devonshire Studies*, 1952, pp. 191–2.
26 W. G. Hoskins, *Provincial England*, 1963, pp. 58, 60.
27 Dorothy M. Owen, *Church and Society in Medieval Lincolnshire*, 1971, p.

104.

28 Such use of church buildings is discussed, with many examples, by J. G. Davies, *The Secular Use of Church Buildings*, 1968, pp. 55–79.

29 J. Gilchrist, *The Church and Economic Activity in the Middle Ages*, 1969, pp. 176–7.

30 John W. Baldwin, *Masters, Princes and Merchants: the Social Views of Peter the Chanter and his Circle*, 1970, 1: 268–9; see also J. Gilchrist, op. cit., pp. 58–62.

31 D. J. Keene, op. cit., p. 520.

32 Ibid., pp. 520–1.

33 Colin Platt, op. cit., pp. 25, 58.

34 Ibid., p. 205.

35 *V.C.H. City of Kingston upon Hull*, pp. 333–5; David Knowles and R. Neville Hadcock, *Medieval Religious Houses, England and Wales*, 1953, p. 282.

36 David Knowles and R. Neville Hadcock, op. cit., pp. 258, 261, 273, 296, 322.

37 Dorothy M. Owen, op. cit., p. 55.

38 David Knowles and R. Neville Hadcock, op. cit., p. 284.

39 J. C. Dickinson, *The Origins of the Austin Canons and their Introduction into England*, 1950, pp. 149–51.

40 A. G. Little (ed.), *Fratris Thomae, vulgo dicti de Eccleston, tractatus De adventu fratrum minorum in Angliam*, 1951, p. xxx.

41 David Knowles and R. Neville Hadcock, op. cit., passim.

42 Dorothy M. Owen, op. cit., p. 85.

43 David Knowles and R. Neville Hadcock, op. cit., passim.

44 Dorothy M. Owen, op. ct loc. cit.

45 Edward Hutton, *The Franciscans in England, 1224–1538*, 1926, pp. 66, 72–3, 78–80.

46 Edward Gillett, *A History of Grimsby*, 1970, p. 78.

47 A. G. Little, op. et loc. cit.; J. W. F. Hill, op. cit., p. 149.

48 Colin Platt, op. cit., p. 66.

49 Ibid., pp. 205–6. For an exact parallel at Chester, see Douglas Jones, op. cit., pp. 93–9.

50 Dorothy M. Owen, op. cit., pp. 128–9.

51 Joyce Youings, *Tuckers Hall, Exeter. The History of a Provincial City Company through Five Centuries*, 1968, pp. 12–13.

52 *V.C.H. City of Kingston upon Hull*, p. 58.

53 *V.C.H. City of York*, p. 96.

54 Elspeth M. Veale, 'Craftsmen and the economy of London in the fourteenth century', in *Studies in London History*, eds A. Hollaender and W. Kellaway, 1969, p. 139.

55 *V.C.H. City of York*, p. 111.

56 A. L. Rowse, *Tudor Cornwall*, 1941, p. 97.

57 Mary Bateson (ed.), *Cambridge Gild Records*, Publications of the Cambridge Antiquarian Society, 39 (1903), pp. xii–xviii.

58 *V.C.H. Warwick*, 8: 211; *V.C.H. Wiltshire*, 6: 97.

59 Toulmin Smith, *English Gilds*, Early English Text Society, 1870, passim.
60 H. F. Westlake, *The Parish Gilds of Mediaeval England*, 1919, pp. 29–30.
61 George Unwin, *The Gilds and Companies of London*, 1963 (4th edition), p. 117.
62 Ibid., p. 121; *V.C.H. City of York*, p. 111.
63 For the term 'cooperative chantry', see H. F. Westlake, op. cit., p. 44; also George Unwin, op. cit., p. 111.
64 K. L. Wood-Legh, 'Some aspects of the history of chantries in the later Middle Ages', *T.R.H.S.*, 4th series, 28 (1946), p. 48; also quoted by Douglas Jones, op. cit., p. 100.
65 K. L. Wood-Legh, *Perpetual Chantries in Britain*, 1965, p. 181.
66 Colin Platt, op. cit., p. 187.
67 Ibid., pp. 186–7; A. B. Wallis Chapman (ed.), *The Black Book of Southampton*, Southampton Record Society, 1912, 2: 98–115, 122–5.
68 Dorothy M. Owen, op. cit., p. 129.
69 There are slighting remarks about the unbeneficed priest in the prologues to both *Canterbury Tales* and *Piers the Plowman*.
70 See the recent studies of Margaret Bowker, *The Secular Clergy in the Diocese of Lincoln 1495–1520*, 1968, chapter 4, and Peter Heath, *The English Parish Clergy on the Eve of the Reformation*, 1969, chapter 7.
71 K. L. Wood-Legh, *Perpetual Chantries in Britain*, 1965, p. 158.
72 A. B. Wallis Chapman, op. cit., 3: 2–9; Colin Platt, op. cit., pp. 188–9.
73 Douglas Jones, op. cit., p. 107 (note 2).
74 Ibid., pp. 14–15.
75 Colin Platt, op. et loc. cit.
76 Peter Heath, op. cit., p. 173.
77 Rosalind Hill, ' "A Chaunterie for Soules": London chantries in the reign of Richard II', in *The Reign of Richard II*, eds F. R. H. Du Boulay and Caroline M. Barron, 1971, p. 247.
78 Dorothy M. Owen, op. cit., p. 134.
79 Rosalind Hill, op. cit., p. 244.
80 William Urry, op. cit., p. 210.
81 Alan Rogers, op. cit., p. 52.
82 *V.C.H. Wiltshire*, 6: 29.
83 Margaret Bowker, op. cit., pp. 126–36.
84 Charlotte Augusta Sneyd (ed.), *A Relation, or rather a True Account, of the Island of England . . . about the year 1500*, Camden Society, 37 (1847), p. 23.
85 Douglas Jones, op. cit., pp. 114–15.
86 Martin Biddle, 'Excavations at Winchester, 1966. Fifth interim report', *Antiquaries Journal*, 47 (1967), pp. 262–3, and 'Excavations at Winchester, 1970. Ninth interim report', ibid., 52 (1972), pp. 111–15; A. Carter and J. P. Roberts, op. cit., pp. 455–7.
87 *V.C.H. City of York*, p. 107.
88 A. R. Myers, *London in the Age of Chaucer*, 1972, p. 161.
89 Colin Platt, op. cit., p. 191.
90 *V.C.H. City of Kingston upon Hull*, pp. 288–9.

91 Ibid., p. 289.

92 Betty R. Masters and Elizabeth Ralph (eds), *The Church Book of St Ewen's, Bristol 1454–1584*, Bristol and Gloucestershire Archaeological Society, Records Section, 6 (1967), pp. 1–11. The inventory is dated 1455.

93 Henry Littlehales (ed.), *The Medieval Records of a London City Church (St Mary at Hill), A.D. 1420–1559*, 2 vols, Early English Text Society, 125 (1904) and 128 (1905), 1: 30–4. The probable date of the inventory is 1496–7.

94 A. R. Myers, op. cit., p. 162.

95 A. G. Little, 'Introduction of the Observant friars into England', *Proceedings of the British Academy*, 10 (1921–3), p. 458.

96 Dorothy M. Owen, op. cit., p. 89.

97 Margaret Bowker, op. cit., p. 153.

98 James Crompton, 'Leicestershire Lollards', *Transactions of the Leicestershire Archaeological and Historical Society*, 44 (1968–9), p. 27.

Chapter 7   The Early-Modern Borough: Continuity and Change

1 For recent discussions of this inflation, see R. B. Outhwaite, *Inflation in Tudor and Early Stuart England*, 1969, pp. 13–14, and Peter H. Ramsey, *The Price Revolution in Sixteenth-Century England*, 1971, p. 4.

2 Julian Cornwall, 'English population in the early sixteenth century', *Ec.H.R.*, 2nd series, 23 (1970), pp. 32–44; see also Ian Blanchard, 'Population change, enclosure, and the early Tudor economy', ibid., pp. 427–45, and Lawrence Stone, *The Causes of the English Revolution, 1529–1642*, 1972, p. 67.

3 J. F. Pound, 'The social and trade structure of Norwich 1525–1575', *Past and Present*, 34 (1966), p. 61.

4 Lawrence Stone, op. cit., p. 70.

5 Ralph Davis, *English Overseas Trade 1500–1700*, 1973, pp. 11–12, 14–17; Alan Everitt, *Change in the Provinces: the Seventeenth Century*, 1972, pp. 16–17.

6 See, for example, F. J. Fisher, 'The development of London as a centre of conspicuous consumption in the sixteenth and seventeenth centuries', *T.R.H.S.*, 4th series, 30 (1948), pp. 37–50.

7 Edward Gillett, *A History of Grimsby*, 1970, pp. 104–5; Colin Platt, *Medieval Southampton*, 1973, pp. 222–3.

8 Alan D. Dyer, *The City of Worcester in the Sixteenth Century*, 1973, pp. 88, 90, 156.

9 J. F. Pound, op. cit., p. 63.

10 Alan Everitt, op. cit., p. 39.

11 Ibid., pp. 40–1.

12 J. U. Nef, 'The progress of technology and the growth of large-scale industry in Great Britain, 1540–1640', *Ec.H.R.*, 5 (1934–5), pp. 3–24.

13 Ralph Davis, op. cit., p. 23.

14 D. M. Woodward, *The Trade of Elizabethan Chester*, 1970, pp. 18–21.

15 H. F. Westlake, *The Parish Gilds of Mediaeval England*, 1919, pp. 133–4.

16 D. M. Palliser, *The Reformation in York 1534–1553*, 1971, p. 6.

17 Edward Gillett, op. cit., p. 88.

18 Colin Platt, op. cit., pp. 190–1.

19 D. M. Palliser, op. cit., p. 29.

20 Lawrence Stone, 'Social mobility in England, 1500–1700', *Past and Present*, 33 (1966), pp. 42–3.

21 Susan Reynolds, 'The rulers of London in the twelfth century', *History*, 57 (1972), p. 346; Sylvia L. Thrupp, *The Merchant Class of Medieval London*, 1948, p. 120.

22 *V.C.H. City of York*, pp. 45–6.

23 Colin Platt, op. cit., pp. 231–2.

24 W. G. Hoskins, 'English provincial towns in the early sixteenth century', *T.R.H.S.*, 5th series, 6 (1956), pp. 10–11.

25 D. J. Keene, *Some Aspects of the History, Topography and Archaeology . . . of Winchester*, Oxford D.Phil., 1972, pp. 155–8; for Southampton, see the urban estates of John Horn and William Soper (Colin Platt, op. cit., pp. 244, 257–8).

26 Levi Fox, 'The administration of gild property in Coventry in the fifteenth century', *E.H.R.*, 55 (1940), pp. 640–1; for the church and the king as landlord, see Eric Kerridge, 'The movement of rent, 1540–1640', *Ec.H.R.*, 2nd series, 6 (1953–4), pp. 33–4.

27 C. H. Williams (ed.), *English Historical Documents 1485–1558*, 1967, pp. 954–5, 969.

28 See, for example, the case of York as studied by D. M. Palliser, op. cit., p. 14.

29 Ian Blanchard, op. cit., p. 435; for the whole question of rising rents, see Eric Kerridge, op. cit., passim.

30 Colin Platt, op. cit., p. 210.

31 W. G. Hoskins, op. cit., p. 11.

32 W. G. Hoskins, 'The rebuilding of rural England, 1570–1640', republished in the same author's *Provincial England*, 1963, pp. 131–48; Lawrence Stone, *The Causes of the English Revolution, 1529–1642*, 1972, p. 73.

33 J. F. Pound, op. cit., p. 62.

34 Vanessa Parker, *The Making of King's Lynn*, 1971, p. 79; Alan D. Dyer, op. cit., p. 163.

35 Alan D. Dyer, op. cit., p. 164; W. G. Hoskins, 'English provincial towns in the early sixteenth century', *T.R.H.S.*, 5th series, 6 (1956), p. 12 (note 1).

36 W. G. Hoskins, *Essays in Leicestershire History*, 1950, pp. 111–12; *V.C.H. City of Leicester*, p. 107.

37 Frederick J. Furnivall (ed.), *Harrison's Description of England in Shakspere's Youth*, 1877, pp. 233–40.

38 Colin Platt, op. cit., p. 217.

39 D. Portman, *Exeter Houses 1400–1700*, 1966, pp. 78–80 and figure xiii.

40 W. A. Pantin, 'The development of domestic architecture in Oxford', *Antiquaries Journal*, 27 (1947), pp. 130–1 and figure 7.

41 Quoted by A. L. Rowse, *Tudor Cornwall*, 1941, p. 433.

42 J. S. Roskell, *The Commons in the Parliament of 1422*, 1954, pp. 46–8.

43 Sylvia L. Thrupp, op. cit., p. 225.

44 *V.C.H. City of York*, p. 86.

45 Lawrence Stone, 'Social mobility in England, 1500–1700', *Past and Present*, 33 (1966), p. 43.

46 Alan Everitt, op. cit., p. 43.

47 Wallace T. MacCaffrey, *Exeter, 1540–1640*, 1958, pp. 262–3; Alan Dyer, op. cit., pp. 186–7.

48 Lawrence Stone, op. cit., p. 24.

49 Colin Platt, op. cit., p. 265.

50 Alan Everitt, op. cit., p. 44.

51 J. S. Roskell, op. cit., p. 127.

52 Ibid., p. 144; May McKisack, *The Parliamentary Representation of the English Boroughs during the Middle Ages*, 1932 (reprinted 1962), p. 61.

53 J. S. Roskell, op. cit., p. 127.

54 Alan D. Dyer, op. cit., p. 214.

55 Edward Gillett, op. cit., p. 62.

56 Ibid., p. 60; May McKisack, op. cit., pp. 62–3.

57 Edward Gillett, op. cit., p. 94.

58 M. D. Lobel, *The Borough of Bury St Edmunds*, 1935, pp. 69–70; Colin Platt, op. cit., p. 222.

59 R. B. Dobson, 'Admissions to the freedom of the city of York in the later Middle Ages', *Ec.H.R.*, 2nd series, 26 (1973), p. 12; *V.C.H. City of York*, p. 86.

60 Colin Platt, op. cit., pp. 208, 226 (note 35).

61 Wallace T. MacCaffrey, op. cit., pp. 257–61.

62 W. C. Hazlitt (ed.), *Inedited Tracts: illustrating the Manners, Opinions and Occupations of Englishmen during the Sixteenth and Seventeenth Centuries*, 1868, p. 78.

Bibliography

Addleshaw, G. W. O., *The Development of the Parochial System from Charlemagne (768–814) to Urban II (1088–1099)*, Borthwick Institute of Historical Research, University of York, St Anthony's Hall Publications, 6 (1970, 2nd edition).

Addyman, P. V. and Hill, D. H., 'Saxon Southampton: a review of the evidence', parts 1 and 2, *Proceedings of the Hampshire Field Club and Archaeological Society*, 25 (1968), pp. 61–93, 26 (1969), pp. 61–96.

Altena, H. H. van Regteren, 'The origins and development of Dutch towns', *World Archaeology*, 2 (1970–1), pp. 128–40.

Baldwin, John W., *Masters, Princes and Merchants: the Social Views of Peter the Chanter and his Circle*, 2 vols, Princeton, 1970.

Ballard, Adolphus, 'The English boroughs in the reign of John', *E.H.R.*, 14 (1899), pp. 93–104.

Ballard, Adolphus (ed.), *British Borough Charters 1042–1216*, Cambridge, 1913.

Ballard, Adolphus and Tait, James (eds), *British Borough Charters 1216–1307*, Cambridge, 1923.

Barley, M. W., 'Medieval town wall, Park Row, Nottingham', *Medieval Archaeology*, 9 (1965), pp. 164–7.

Barlow, Frank, *The English Church 1000–1066*, London, 1963.

Bartlett, John, 'The medieval walls of Hull', *Bulletin of the Kingston upon Hull Museums*, 3–4 (1969–70, revised 1971).

Bartlett, John, 'Medieval Hull. Excavations in High St. 1971', *Bulletin of the Kingston upon Hull Museums*, 7 (1971).

Bartlett, J. N., 'The expansion and decline of York in the later Middle Ages', *Ec.H.R.*, 2nd series, 12 (1959–60), pp. 17–33.

Barton, K. J., 'Excavations at Back Hall, Bristol, 1958', *Transactions of the Bristol and Gloucestershire Archaeological Society*, 79 (1960), pp. 251–86.

Bateson, Mary (ed.), *Records of the Borough of Leicester*, 3 vols, London and Cambridge, 1899–1905.

Bateson, Mary (ed.), *Cambridge Gild Records*, Publications of the Cambridge Antiquarian Society, 39 (1903).

Bean, J. M. W., 'Plague, population and economic decline in England in the later Middle Ages', *Ec.H.R.*, 2nd series, 15 (1962–3), pp. 423–37.

Beresford, Maurice, *New Towns of the Middle Ages: Town Plantation in England, Wales and Gascony*, London, 1967.

Beresford, Maurice and Hurst, John G. (eds), *Deserted Medieval Villages*, London, 1971.

Biddle, Martin, 'Excavations at Winchester, 1966. Fifth interim report', *Antiquaries Journal*, 47 (1967), pp. 251–79.

Biddle, Martin, 'Excavations at Winchester, 1967. Sixth interim report', *Antiquaries Journal*, 48 (1968), pp. 250–84.

Biddle, Martin, 'Excavations at Winchester, 1969. Eighth interim report', *Antiquaries Journal*, 50 (1970), pp. 277–326.

Biddle, Martin, 'Excavations at Winchester, 1970. Ninth interim report', *Antiquaries Journal*, 52 (1972), pp. 93–131.

Biddle, Martin, 'Archaeology and the beginnings of English society', in *England before the Conquest. Studies in Primary Sources presented to Dorothy Whitelock*, eds Peter Clemoes and Kathleen Hughes, Cambridge, 1971, pp. 391–408.

Biddle, Martin and Hill, David, 'Late Saxon planned towns', *Antiquaries Journal*, 51 (1971), pp. 70–85.

Blanchard, Ian, 'Population change, enclosure, and the early Tudor economy', *Ec.H.R.*, 2nd series, 23 (1970), pp. 427–45.

Bonney, Helen, ' "Balle's Place", Salisbury: a 14th-century merchant's house', *Wiltshire Archaeological and Natural History Magazine*, 56 (1964), pp. 155–67.

Bowker, Margaret, *The Secular Clergy in the Diocese of Lincoln 1495–1520*, Cambridge, 1968.

Bridbury, A. R., *England and the Salt Trade in the Later Middle Ages*, Oxford, 1955.

Bridbury, A. R., *Economic Growth: England in the Later Middle Ages*, London, 1962.

Bridbury, A. R., 'The Dark Ages', *Ec.H.R.*, 2nd series, 22 (1969), pp. 526–37.

Brooke, C. N. L., 'The missionary at home: the church in the towns, 1000–1250', in *The Mission of the Church and the Propagation of the Faith. Studies in Church History 6*, ed. G. J. Cuming, Cambridge, 1970, pp. 59–83.

Brothwell, Don, 'Palaeodemography and earlier British populations',

World Archaeology, 4 (1972), pp. 75–87.

Cam, Helen M., *Liberties and Communities in Medieval England*, Cambridge, 1944.

Carter, A. and Roberts, J. P., 'Excavations in Norwich – 1972. The Norwich Survey – second interim report', *Norfolk Archaeology*, 35 (1973), pp. 443–68.

Carus-Wilson, E. M., 'An industrial revolution of the thirteenth century', *Ec.H.R.*, 11 (1941), pp. 39–60.

Carus-Wilson, E. M., 'The medieval trade of the ports of the Wash', *Medieval Archaeology*, 6–7 (1962–3), pp. 182–201.

Carus-Wilson, E. M., 'The first half-century of the borough of Stratford-upon-Avon', *Ec.H.R.*, 2nd series, 18 (1965), pp. 46–63.

Carus-Wilson, E. M., *Medieval Merchant Venturers*, London, 1967 (2nd edition).

Carus-Wilson, E. M. and Coleman, Olive, *England's Export Trade, 1275–1547*, Oxford, 1963.

Chapman, A. B. Wallis (ed.), *The Black Book of Southampton*, 3 vols, Southampton Record Society, 1912–15.

Chew, Helena M., 'Mortmain in medieval London', *E.H.R.*, 60 (1945), pp. 1–15.

Coates, Bryan E., 'The origin and distribution of markets and fairs in medieval Derbyshire', *Derbyshire Archaeological Journal*, 85 (1965), pp. 92–111.

Colvin, H. M., 'Domestic architecture and town-planning', in *Medieval England*, ed. Austin Lane Poole, Oxford, 1958, 1: 37–97.

Conzen, M. R. G., *Alnwick, Northumberland, a Study in Town Plan Analysis*, Transactions and Publications of the Institute of British Geographers, 27 (1960).

Conzen, M. R. G., 'The use of town plans in the study of urban history', in *The Study of Urban History*, ed. H. J. Dyos, London, 1968, pp. 113–30.

Coornaert, Emile, 'Les ghildes médiévales (v^e–xive siècles)', *Revue Historique*, 199 (1948), pp. 22–55, 208–43.

Cornwall, Julian, 'English country towns in the fifteen twenties', *Ec.H.R.*, 2nd series, 15 (1962–3), pp. 54–69.

Cornwall, Julian, 'English population in the early sixteenth century', *Ec.H.R.*, 2nd series, 23 (1970), pp. 32–44.

Coulton, G. C., *Social Life in Britain from the Conquest to the Reformation*, Cambridge, 1918.

Crompton, James, 'Leicestershire Lollards', *Transactions of the*

Leicestershire Archaeological and Historical Society, 44 (1968–9), pp. 11–44.

Cronne, H. A. (ed.), *Bristol Charters 1378–1499*, Bristol Record Society, 11 (1946).

Cronne, H. A., *The Borough of Warwick in the Middle Ages*, Dugdale Society Occasional Papers, 10 (1951).

Dallaway, James, *Antiquities of Bristow in the Middle Centuries; including the Topography of William Wyrcestre, and the Life of William Canynges*, Bristol, 1834.

Darby, H. C., *An Historical Geography of England before A.D. 1800*, Cambridge, 1936.

Davies, J. G., *The Secular Use of Church Buildings*, London, 1968.

Davis, Ralph, *English Overseas Trade 1500–1700*, London, 1973.

Davis, R. H. C., 'An Oxford charter of 1191 and the beginnings of municipal freedom', *Oxoniensia*, 33 (1968), pp. 53–65.

Dickinson, J. C., *The Origins of the Austin Canons and their Introduction into England*, London, 1950.

Dobson, R. B., 'Admissions to the freedom of the city of York in the later Middle Ages', *Ec.H.R.*, 2nd series, 26 (1973), pp. 1–22.

Douch, Robert, *Visitors' Descriptions of Southampton, 1540–1956*, Southampton Papers, 2 (1961).

Douglas, D. C. and Greenaway, G. W. (eds), *English Historical Documents 1042–1189*, London, 1953.

Down, Alec and Rule, Margaret, *Chichester Excavations I*, Chichester, 1971.

Duby, Georges, *The Early Growth of the European Economy. Warriors and Peasants from the Seventh to the Twelfth Century*, London, 1974.

Dyer, Alan D., *The City of Worcester in the Sixteenth Century*, Leicester, 1973.

Everitt, Alan, *Change in the Provinces: the Seventeenth Century*, Occasional Papers of the Department of English Local History, University of Leicester, 2nd series, 1 (1972).

Faulkner, P. A., 'Medieval undercrofts and town houses', *Archaeological Journal*, 123 (1966), pp. 120–35.

Finberg, H. P. R. (ed.), *Gloucestershire Studies*, Leicester, 1957.

Fisher, F. J., 'The development of London as a centre of conspicuous consumption in the sixteenth and seventeenth centuries', *T.R.H.S.*, 4th series, 30 (1948), pp. 37–50.

Foote, Peter and Wilson, David M., *The Viking Achievement*, London, 1970.

Fox, Aileen, 'The underground conduits in Exeter, exposed during reconstruction in 1950', *Reports and Transactions of the Devonshire Association*, 83 (1951), pp. 172–8.

Fox, Levi, 'The administration of gild property in Coventry in the fifteenth century', *E.H.R.*, 55 (1940), pp. 634–47.

Fraser, Constance M., 'The pattern of trade in the north-east of England, 1265–1350', *Northern History*, 4 (1969), pp. 44–67.

Furnivall, Frederick J. (ed.), *Harrison's Description of England in Shakspere's Youth*, The New Shakspere Society, London, 1877.

Ganshof, F. L., *Étude sur le Développement des Villes entre Loire et Rhin au Moyen Age*, Paris and Brussels, 1943.

Geremek, Bronislaw, *Le Salariat dans l'Artisanat Parisien aux xiiie–xve siècles*, Paris, 1968.

Gilchrist, J., *The Church and Economic Activity in the Middle Ages*, London, 1969.

Gillett, Edward, *A History of Grimsby*, Oxford, 1970.

Godfrey, John, *The Church in Anglo-Saxon England*, Cambridge, 1962.

Gooder, Eileen, *Coventry's Town Wall*, Coventry and North Warwickshire History Pamphlets, 4 (1971: revised edition).

Grierson, Philip, 'Commerce in the Dark Ages: a critique of the evidence', *T.R.H.S.*, 5th series, 9 (1959), pp. 123–40.

Gross, Charles (ed.), *Select Cases Concerning the Law Merchant, A.D. 1270–1638*, Publications of the Selden Society, 23 (1908).

Hassall, T. G., 'Excavations at Oxford 1970: third interim report', *Oxoniensia*, 36 (1971), pp. 1–14.

Hassall, T. G., *Oxford: the City beneath your Feet*, Oxford, 1972.

Hazlitt, W. C. (ed.), *Inedited Tracts: illustrating the Manners, Opinions and Occupations of Englishmen during the Sixteenth and Seventeenth Centuries*, Roxburghe Club, 1868.

Heath, Peter, *The English Parish Clergy on the Eve of the Reformation*, London, 1969.

Hemmeon, Morley de Wolf, *Burgage Tenure in Mediaeval England*, Cambridge (Mass.), 1914.

Herlihy, David, *Medieval and Renaissance Pistoia. The Social History of an Italian Town, 1200–1430*, New Haven and London, 1967.

Hewitt, H. J., *Medieval Cheshire. An Economic and Social History of Cheshire in the Reigns of the Three Edwards*, Chetham Society, new series, 88 (1929).

Hibbert, A. B., 'The origins of the medieval town patriciate', *Past and Present*, 3 (1953), pp. 15–27.

Hill, J. W. F., *Medieval Lincoln*, Cambridge, 1948.

Hill, Rosalind, ' "A Chaunterie for Soules": London chantries in the reign of Richard II', in *The Reign of Richard II*, eds F. R. H. Du Boulay and Caroline M. Barron, 1971, pp. 242–55.

Hilton, R. H., *A Medieval Society. The West Midlands at the End of the Thirteenth Century*, London, 1966.

Hodgett, Gerald A. J., *The Cartulary of Holy Trinity, Aldgate*, London Record Society Publications, 7 (1971).

Honeybourne, Marjory, 'The leper hospitals of the London area', *Transactions of the London and Middlesex Archaeological Society*, 21 (1967), pp. 3–61.

Hoskins, W. G., *Essays in Leicestershire History*, Liverpool, 1950.

Hoskins, W. G., 'An Elizabethan provincial town: Leicester', in *Studies in Social History: a tribute to G. M. Trevelyan*, ed. J. H. Plumb, London, 1955, pp. 35–67.

Hoskins, W. G., 'English provincial towns in the early sixteenth century', *T.R.H.S.*, 5th series, 6 (1956), pp. 1–19.

Hoskins, W. G., *Two Thousand Years in Exeter*, Exeter, 1960.

Hoskins, W. G., *Provincial England. Essays in Social and Economic History*, London, 1963.

Hoskins, W. G. and Finberg, H. P. R., *Devonshire Studies*, London, 1952.

Hunnisett, R. F., *The Medieval Coroner*, Cambridge, 1961.

Hurst, Henry, 'Excavations at Gloucester, 1968–1971: first interim report', *Antiquaries Journal*, 52 (1972), pp. 24–69.

Hutton, Edward, *The Franciscans in England, 1224–1538*, London, 1926.

James, Margery Kirkbride, *Studies in the Medieval Wine Trade*, Oxford, 1971.

Jones, Douglas, *The Church in Chester, 1300–1540*, Chetham Society, 3rd series, 7 (1957).

Jones, S. R. and Smith, J. T., 'The Wealden houses of Warwickshire and their significance', *Transactions and Proceedings of the Birmingham Archaeological Society*, 79 (1960–1), pp. 24–35.

Jusserand, J. J., *English Wayfaring Life in the Middle Ages*, London, 1889 (re-issued 1961).

Keene, D. J., *Some Aspects of the History, Topography and Archaeology of the North-Eastern Part of the Medieval City of Winchester with Special Reference to the Brooks Area*, Oxford D.Phil. thesis, 1972.

Kerridge, Eric, 'The movement of rent, 1540–1640', *Ec.H.R.*, 2nd series, 6 (1953–4), pp. 16–34.

Kissan, B. W., 'An early list of London properties', *Transactions of the London and Middlesex Archaeological Society*, new series, 8 (1938), pp. 57–69.

Knowles, David and Hadcock, R. Neville, *Medieval Religious Houses, England and Wales*, London, 1953.

Lipman, V. D., *The Jews of Medieval Norwich*, The Jewish Historical Society of England, London, 1967.

Little, A. G., 'Introduction of the Observant friars into England', *Proceedings of the British Academy*, 10 (1921–3), pp. 455–71.

Little, A. G. (ed.), *Fratris Thomae, vulgo dicti de Eccleston, tractatus De adventu fratrum minorum in Angliam*, Manchester, 1951.

Littlehales, Henry (ed.), *The Medieval Records of a London City Church (St Mary at Hill), A.D. 1420–1559*, 2 vols, Early English Text Society, 125 (1904) and 128 (1905).

Lloyd, T. H., *The Movement of Wool Prices in Medieval England*, The Economic History Review Supplements 6, Cambridge, 1973.

Lobel, M. D., *The Borough of Bury St Edmunds*, Oxford, 1935.

Lobel, M. D. (ed.), *Historic Towns. Maps and plans of towns and cities in the British Isles, with historical commentaries, from earliest times to 1800*, volume 1, London and Oxford, 1969.

Loyn, Henry, *The Norman Conquest*, London, 1967 (2nd edition).

Loyn, Henry, 'Towns in late Anglo-Saxon England: the evidence and some possible lines of enquiry', in *England before the Conquest. Studies in Primary Sources presented to Dorothy Whitelock*, eds Peter Clemoes and Kathleen Hughes, Cambridge, 1971, pp. 115–28.

MacCaffrey, Wallace T., *Exeter, 1540–1640. The Growth of an English County Town*, Cambridge (Mass.), 1958.

McKisack, May, *The Parliamentary Representation of the English Boroughs during the Middle Ages*, Oxford, 1932 (reprinted 1962).

McNeill, John T. and Gamer, Helena M., *Medieval Handbooks of Penance*, New York, 1938 (reprinted 1965).

Maitland, F. W. and Bateson, M. (eds), *The Charters of the Borough of Cambridge*, Cambridge, 1901.

Malden, Henry Elliott (ed.), *The Cely Papers: Selections from the Correspondence and Memoranda of the Cely Family, Merchants of the Staple, A.D. 1475–1488*, Camden Society, 3rd series, 1 (1900).

Martin, G. H., *The Early Court Rolls of the Borough of Ipswich*, Occasional Papers of the Department of English Local History, University of Leicester, 5 (1954).

Martin, G. H., *The Borough and the Merchant Community of Ipswich, 1317–1422*, Oxford D.Phil. thesis, 1955.

Martin, G. H., 'The English borough in the thirteenth century', *T.R.H.S.*, 5th series, 13 (1963), pp. 123–44.

Martin, G. H. (ed.), *The Royal Charters of Grantham, 1463–1688*, Leicester, 1963.

Martin, G. H., 'Church life in medieval Leicester', in *The Growth of Leicester*, ed. A. E. Brown, Leicester, 1970, pp. 27–37.

Martin, G. H., 'The registration of deeds of title in the medieval borough', in *The Study of Medieval Records. Essays in Honour of Kathleen Major*, eds D. A. Bullough and R. L. Storey, Oxford, 1971, pp. 151–73.

Masters, Betty R., 'The town clerk', *The Guildhall Miscellany*, 3 (1969), pp. 55–74.

Masters, Betty R. and Ralph, Elizabeth (eds), *The Church Book of St Ewen's, Bristol 1454–1584*, Publications of the Bristol and Gloucestershire Archaeological Society, Records Section, 6 (1967).

Miles, Henrietta, 'Rhuddlan', *Current Archaeology*, 32 (1972), pp. 245–8.

Miller, Edward, 'The fortunes of the English textile industry during the thirteenth century', *Ec.H.R.*, 2nd series, 18 (1965), pp. 64–82.

Murray, K. M. E., *The Constitutional History of the Cinque Ports*, Manchester, 1935.

Myers, A. R. (ed.), *English Historical Documents 1327–1485*, London, 1969.

Myers, A. R., *London in the Age of Chaucer*, Oklahoma, 1972.

Nef, J. U., 'The progress of technology and the growth of large-scale industry in Great Britain, 1540–1640', *Ec.H.R.*, 5 (1934–5), pp. 3–24.

Outhwaite, R. B., *Inflation in Tudor and Early Stuart England*, London, 1969.

Owen, Dorothy M., *Church and Society in Medieval Lincolnshire*, Lincolnshire Local History Society, History of Lincolnshire, vol. 5, 1971.

Owst, G. R., *Literature and Pulpit in Medieval England*, Cambridge, 1933.

Palliser, D. M., *The Reformation in York 1534–1553*, Borthwick Institute of Historical Research, University of York, Borthwick Papers 40 (1971).

Palliser, D. M. and Pinnock, A. C., 'The markets of medieval Staffordshire', *North Staffordshire Journal of Field Studies*, 11 (1971), pp. 49–59.

Pantin, W. A., 'The development of domestic architecture in Oxford', *Antiquaries Journal*, 27 (1947), pp. 120–50.

Pantin, W. A., 'Medieval English town-house plans', *Medieval Archaeology*, 6–7 (1962–3), pp. 202–39.

Pantin, W. A., 'Some medieval English town houses: a study in adaptation', in *Culture and Environment, Essays in Honour of Sir Cyril Fox*, eds I. Ll. Foster and L. Alcock, London, 1963, pp. 445–78.

Parker, Vanessa, *The Making of King's Lynn*, Chichester and London, 1971.

Pelham, R. A., 'The urban population of Sussex in 1340', *Sussex Archaeological Collections*, 78 (1937), pp. 211–23.

Phelps Brown, E. H. and Hopkins, Sheila V., 'Seven centuries of the prices of consumables, compared with builders' wage-rates', *Economica*, new series, 23 (1956), pp. 296–314.

Platt, Colin, 'Southampton, 1000–1600 A.D.: wealth and settlement patterns in a major medieval seaport', *Hansische Geschichtsblätter*, 91 (1973), pp. 12–23.

Platt, Colin, *Medieval Southampton: the Port and Trading Community, A.D. 1000–1600*, London, 1973.

Platt, Colin and Coleman-Smith, Richard, *Excavations in Medieval Southampton, 1953–1969*, Leicester, 1975.

Pollock, Sir Frederick and Maitland, Frederic William, *The History of English Law before the Time of Edward I*, Cambridge, 1898 (reissued 1968).

Portman, D., *Exeter Houses 1400–1700*, Exeter, 1966.

Postan, M. M., *The Medieval Economy and Society. An Economic History of Britain 1100–1500*, London, 1972.

Pound, J. F., 'The social and trade structure of Norwich 1525–1575', *Past and Present*, 34 (1966), pp. 49–69.

Power, Eileen, *The Wool Trade in English Medieval History*, Oxford, 1941.

Pugh, Ralph B., *Imprisonment in Medieval England*, Cambridge, 1968.

Pugh, T. B. (ed.), *The Middle Ages: Glamorgan County History 3*, Cardiff, 1971.

Raine, Angelo, *Medieval York: a Topographical Survey based on Original Sources*, London, 1955.

Ramsey, Peter H., *The Price Revolution in Sixteenth-Century England*, London, 1971.

Reynolds, Susan, 'The rulers of London in the twelfth century',

History, 57 (1972), pp. 337–53.

Riley, Henry Thomas (ed.), *Munimenta Gildhallae Londoniensis: Liber Albus, Liber Custumarum et Liber Horn*, 3 vols, Rolls Series, London, 1859–62.

Rogers, Alan (ed.), *The Making of Stamford*, Leicester, 1965.

Rogers, Alan, *The Medieval Buildings of Stamford*, Stamford Survey Group Report 1, Nottingham, 1970.

Roskell, J. S., 'The social composition of the Commons in a fifteenth-century parliament', *Bulletin of the Institute of Historical Research*, 24 (1951), pp. 152–72.

Roskell, J. S., *The Commons in the Parliament of 1422. English Society and Parliamentary Representation under the Lancastrians*, Manchester, 1954.

Rowe, Margery M. and Jackson, Andrew M. (eds), *Exeter Freemen 1266–1967*, Devon and Cornwall Record Society, extra series, 1 (1973).

Rowse, A. L., *Tudor Cornwall. Portrait of a Society*, London, 1941.

Ruddock, Alwyn, *Italian Merchants and Shipping in Southampton, 1270–1600*, Southampton Records Series, 1 (1951).

Russell, J. C., 'Population in Europe 500–1500', in *The Fontana Economic History of Europe. The Middle Ages*, ed. Carlo M. Cipolla, London, 1972, pp. 25–70.

Rye, William Brenchley (ed.), *England as Seen by Foreigners in the Days of Elizabeth and James the First*, London, 1865.

Sabine, Ernest L., 'Latrines and cesspools in mediaeval London', *Speculum*, 9 (1934), pp. 303–21.

Sabine, Ernest L., 'City cleaning in mediaeval London', *Speculum*, 12 (1937), pp. 19–43.

Salter, H. E., *Medieval Oxford*, Oxford, 1936.

Salzman, L. F., *Building in England down to 1540. A Documentary History*, Oxford, 1967 (2nd edition).

Savage, Sir William, 'Somerset towns. I. Origins and early government', *Proceedings of the Somersetshire Archaeological and Natural History Society*, 99–100 (1954–5), pp. 49–74.

Sawyer, P. H., 'The wealth of England in the eleventh century', *T.R.H.S.*, 5th series, 15 (1965), pp. 145–64.

Scarfe, Norman, *The Suffolk Landscape*, London, 1972.

Schofield, R. S., 'The geographical distribution of wealth in England, 1334–1649', *Ec.H.R.*, 2nd series, 18 (1965), pp. 483–510.

Shoesmith, Ron, 'Hereford', *Current Archaeology*, 33 (1972), pp. 256–8.

Smith, Terence Paul, 'The medieval town defences of King's Lynn', *Journal of the British Archaeological Association*, 3rd series, 33 (1970), pp. 57–88.

Smith, Toulmin (ed.), *English Gilds*, Early English Text Society, 1870.

Sneyd, C. A. (ed.), *A Relation, or rather a True Account, of the Island of England; with sundry particulars of the customs of these people, and of the royal revenues under King Henry the Seventh, about the year 1500*, Camden Society, 37 (1847).

Stenton, F. M., 'The road system of medieval England', *Ec.H.R.*, 7 (1936), pp. 1–21.

Stephens, W. B. (ed.), *History of Congleton*, Manchester, 1970.

Stephenson, Carl, *Borough and Town. A Study of Urban Origins in England*, Cambridge (Mass.), 1933.

Stone, Lawrence, 'Social mobility in England, 1500–1700', *Past and Present*, 33 (1966), pp. 16–55.

Stone, Lawrence, *The Causes of the English Revolution, 1529–1642*, London, 1972.

Studer, Paul (ed.), *The Oak Book of Southampton of c. A.D. 1300*, 3 vols, Southampton Record Society, 1910–11.

Tait, James, *Mediaeval Manchester and the Beginnings of Lancashire*, Manchester, 1904.

Tait, James, *The Medieval English Borough*, Manchester, 1936.

Taylor, M. V. (ed.), *Liber Luciani de Laude Cestrie*, Lancashire and Cheshire Record Society, 64 (1912).

Thrupp, Sylvia L., 'Social control in the medieval town', *Journal of Economic History*, 1: supplement (1941), pp. 39–52.

Thrupp, Sylvia L., *The Merchant Class of Medieval London, 1300–1500*, Chicago, 1948.

Thrupp, Sylvia L., 'The Gilds', in *The Cambridge Economic History of Europe*, volume 3, eds M. M. Postan, E. E. Rich and Edward Miller, Cambridge, 1965, pp. 230–80.

Thrupp, Sylvia L., 'The problem of replacement-rates in late medieval English population', *Ec.H.R.*, 2nd series, 18 (1965–6), pp. 101–19.

Thrupp, Sylvia L., 'Plague effects in medieval Europe', *Comparative Studies in Society and History*, 8 (1965–6), pp. 474–83.

Thrupp, Sylvia L. and Johnson, Harold B., 'The earliest Canterbury freemen's rolls 1298–1363', *Kent Record Society* 18 (1964), pp. 173–213.

Trenholme, N. M., *The English Monastic Borough. A Study in Medieval History*, University of Missouri Studies, volume 2, number 3, Columbia, 1927.

Trexler, Richard C., 'Une table florentine d'espérance de vie', *Annales: Économies, Sociétés, Civilisations*, 26 (1971), pp. 137–9.

Turner, Hilary L., *Town Defences in England and Wales; an Architectural and Documentary Study, A.D. 900–1500*, London, 1971.

Unwin, George, *The Gilds and Companies of London*, London, 1963 (4th edition).

Urry, William, *Canterbury under the Angevin Kings*, London, 1967.

Veale, Elspeth M., *The English Fur Trade in the Later Middle Ages*, Oxford, 1966.

Veale, Elspeth M., 'Craftsmen and the economy of London in the fourteenth century', in *Studies in London History*, eds A. Hollaender and W. Kellaway, London, 1969, pp. 133–51.

Verlinden, C., 'Markets and fairs', in *The Cambridge Economic History of Europe*, volume 3, eds M. M. Postan, E. E. Rich and Edward Miller, Cambridge, 1965, pp. 119–53.

Wade-Martins, Peter, 'North Elmham', *Current Archaeology*, 36 (1973), pp. 22–5.

Walker, David, *Bristol in the Early Middle Ages*, Historical Association, Bristol, 1971.

Weinbaum, Martin, *The Incorporation of Boroughs*, Manchester, 1937.

West, S. E., 'Excavations at Cox Lane (1958) and at the town defences, Shire Hall yard, Ipswich (1959)', *Proceedings of the Suffolk Institute of Archaeology*, 29 (1961–3), pp. 233–303.

Westlake, H. F., *The Parish Gilds of Mediaeval England*, London, 1919.

Williams, C. H. (ed.), *English Historical Documents 1485–1558*, London, 1967.

Williams, Gwyn, *Medieval London: from Commune to Capital*, London, 1963.

Wood, Margaret, *The English Mediaeval House*, London, 1965.

Wood-Legh, K. L., 'Some aspects of the history of chantries in the later Middle Ages', *T.R.H.S.*, 4th series, 28 (1946), pp. 47–60.

Wood-Legh, K. L., *Perpetual Chantries in Britain*, Cambridge, 1965.

Woodward, D. M., *The Trade of Elizabethan Chester*, Occasional Papers in Economic and Social History 4, University of Hull, 1970.

Youings, Joyce, *Tuckers Hall, Exeter. The History of a Provincial City Company through Five Centuries*, Exeter, 1968.

Index

Alnwick, 33, 35, 54, 57, 65
Apothecaries, 94
Arundel, 164
Ashburton, 113

Baker, Robert, 47
Bakers, 95
Banbury, 65
Barnstaple, 29
Bath, 37
Battle, 189
Baudas, 50
Bede, 23
Beverley, 141, 153
Black Death, 120
Bodmin, 199
Boston, 31, 95, 97, 180, 195, 204
Bracton, Henry, 93
Bradford-on-Avon, 131
Brand, Robert, 155
Bretford, 31
Bridgwater, 168
Bristol, 45, 53, 62, 80, 87, 125, 142,
    169, 171, 180, 188, 208, 213
Broadway, 31
Burgage tenure, 156
Burgess aristocracy, 27–8
Burgess origins, 115–17
Burton-upon-Trent, 65
Bury St Edmunds, 37, 71, 162, 163,
    170

Cambridge, 28, 43, 45, 98, 115, 122–5,
    199, 206, 223
Campision, 50
Canterbury, 28, 37, 43, 46, 50, 71, 73,
    80, 117, 118, 122, 125, 136, 152,
    160, 164, 183, 184

Canynges, William, 130
Caxton, William, 119
Cely, Richard, 122
Chantries, 200–2, 204–5, 207
Charters, borough, 155–62
Chester, 37, 188, 208, 215
Chich, Arnold, 125
Chichester, 37, 40, 43, 58
Chipping Campden, 31, 128
Chipping Sodbury, 31
Church and the boroughs, 157–9,
    179–210
Church property, 183–8, 216–17
Cinque ports, 148
Cirencester, 170
Class differences, 141–2, 143, 148–50,
    217–19
Clergy: chantries, 200–2, 204–5, 207;
    see also Church
Cloth trade, 102–11, 112
Coggeshall, 130
Colchester, 37, 50
Common land, 149
Congleton, 114
Constitution, borough, 151–78
Coroners, election of, 164
County status, 171
Coventry, 45, 50, 51, 52, 54, 82, 84,
    94, 95, 114, 115, 130, 131, 149,
    168–9, 170, 171, 199, 206, 216
Craftsmen, 133, 134, 135–9, 141, 150,
    197–9
Crediton, 113

Dartmouth, 112
Deeds, enrolment, 166
Derbyshire, 31, 92, 97
Devonshire, 29, 30, 113

Dissolution, 209, 216–17, 219, 221
Domesday Book, 21, 28, 29, 31–2, 43
Doncaster, 58, 148
Durham, 95, 97

Economy, 93–114
Elections, 142, 144–5, 157
Exeter, 24, 29, 37, 40, 46, 80, 81–2, 86, 87, 89, 95, 113, 127, 129, 132, 144, 148, 197, 221, 224, 225, 226, 229

Fairs: *see* Markets
Family life, 29; alliances, 124
Fee farms, 154–5, 156, 162
Flamesbury, Robert, 187
Flemish trade,104–6, 111
Flint, 188
Fortifications, town, 50–5
Forty, John, 123
Franciscius, Andreas, 59–60
Friars, 194–7, 209–10

Garderobe, 86, 89
Gentry, 227–9, 230–1
Gilds, 25, 137–42, 149, 152, 153, 155, 161–2
Glamorgan, 25
Gloucester, 37, 39, 45, 46, 53, 87, 125, 154, 155, 157
Gotson, Peter, 20
Grantham, 147, 168, 180, 195
Great Yarmouth, 199
Grevel, William, 128–9
Grimsby, 46, 113, 154, 195, 196, 213, 227–8, 231

Hanseatic trade, 111–12, 117
Hedon, 171
Hereford, 33, 34, 35, 36, 45, 51
Holbeach, 190
Holmhegge, Joan, 205
Honiton, 95
Horton, Thomas, 131
Hospitals, 191–4
Housing, 64, 65, 66, 67, 68, 74–5, 77, 222–6; furniture, 88, 90–1

Hull, 50, 51, 87, 96, 111, 112, 115, 117, 126, 127, 165, 167, 168, 171, 172–3, 176, 177, 191, 192, 198, 208

Infant mortality, 119–21
Inflation, 211, 212, 215–17
Ipswich, 51, 55, 74, 142, 157–9, 164, 165, 173, 189, 230

Jannys, Robert, 130

Kings Lynn, 31, 45, 51, 55, 56, 57, 68, 75, 77–8, 81, 83, 97, 111, 216

Land: transferability, 28, 153–4, 166; *see also* Common land *and* Property
Lando, Girolamo, 20, 53
Lavenham, 106, 108, 109, 110
Lawyers, 226–7
Leeds, 61
Leicester, 27, 46, 47, 95, 97, 130, 131, 132, 141, 149, 161–2, 184
Lemnius, Levinus, 89–90
Leper hospitals, 45–6
Life expectancy, 119–21
Lincoln, 71, 97, 104, 105, 110, 117, 127, 141–2, 154, 160, 177, 183, 186, 195, 204
Liskeard, 144
Lollards, 209, 210
London, 19, 46, 50, 55, 57, 59, 80, 87, 89, 94, 96, 105, 117, 121, 127, 136, 137, 141, 152, 153, 154, 155, 159, 161, 176, 183, 184, 207, 208, 211, 213
Lucian, 37
Ludlow, 37, 43, 44, 105, 228
Lydford, 29
Lyster, Richard, 131
Lyster, Thomas, 146

Maghfeld, Gilbert, 129
Market Harborough, 35, 115, 189
Markets and fairs, 31–2, 61, 92–4, 97–8, 100, 102, 114
Marlborough, 141
Marriage, 121–2, 124, 127
Mayors, 148–9, 159, 160, 161, 178

Middlewich, 113
Mille, John, 146
Modbury, 113
Moreton-in-the-Marsh, 31
Murage, 54

Newark, 198
Newbury, 154
Newcastle-upon-Tyne, 152–3, 171
Norman Conquest, 25, 27
Northampton, 79, 149, 159, 161
Northleach, 31, 114, 123
Norwich, 45, 57, 58, 69, 70–1, 79, 130,
    131, 132, 171, 181, 187, 188, 192,
    194, 208, 211, 213, 214
Nottingham, 33, 35, 45, 159, 184

Okehampton, 29, 113
Orford, 154
Ouse, river, 95–6
Overseas trade, 101–11
Oxford, 43, 50, 57, 59, 60, 66, 76, 78,
    85, 95, 108, 136, 141, 155, 157, 193,
    194, 225

Paris, Simon de, 117
Parish church, 45, 179–210; financing,
    208
Parish gilds, 199–204
Parliamentary burgesses, 147, 226–7
Paycocke, Thomas, 130
Peterborough, 27
Plague, 120
Planning of towns, 33–45
Plymouth, 112
Plympton, 113
Poole, 113
Population, 19, 21, 118–21, 211–13;
    movements, 122, 123
Poverty, 134–5
Prices, 211–12
Professions, 227
Property, 122, 125, 219–21, 226
Property, community, 172–6
Provincial towns, 213–15
Pultney, Sir John, 117
Public services, 85, 87, 89

Reading, 45, 195
Record-keeping, 164–6
Recorders, 177, 178
Reeves, 159–60
Rentier class, 219–21
Roads, 58–9, 87
Roman towns, 23

St Albans, 40
St Ives, 97
St Neots, 31, 32
Salford, 166
Salisbury, 33, 37, 41, 42, 45, 55, 57,
    129, 140, 199, 201
Saunders, Laurence, 149
Scarborough, 65, 154, 218
Seals, town, 157–8
Seigneurial foundations, 31
Shrewsbury, 50, 105, 112, 140, 172,
    216
Society, borough, 115–50
Soper, William, 203–4
Southampton, 23, 28, 32, 43, 47, 48,
    49, 52, 53, 54, 55, 57, 58, 60, 61, 62,
    63, 67, 68, 69, 70, 71, 72, 73, 74, 77,
    87, 94, 98, 100, 105, 109, 127, 129,
    130, 131, 132, 133, 134, 140–1, 142,
    146, 147, 148, 149, 150, 160, 184,
    185, 191, 197, 202, 203, 204, 205,
    217, 219, 221, 222, 224, 228, 229
Spalding, 199
Spring, Thomas, 130
Staffordshire, 31
Stamford, 27, 46, 48, 67, 147, 185, 195
Stockport, 166
Stratford-upon-Avon, 31, 55, 61, 65,
    93, 115
Suburbs, 46–9
Suffolk, 26
Swansea, 74
Sworn commune, 154–5

Tavistock, 113, 169, 170, 189
Tenement plots, 63, 65
Tiverton, 110, 112, 200
Tokey, Richard, 91
Tolls, 156, 157, 177
Torrington, 113, 114

Totnes, 29, 110, 112
Town clerk, 177–8
Town planning, 33–45, 55–6
Trading, 21–3, 55–8, 102–10, 213–15
Transport, 94–7
Troy, 49
Truro, 226
Tucker, Richard, 118

Urbanization, 19–21, 23–4, 25, 29, 32

Wallingford, 43
Wareham, 43
Warwick, 28, 46, 114, 168
Wealth, distribution of, 107, 110–11, 129, 131–3

Wharram Percy, 119, 121
Wigstons, William, 131
Wilton, 33, 147
Winchelsea, 37, 41, 117
Winchester, 23, 24, 37, 43, 46, 54–5, 57, 59, 62, 67, 78, 84, 85, 87, 97, 141, 174, 181, 182, 183, 191, 199, 208, 219
Worcester, 24, 115, 213, 214, 231

York, 19, 21, 52, 58, 64, 78, 82, 87, 95–6, 112, 115, 117, 118, 125, 127, 132, 133, 135, 143, 148, 154, 175, 180, 183, 188, 192, 198–9, 208, 217, 219, 229